A TREATISE ON MONEY

BY

JOHN MAYNARD KEYNES
FELLOW OF KING'S COLLEGE CAMBRIDGE

IN TWO VOLUMES

VOLUME I
THE PURE THEORY OF MONEY

HARCOURT, BRACE AND COMPANY
NEW YORK

Library of Congress Cataloging in Publication Data

Keynes, John Maynard, 1883-1946.
　A treatise on money.

　　Reprint of the 1930 ed. published by Harcourt, Brace, New York.
　　CONTENTS: v. 1. The pure theory of money.—v. 2. The applied theory of money.
　　1. Money.　2. Monetary policy.　3. Banks and banking.
I. Title.
HG221.K45　1976　　　332.4　　　75-41162
ISBN 0-404-15000-4

Reprinted from an original copy in the collections of the Library of the City College of New York

From the edition of 1930, New York
First AMS edition published in 1976
Manufactured in the United States of America

International Standard Book Number:
Complete Set: 0-404-15000-4
Volume I: 0-404-15001-2

AMS PRESS INC.
NEW YORK, N. Y.

PREFACE

IN Books III. and IV. of this Treatise I propose a novel means of approach to the fundamental problems of monetary theory. My object has been to find a method which is useful in describing, not merely the characteristics of static equilibrium, but also those of disequilibrium, and to discover the dynamical laws governing the passage of a monetary system from one position of equilibrium to another. This discussion constitutes the kernel of Volume I. on "The Pure Theory of Money". In Volume II., on "The Applied Theory of Money", I have endeavoured to combine the quantitative method with the qualitative, and have made as good an estimate as I can of the order of magnitude of the quantities entering into the argument, on the basis, mainly, of present-day facts in Great Britain and the United States. In this volume I have also described the salient features of modern banking and monetary systems, and have discussed the objects and methods of Monetary Management in the practical sphere.

As I read through the page proofs of this book I am acutely conscious of its defects. It has occupied me for several years, not free from other occupations, during which my ideas have been developing and changing, with the result that its parts are not all entirely harmonious with one another. The ideas with which I have finished up are widely different from those with which I began. The result is, I am afraid, that there is a good deal in this book which represents the process of getting rid of the ideas which I used to have and of finding my way to those which I now have. There are many skins which I have sloughed still littering these pages. It follows that I could do it better and much shorter if I were to start over again. I feel like someone who has been forcing his way through a confused jungle. Now that I have emerged from it, I see that I might have taken a more direct route and that many problems and perplexities which beset me during the journey had not precisely the significance which I supposed at the time. Nevertheless, I expect that I shall do well to offer my book to the world for what it is worth at the stage it has now reached, even if it represents a collection of material rather than a finished work.

In the second place, I have attempted, perhaps foolishly, to combine a systematic Treatise, both Pure and Applied, with a number of discussions which might have been the subject of separate monographs. The most important of these quasi-digressions are Book II. on Index Numbers and Book VI. on Fluctuations in the Rate of Investment. Book II., in particular, holds back for many pages the main progression of the argument towards the fundamental theory which occupies Books III. and IV.; perhaps some readers may prefer to omit these chapters or to return to them later on.

Another disadvantage from which I have suffered has been the absence of any models to guide me to the right order and arrangement of the various topics.

PREFACE

The best way to expound a subject of this kind can only be discovered gradually as the result of the experience of successive authors. But although my field of study is one which is being lectured upon in every University in the world, there exists, extraordinarily enough, no printed Treatise in any language — so far as I am aware—which deals systematically and thoroughly with the theory and facts of Representative Money as it exists in the modern world. I hope to use the experience, which I have now gained, to prepare something on a smaller scale which will try to find the best way to explain the subject.

I believe that a right understanding of the topics of this book is of enormous practical importance to the well-being of the world. If I am able to make a contribution to it, I owe this to the atmosphere of discussion and conversation in which I have worked at Cambridge. Mr. D. H. Robertson has cast a penetrating light on certain fundamental matters, and this book would never have taken its present shape without the help of his ideas. In the gradual evolution of the book into its final form and in the avoidance of errors my greatest debt is to Mr. R. F. Kahn of King's College, Cambridge, whose care and acuteness have left their trace on many pages, and to whom I am also indebted for the Index. Amongst several others from whom I have had help at different stages I would particularly mention Mr. H. D. Henderson.

When the greater part of what follows was already in print I was appointed to serve on the Treasury Committee on Finance and Industry of which Lord Macmillan is the Chairman. Thus the practical suggestions contained in Volume II. represent my opinions as they stood before the work of the Committee commenced rather than what they may be when the time comes for the Committee to report.

I must mention my obligation to the printers of this book, Messrs. R. & R. Clark of Edinburgh, for their great patience and accuracy with proof-sheets which they have had to keep in type for a long period subject to continual alterations and additions.

J. M. KEYNES.

KING'S COLLEGE, CAMBRIDGE,
September 14, 1930.

CONTENTS

VOLUME I

THE PURE THEORY OF MONEY

BOOK I

THE NATURE OF MONEY

CHAPTER 1

	PAGE
THE CLASSIFICATION OF MONEY	3
(i.) Money and Money-of-Account	3
(ii.) Money-Proper and Bank-Money	5
(iii.) Representative Money	6
(iv.) The Forms of Money	7
(v.) Current Money	9
(vi.) Illustrations from History	11
(vii.) The Evolution of Managed Money	15

CHAPTER 2

BANK-MONEY	23
(i.) The "Creation" of Bank-Money	23
(ii.) Current Money is predominantly Bank-Money	31

CHAPTER 3

THE ANALYSIS OF BANK-MONEY	34
(i.) Income-deposits, Business-deposits and Savings-deposits	34
(ii.) Demand-deposits and Time-deposits	36
(iii.) Deposits and Overdrafts	41
(iv.) The Volume of Deposits in relation to the Volume of Transactions	43

BOOK II

THE VALUE OF MONEY

CHAPTER 4

	PAGE
THE PURCHASING POWER OF MONEY	53
(i.) The Meaning of Purchasing Power	53
(ii.) The Consumption Standard	57
(iii.) The Earnings Standard	63
(iv.) Working-class Index Numbers	64

CHAPTER 5

THE PLURALITY OF SECONDARY PRICE-LEVELS	65
(i.) The Wholesale Standard	66
(ii.) International Standards	69

CHAPTER 6

CURRENCY STANDARDS	76
(i.) The Cash-Transactions Standard and the Cash-Balances Standard	76
(ii.) Is there such a thing as an "Objective Mean Variation of General Prices"?	79

CHAPTER 7

THE DIFFUSION OF PRICE-LEVELS	89

CHAPTER 8

THE THEORY OF COMPARISONS OF PURCHASING POWER	95
(i.) The Meaning of Comparisons of Purchasing Power	95
(ii.) Methods of Approximation	99
a. The Direct Method	100
b. The Indirect Method	102
1. The "Highest Common Factor" Method	105
2. The Method of Limits	109
3. The "Crossing of Formulae"	111
4. The Chain Method	116

CONTENTS xi

BOOK III

THE FUNDAMENTAL EQUATIONS OF MONEY

CHAPTER 9

	PAGE
CERTAIN DEFINITIONS	123
(i.) Income, Profits, Savings and Investment	123
(ii.) Available and Non-available Output	127
(iii.) The Classification of Capital	128
(iv.) Foreign Lending and the Foreign Balance	131

CHAPTER 10

THE FUNDAMENTAL EQUATIONS FOR THE VALUE OF MONEY.	133
(i.) The Fundamental Equations for the Value of Money	135
(ii.) The Characteristics of Profit	137
(iii.) The Price-level of New Investment-goods	140
(iv.) The Relation of the Price-level to the Quantity of Money	146

CHAPTER 11

THE CONDITIONS OF EQUILIBRIUM	151
(i.) The Condition of Zero-profits	151
(ii.) The Rate of Interest, or Bank-rate	154
(iii.) Inflation and Deflation	155
(iv.) The Causal Direction of Change	156
(v.) The Behaviour of Entrepreneurs	159
(vi.) The Condition of External Equilibrium	161
(vii.) Changes in Price-Levels due to Spontaneous Changes in Earnings	166

CHAPTER 12

THE DISTINCTION BETWEEN SAVINGS AND INVESTMENT	171
(i.) Savings and Investment	171
(ii.) An Illustration	176
(iii.) Theories of Over-Saving	178
(iv.) A Summary of the Argument	179

xii A TREATISE ON MONEY

CHAPTER 13

	PAGE
The "Modus Operandi" of Bank-rate	185
(i.) The Traditional Doctrine	185
(ii.) The General Theory of Bank-rate	200
(iii.) Some Special Aspects of Bank-rate	209
(iv.) The Function of Bank-rate in Relation to External Equilibrium	213
(v.) The Relation of Bank-rate to the Quantity of Money	216

CHAPTER 14

Alternative Forms of the Fundamental Equation	221
(i.) The "Real Balances" Quantity Equation	222
(ii.) The "Cambridge" Quantity Equation	229
(iii.) The "Fisher" Quantity Equation	233
(iv.) The Relationship between the "Cambridge" and the "Fisher" Equations	237
(v.) The Relationship between the "Fisher" Equation and the Fundamental Equations of Chapter 10	239

BOOK IV

THE DYNAMICS OF THE PRICE-LEVEL

CHAPTER 15

The Industrial Circulation and the Financial Circulation	243
(i.) Industry and Finance distinguished and defined	243
(ii.) Factors determining the Volume of the Industrial Circulation	244
(iii.) Factors determining the Volume of the Financial Circulation	248

CHAPTER 16

A Classification of the Causes of a Disequilibrium in the Purchasing Power of Money	258
I. Changes due to Monetary Factors	259
II. Changes due to Investment Factors	260
III. Changes due to Industrial Factors	260

CONTENTS

CHAPTER 17

	PAGE
CHANGES DUE TO MONETARY FACTORS	262
(i.) The Industrial Consequences of Changed Supply of Money	262
(ii.) The Diffusion of a Change in the Total Deposits between the Different Kinds of Deposits	265
(iii.) The Problems of the Transition	269

CHAPTER 18

CHANGES DUE TO INVESTMENT FACTORS	276
(i.) The Definition of the Credit Cycle	277
(ii.) The Genesis and Life-history of a Credit Cycle	279

CHAPTER 19

SOME SPECIAL ASPECTS OF THE CREDIT CYCLE	293
(i.) The " Justification " of Commodity Inflation	293
(ii.) The Incidence of Commodity Inflation	298
(iii.) The Normal Course of a Credit Cycle	302

CHAPTER 20

AN EXERCISE IN THE PURE THEORY OF THE CREDIT CYCLE	305
(i.) The Standard Case	306
(ii.) Eight Epilogues	312
(iii.) The Generalised Case	317

CHAPTER 21

CHANGES DUE TO INTERNATIONAL DISEQUILIBRIUM	326
(i.) Relative Price-levels and Relative Interest-rates as causes of Monetary Disequilibrium	326
(ii.) The Relationships between Foreign Lending and Movements of Gold	329
(iii.) The Net National Advantages of Foreign Investment	343
(iv.) The Awkwardness of Changes due to International Factors	346
(v.) The same Phenomena under Gold-Exchange Management	350
(vi.) The same Phenomena in the Absence of an International Standard	356

A TREATISE ON MONEY

VOLUME II
THE APPLIED THEORY OF MONEY

BOOK V
MONETARY FACTORS AND THEIR FLUCTUATIONS

CHAPTER 22

	PAGE
THE APPLIED THEORY OF MONEY	3

CHAPTER 23

THE PROPORTION OF SAVINGS-DEPOSITS TO CASH-DEPOSITS	7
1. England	8
2. The United States	14
3. Elsewhere	18

CHAPTER 24

THE VELOCITIES OF CIRCULATION	20
(i.) The Conception of "Velocity" as applied to Bank Money	20
(ii.) The Velocities of the Income-deposits and of the Business-deposits distinguished	22
(iii.) The Velocity of the Income-deposits	25
(iv.) The Velocity of the Business-deposits	30
1. Great Britain	31
2. The United States	35
(v.) The Variability of the Velocity of the Business-deposits	39
(vi.) Factors determining True Velocities	43

CHAPTER 25

THE RATIO OF BANK MONEY TO RESERVE MONEY	49
(i.) The Stability of Reserve-ratios	53
1. England	55
2. The United States	61
3. Elsewhere	64
(ii.) The Interchangeability of Non-Reserve Bank Assets	66
(iii.) How ought the Reserve-ratio to be fixed?	68

CONTENTS

CHAPTER 26

	PAGE
THE ACTIVITY OF BUSINESS	79
(i.) The Influence of Business Activity on the Velocity of the Business-deposits	79
(ii.) The Relation between the Bank Clearings and the Volume of Trade	82
(iii.) Statistical Summary	88

BOOK VI

THE RATE OF INVESTMENT AND ITS FLUCTUATIONS

CHAPTER 27

FLUCTUATIONS IN THE RATE OF INVESTMENT—I. FIXED CAPITAL	95
(i.) The Statistical Indications	97
(ii.) Theories of the Credit Cycle based on Fluctuations in Fixed Capital Investment	99

CHAPTER 28

FLUCTUATIONS IN THE RATE OF INVESTMENT—II. WORKING CAPITAL	102
(i.) The Statistical Indications	103
(ii.) The Theory of Working Capital	116
(iii.) Productive and Unproductive Consumption	124
(iv.) The True Wages Fund	127

CHAPTER 29

FLUCTUATIONS IN THE RATE OF INVESTMENT—III. LIQUID CAPITAL	130
(i.) Mr. Hawtrey's Theory of Liquid Stocks	131
(ii.) The Obstacles to an Accumulation of Liquid Capital	133
(iii.) The " Carrying " Costs	135
(iv.) The Equation relating Price Fluctuations to " Carrying " Costs	140
(v.) The Theory of the " Forward Market "	142
(vi.) Conclusion	145

CHAPTER 30

	PAGE
HISTORICAL ILLUSTRATIONS	148
(i.) Spanish Treasure	152
(ii.) The Depression of the Eighteen Nineties	164
(iii.) The War Boom, 1914–18	170
(iv.) The Post-war Boom, 1919–20	176
(v.) Great Britain's Return to the Gold Standard	181
(vi.) British Home and Foreign Investment after the Return to Gold	184
(vii.) The United States, 1925–30	190
(viii.) The "Gibson Paradox"	198

BOOK VII

THE MANAGEMENT OF MONEY

CHAPTER 31

THE PROBLEM OF THE MANAGEMENT OF MONEY	211
(i.) Control of Prices through the Rate of Investment	211
(ii.) The Dual Functions of Bankers	213

CHAPTER 32

METHODS OF NATIONAL MANAGEMENT—I. THE CONTROL OF THE MEMBER BANKS	225
(i.) The British System	227
(ii.) The Continental System	233
(iii.) The United States Federal Reserve System	234
(iv.) Will Member Banks borrow from the Central Bank at a Rate above the Market?	243
(v.) Open-market Policy further analysed	250
(vi.) The Method of Varying Member Bank Reserve-ratios	260

CHAPTER 33

METHODS OF NATIONAL MANAGEMENT—II. THE REGULATION OF THE CENTRAL RESERVES	262
(i.) Existing Methods of Regulating Note Issues	265
(ii.) The Right Principles of Regulation	272

CONTENTS xvii

CHAPTER 34

PROBLEMS OF INTERNATIONAL MANAGEMENT—I. THE RELATIONS OF CENTRAL BANKS TO ONE ANOTHER 279

CHAPTER 35

PROBLEMS OF INTERNATIONAL MANAGEMENT—II. THE GOLD STANDARD 289
  (i.) *Auri sacra Fames* 289
  (ii.) The Case for the Gold Standard 293

CHAPTER 36

PROBLEMS OF INTERNATIONAL MANAGEMENT—III. THE PROBLEM OF NATIONAL AUTONOMY 302
  (i.) The Dilemma of an International System . . . 302
  (ii.) Methods of Regulating the Rate of Foreign Lending . 306
  (iii.) The Significance of the Gold Points 319
  (iv.) Should Standards of Value be International ? . . 332

CHAPTER 37

PROBLEMS OF NATIONAL MANAGEMENT—III. THE CONTROL OF THE RATE OF INVESTMENT 339
  (i.) Can the Banking System Control the Price-level ? . . 339
  (ii.) Short-term Rates of Interest and Long-term Rates . 352
  (iii.) Can the Banking System control the Rate of Investment ? 362
    a. The Direct Influence of the Short-term Rate of Interest 363
    b. The Fringe of Unsatisfied Borrowers . . . 364
    c. Issue Houses and Underwriters 367
    d. Open-market operations to the point of Saturation . 369
    e. International Complications 374
  (iv.) The Slump of 1930 377

CHAPTER 38

PROBLEMS OF SUPERNATIONAL MANAGEMENT 388
  (i.) The Dual Problem of Supernational Management . . 389
  (ii.) Methods of Supernational Management . . . 395
  (iii.) The Bank of International Settlements . . . 402
  (iv.) Conclusion 405

INDEX 409

BOOK I
THE NATURE OF MONEY

CHAPTER 1

THE CLASSIFICATION OF MONEY

(i.) Money and Money-of-Account

Money-of-Account, namely that in which Debts and Prices and General Purchasing Power are *expressed*, is the primary concept of a Theory of Money.

A Money-of-Account comes into existence along with Debts, which are contracts for deferred payment, and Price-Lists, which are offers of contracts for sale or purchase. Such Debts and Price-Lists, whether they are recorded by word of mouth or by book entry on baked bricks or paper documents, can only be expressed in terms of a Money-of-Account.

Money itself, namely that by delivery of which debt-contracts and price-contracts are *discharged*, and in the shape of which a store of General Purchasing Power is *held*, derives its character from its relationship to the Money-of-Account, since the debts and prices must first have been expressed in terms of the latter. Something which is merely used as a convenient medium of exchange on the spot may approach to being Money, inasmuch as it may represent a means of holding General Purchasing Power. But if this is all, we have scarcely emerged from the stage of Barter. Money-Proper in the full sense of the term can only exist in relation to a Money-of-Account.

Perhaps we may elucidate the distinction between *money* and *money-of-account* by saying that the money-of-account is the *description* or *title* and the money is the *thing* which answers to the description. Now if the same thing always answered to the same description, the distinction would have no practical interest. But if the thing can change, whilst the description remains the same, then the distinction can be highly significant. The difference is like that between the King of England (whoever he may be) and King George. A contract to pay ten years hence a weight of gold equal to the weight of the King of England is not the same thing as a contract to pay a weight of gold equal to the weight of the individual who is now King George. It is for the State to declare, when the time comes, who the King of England is.

Now by the mention of contracts and offers, we have introduced Law or Custom, by which they are enforceable; that is to say, we have introduced the State or the Community. Furthermore it is a peculiar characteristic of money contracts that it is the State or Community not only which enforces delivery, but also which decides what it is that must be delivered as a lawful or customary discharge of a contract which has been concluded in terms of the money-of-account. The State, therefore, comes in first of all as the authority of law which enforces the payment of the thing which corresponds to the name or description in the contract. But it comes in doubly when, in addition, it claims the right to determine and declare *what thing* corresponds to the name, and to vary its declaration from time to time—when, that is to say, it claims the right to re-edit the dictionary. This right is claimed by all modern States and has been so claimed for some four thousand years at least. It is when this stage in the evolution of Money has been reached that Knapp's Chartalism—the doctrine that money is peculiarly a creation of the State—is fully realised.

Thus the Age of Money had succeeded to the Age

of Barter as soon as men had adopted a money-of-account. And the Age of Chartalist or State Money was reached when the State claimed the right to declare what thing should answer as money to the current money-of-account—when it claimed the right not only to enforce the dictionary but also to write the dictionary. To-day all civilised money is, beyond the possibility of dispute, chartalist.

It will be noticed that the money-of-account must be *continuous*. When the name is changed—which may or may not be coincident with a change in the money which answers to it—the new unit must bear a definite relation to the old. The State will, as a rule, promulgate a formula which defines the new money-of-account in terms of the old. If, however, failing a decree by the State, all contracts prior to a certain date are worked out in the old currency, and all contracts subsequent to that date are made in the new, even so the market cannot help establishing for itself a parity between the two. Thus there can be no real breach in the continuity of descent in the pedigree of the money-of-account, except by a catastrophe in which all existing contracts are simultaneously wiped out.

(ii.) MONEY-PROPER AND BANK-MONEY

We have seen that the introduction of a Money-of-Account gives rise to two derived categories— Offers of Contracts, Contracts and Acknowledgments-of-Debt, which are in terms of it, and Money-Proper, answering to it, delivery of which will discharge the Contract or the Debt. The first of these prepares the way for the next development, namely the discovery that for many purposes the acknowledgments of debt are themselves a serviceable substitute for Money-Proper in the settlement of transactions. When acknowledgments of debt are used in this way, we may call them Bank-Money—not forgetting, however, that they are not Money-Proper. Bank-Money is simply an acknowledgment of a private debt, expressed in the money-of-account, which is used by passing from one hand to another, alternatively with Money-Proper, to settle a transaction. We thus have side by side State-Money or Money-Proper and Bank-Money or Acknowledgments-of-Debt.

(iii.) REPRESENTATIVE MONEY

This, in its turn, leads the way to a further evolution of State-Money itself. The Bank-Money may represent no longer a private debt, as in the above definition, but a debt owing by the State; and the State may then use its chartalist prerogative to declare that the debt itself is an acceptable discharge of a liability. A particular kind of Bank-Money is then transformed into Money-Proper—a species of Money-Proper which we may call Representative Money. When, however, what was merely a debt has become money-proper, it has changed its character and should no longer be reckoned as a debt, since it is of the essence of a debt to be enforceable in terms of something other than itself. To regard Representative Money, even when it conforms to an objective standard, as being still a debt will suggest false analogies.

At the cost of not conforming entirely with current usage, I propose to include as State-Money not only money which is itself compulsory legal-tender but also money which the State or the Central Bank undertakes to accept in payments to itself or to exchange for compulsory legal-tender money.[1] Thus

[1] The exact legal status of various moneys is susceptible of considerable variety. For example, the Federal Reserve Bank Notes in the United States are only "optional" money. Knapp accepts as "Money"—rightly,

most present-day Bank Notes, and even Central Bank Deposits, are here classified as State-Money, whilst Bank-Money (or non-legal-tender money) is mainly composed, nowadays, of Member Bank Deposits.[1] Historically a good many examples of Representative State-Money are descended from some kind of Bank-Money, which by being adopted by the State has subsequently passed over from the one category to the other.

(iv.) The Forms of Money

We are now in a position to proceed to a further analysis having an object different from the above, namely, to classify the three *forms* which State-Money can take, which we may call, for short, *Commodity Money*, *Fiat Money* and *Managed Money*, the last two being sub-species of *Representative Money*.

Commodity Money is composed of actual units of a particular freely-obtainable, non-monopolised commodity[2] which happens to have been chosen for the familiar purposes of money, but the supply of which is governed—like that of any other commodity —by scarcity and cost of production.

Fiat Money is Representative (or token) Money (*i.e.* something the intrinsic value of the material substance of which is divorced from its monetary face value)—now generally made of paper except in the case of small denominations—which is created and issued by the State, but is not convertible by law into anything other than itself, and has no fixed value in terms of an objective standard.

I think—anything which the State undertakes to accept at its pay-offices, whether or not it is declared legal-tender between citizens.

[1] See below (p. 10) for the explanation of this term.

[2] Or of warehouse warrants for actually existing units of the commodity. *E.g.* American Gold Certificates are best regarded as Commodity Money.

Managed Money is similar to Fiat Money, except that the State undertakes to manage the conditions of its issue in such a way that, by convertibility or otherwise, it shall have a determinate value in terms of an objective standard.

Commodity Money and Managed Money are alike in that they are related to an objective standard of value. Managed Money and Fiat Money are alike in that they are representative or paper money, having relatively little or no intrinsic value apart from the law or practice of the State.

Thus Managed Money is in a sense a hybrid between the other two; and, perhaps for this reason, its qualities are not so easily understood. The public knows Commodity Money and it knows Fiat Money; but, readier to recognise the Standard than the Form, it is apt to consider a Managed Money which has a familiar commodity as its standard as the same thing as a Commodity Money, and a Managed Money which has an unfamiliar standard as a Fiat Money in disguise. In fact, however, the best typical modern Moneys, whilst many of them still remain mixtures of Commodity Money and Managed Money, approximate more and more to the form of Managed Money. Moreover, Managed Money is, in a sense, the most generalised form of Money—which may be considered to degenerate into Commodity Money on the one side when the managing authority holds against it a hundred per cent of the objective standard, so that it is in effect a warehouse warrant, and into Fiat Money on the other side when it loses its objective standard. For these reasons the theory which will be developed in the following chapters is expressed with primary reference to a Managed Money; but the formulas reached will be easily modifiable, if necessary, to suit the special conditions either of a Commodity Money or of a Fiat Money.

THE CLASSIFICATION OF MONEY

The scheme of conceptions and forms, set forth above, and their inter-relations, can be displayed in a diagram thus:

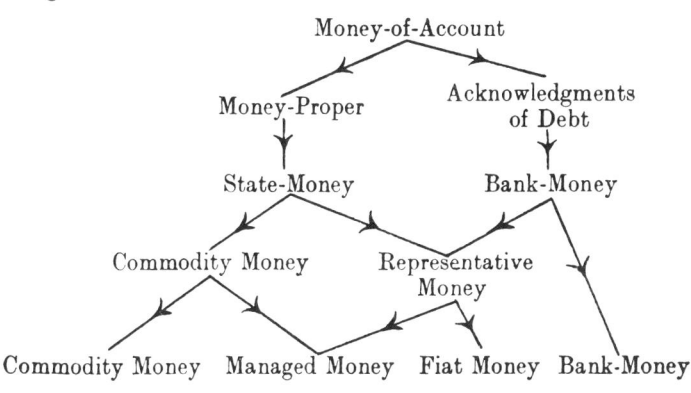

```
                    Money-of-Account
                   ╱              ╲
           Money-Proper      Acknowledgments
               ↓                of Debt
                                   ↓
           State-Money          Bank-Money
           ╱        ╲           ╱
   Commodity Money   Representative
                         Money
       ╱      ╲         ╱      ╲
Commodity  Managed   Fiat    Bank-Money
  Money     Money    Money
```

Thus we are left with four kinds of instruments of exchange, of which three are Money-Proper and the fourth is not Money-Proper but an acknowledgment of debt.

(v.) CURRENT MONEY

One of the fundamental elements in the Theory of Money is the total quantity of Money of all kinds in the hands of the public; and it often makes but little difference whether the money in question is State-Money or Bank-Money. The aggregate of both may be called *Current Money*. The relationship between Current Money and State-Money is as follows.

The typical modern Banking System consists of a Sun, namely the Central Bank, and Planets, which, following American usage, it is convenient to call the Member Banks. The total stock of State-Money is held partly by the Public, partly by the Member Banks, and partly by the Central Bank. The State-Money held by the Central Bank constitutes its

" reserve " against its deposits. These deposits we may term *Central Bank-Money*. It is convenient to assume that all the Central Bank-Money is held by the Member Banks—in so far as it may be held by the public, it may be on the same footing as State-Money or as Member Bank-Money, according to circumstances. This Central Bank-Money *plus* the State-Money held by the Member Banks makes up the Reserves of the Member Banks, which they, in turn, hold against their Deposits. These Deposits constitute the *Member Bank-Money* in the hands of the Public, and make up, together with the State-Money (and Central Bank-Money, if any) held by the Public, the aggregate of *Current Money*.

We can, therefore, continue our genealogical tree so as to exhibit the relationships thus :

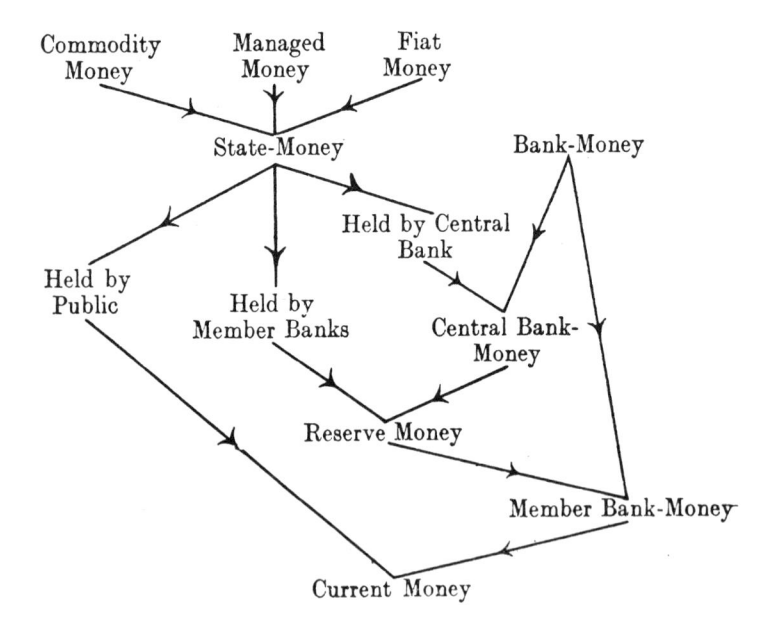

```
Commodity      Managed       Fiat
 Money          Money        Money
     \            |           /
      \           v          /
       →     State-Money    ←
                  |            Bank-Money
                  v                |
              Held by Central      |
                 Bank              |
      /           |                |
Held by           v                v
Public       Held by         Central Bank-
             Member Banks       Money
      \           |                |
       \          v                |
            Reserve Money          |
                  |                |
                  v                v
                  Member Bank-Money
                         |
                         v
                   Current Money
```

THE CLASSIFICATION OF MONEY

Finally in Chapter 3 we shall further analyse Current Money as follows :

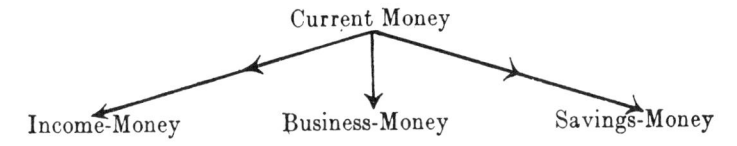

```
              Current Money
        ↙          ↓         ↘
Income-Money  Business-Money  Savings-Money
```

(vi.) ILLUSTRATIONS FROM HISTORY

Some historical examples will serve to illustrate the argument. The beginning of Money-Proper is often associated by historians with the first coinage, in regard to which the statement of Herodotus that it began in Lydia in the sixth or seventh century B.C. may still be credited. But I do not think that the act of coinage effected so significant a change as is commonly attributed to it. It was, perhaps, the first step towards Representative Money, or at any rate a step which made easier the subsequent transitions to Representative Money and to Fiat Money. But it is probable that the fundamental transition, namely the transition to Chartalist or State Money, long preceded it ; just as the next important step, namely to Representative Money, was long subsequent.

For Chartalism begins when the State *designates* the objective standard which shall correspond to the money-of-account. Representative Money begins when money is no longer composed of its objective standard. Fiat Money only appears when the State goes a step further and abandons the objective standard. Coined Money, which the State alone can mint and which may have a value superior to that of the commodity of which it is composed, is at the most a first step in the direction of Representative Money. Thus Coinage is not one of the three vital innovations in the evolution of Money, and truly Representative Money was not in fact issued until many centuries after the first coinage. On the other hand, it is by no means essential to Chartalism, that is to say the designation of the standard by the State, that the State should mint the standard; the essential characteristics of Chartalism are already present, even when money passes by weight and not by tale, provided that it is the State which designates the commodity and the standard of weight.

When the Kings of Lydia first struck coins, it may have been as a convenient certificate of fineness and weight, or a mere act of ostentation appropriate to the offspring of Crœsus and the neighbours of Midas. The stamping of pieces of metal with a trade-mark was just a piece of local vanity, patriotism or advertisement, with no far-reaching importance. It is a practice which has never caught on in some important commercial areas. Egypt never coined money before the Ptolemies, and China (broadly speaking) has never coined silver, which is its standard of value, until the most recent times. The Carthaginians were reluctant coiners, and perhaps never coined except for foreign activities. The Semitic races, whose instincts are keenest for the essential qualities of Money, have never paid much attention to the deceptive signatures of Mints, which content the financial amateurs of the North, and have cared only for the touch and weight of the metal. It was not necessary, therefore, that talents or shekels should be minted; it was sufficient that these units should be State-created in the sense that it was the State which defined (with the right to vary its definition from time to time) *what* weight and fineness of silver would, in the eyes of the law, satisfy a debt or a customary payment expressed in talents or in shekels of silver.

The first State reform of the standard of weight, of which we have definite record, was the Babylonian reform towards the end of the third millennium B.C.

But this was not the beginning. Earlier standards existed. And in the primitive age, before man had attained to the conception of weight or to the technical contrivance of the scales, when he had to depend for measurement upon *counting* barley-corns or carats or cowries, it may still have been the State or the Community which determined what kind or quality of unit should be a due discharge of an obligation to pay which had been expressed by the numerals one or two or ten—as when, so late as the thirteenth century, the English Government defined a penny sterling to be the weight of " 32 wheat corns in the midst of the ear ". A District Commissioner in Uganda to-day, where goats are the customary native standard, tells me that it is a part of his official duties to decide, in cases of dispute, whether a given goat is or is not too old or too scraggy to constitute a standard goat for the purposes of discharging a debt.

Money, like certain other essential elements in civilisation, is a far more ancient institution than we were taught to believe some few years ago. Its origins are lost in the mists when the ice was melting, and may well stretch back into the paradisaic intervals in human history of the interglacial periods, when the weather was delightful and the mind free to be fertile of new ideas—in the Islands of the Hesperides or Atlantis or some Eden of Central Asia.

The Solonic Reform of the Athenian currency in the sixth century B.C. was an exercise of the chartalist prerogative which was contemporary with, but in no way dependent upon, the existence of coined money. It was just a change of standard. Nor am I aware of any chartalist change of standard, expressly designed to benefit the State at the expense of the public, earlier than the second Punic War—Rome being the first original to add this instrument to the armoury of statecraft. From that time on chartalist changes of standard, generally in the form of debasements, sometimes for one purpose and sometimes for another, are the familiar theme of historians.

Nevertheless these changes of standard do not, so far as affects the *form* of Money, carry us beyond the stage of Commodity Money. The *debasement* of the standard, *i.e.* a change of standard which abruptly diminishes the value of the money-of-account, does not, in itself, carry us a single step towards Representative Money. Commodity Money does not cease to be such merely because the unit of commodity is changed in kind or diminished in quantity. There is no evidence, until long subsequently, of money which was, in any significant degree, representative or token. A coin might have a value somewhat superior to that of its metal content, because of the convenience and prestige of the coin, or because the stamp was a guarantee of fineness and acceptability, or merely because of its æsthetic qualities—as the dollar of Maria Theresa has, in modern times, commended itself to the nomadic Arabs of Africa. A seigniorage, too, might be charged for the service of mintage. There were token coins for very small denominations of currency. And clipt or worn money might circulate amongst the vulgar at its face value. But the characteristics of these examples are not enough to constitute Representative Money in the proper sense of the term. The true link between Commodity Money and Representative Money is to be found, perhaps, in Commodity Money, the supply of which is limited by absolute scarcity rather than by cost of production, and the demand for which is wholly dependent upon the fact that it has been selected by law or convention as the material of money and not upon its intrinsic value in other uses—as, for example, in the case of the primitive stone moneys of Polynesia.

Leaving on one side the paper moneys, which are

alleged to have been anciently current in China, and also those of John Law and other precursors, the historical importance of Representative Money dates from so recent an epoch as that of the French Revolution, the exigent consequences of which led to the adoption not merely of Representative Money but of Fiat Money for many years in what were then the leading financial centres of the world, France and England.

Nevertheless, whilst Representative Money is a relatively modern device, it was, as we have seen, adapted and taken over by the State from a far more ancient contrivance of private finance—namely Bank-Money. The earliest beginnings of Bank-Money, like those of Chartalist Money, are lost in antiquity. Perhaps Bank-Money, especially in the shape of Bills of Exchange and letters of credit for travellers abroad, may have existed almost as long as Money-Proper. For the use of Bank-Money depends on nothing except the discovery that, in many cases, the transference of the debts themselves is just as serviceable for the settlement of transactions as is the transference of the money in terms of which they are expressed. A title to a debt is a title to money at one remove, and, to the extent and within the field that confidence is felt in the prompt convertibility of the debt into the money, the element of remoteness is irrelevant to the serviceability of Bank-Money for settling transactions. Bank-Money in the shape of Bills of Exchange was not less useful and necessary in the ancient world than to-day for the purpose of settling transactions at a distance, owing to the cheapness of its cost of transmission as compared with the costs and risks of transporting Money-Proper.

(vii.) THE EVOLUTION OF MANAGED MONEY

That species of Representative Money which I have called Managed Money is, as the diagram shows, the most mixed form of all and, alone of the four forms, has relationships to each of the other three. It has come into existence by easy stages, and many existing monetary systems are still composite in character, made up partly of Managed Money and partly of Commodity Money.

The first important attempt to lay down scientific principles for the management of a managed money, so as to make it conform to its standard (whatever that standard may be), arose out of the controversy which culminated in the British Bank Charter Act of 1844. In the eighteenth century Commodity Money was still the rule; but the evolution of Bank-Money in the shape of Bank Notes was showing the way towards Representative Money.[1] The consequences of the French Revolution swung the currencies of France and England right over into Fiat Money; and when in England this stage was brought to an end by the introduction of the Gold Standard, the uses of Representative Money had become so familiar and acceptable to the public, and so profitable to the Treasury and the Bank of England, that the new system was not a pure Commodity Money but a mixed Managed System. If Ricardo had had his way with his Ingot Proposals, Commodity Money would never have been restored, and a pure Managed Money would have come into force in England in 1819.

But whilst a Managed Money came into force as from that date, the principles and methods of currency management were but ill understood by those responsible for its management, namely, the Governors and Court of the Bank of England—indeed it may be said that they were not understood at all. Twenty-five years of trouble and threatened collapse of the standard ensued, until the reformers of that day brought in a

[1] By the middle of the eighteenth century the circulation of Bank Notes was already predominant in Scotland, the glittering economies of *not* holding metal being as characteristically attractive to North Britain as the glittering certainties of holding it to Nearer Asia.

new era of management methods with the Act of 1844. This Act was compounded of one sound principle and one serious confusion. The sound principle consisted in the stress laid on the limitation of the quantity of the representative money as a means of ensuring the maintenance of the standard. The confusion lay in the futile attempt to ignore the existence of Bank-Money and consequently the inter-relationships of Money and Bank-Credit, and to make Representative Money behave exactly as though it were Commodity Money. Indeed the confusion was so serious that it would probably have led to an actual breakdown if it had not been for a second sound principle which, whilst not actually embodied in the Act, swam into the consciousness of the best practical financiers at about the same date, namely the principle of Bank-rate. The efficacy of Bank-rate for the management of a managed money was a great discovery and also a most novel one—a few years earlier the Bank of England had not had the slightest understanding of any connection between bank-rate policy and the maintenance of the standard.

The gradual evolution of bank-rate policy under conditions, in London, peculiarly well adapted to it, coupled with a prodigious growth of Bank-Money, characterised British monetary developments for the next seventy years. But, whilst the practical efficacy of bank-rate became not merely familiar but an article of faith and dogma, its precise *modus operandi* and the varying results to be expected from its application in varying conditions were not clearly understood —and have not been clearly understood, in my opinion, down to this day.

Meanwhile other variants of Managed Money were coming into vogue, particularly those which have been discussed under the generic name of Exchange Standards, of which the Indian Rupee has been the classic instance—the Indian Rupee being the subject of the leading theoretical discussions of this method of management and also of its actual operation on the largest scale. Some years ago (in my *Indian Currency and Finance*, 1913) I wrote at length on the subject of Exchange Standards. But a brief digression may be in place here, bringing up to date my views as to how this type of standard is most conveniently classified.

There is, I think, an ambiguity in some discussions of this topic between *Exchange Standards* and what it would be more correct to call *Exchange Management*. I define an *Exchange Standard* as a Managed Representative Money the objective standard of which is the legal-tender money of some other country. The controversy as to whether the Indian Rupee should be fixed in terms of sterling or in terms of gold was a controversy as to whether or not the rupee should be an Exchange Standard. One of the transitional standards in the process of stabilising the German mark was an Exchange Standard, whereas the mark as finally established is on a Gold Standard. On the other hand, where the objective standard is not a foreign money but (*e.g.*) gold, but where, nevertheless, the method of managing the Money in question so as to conform to this standard consists, wholly or mainly, in maintaining reserves at foreign centres and in buying or selling foreign exchange at stated rates rather than in buying or selling gold on the spot at stated rates, this I should designate as *Exchange Management*. The objective standard at which Exchange Management aims may be an Exchange Standard; but not necessarily so. The characteristic of Exchange Management Moneys is to be found not in their Standard but in their Form.

For countries which are small compared with their neighbours, or do not contain independent financial centres of international importance, an

Exchange Standard may be ideal. But it does undoubtedly involve some measure of dependence on the country whose money is chosen as the basis of the Exchange Standard, which may be hurtful to the national pride. Exchange Management, on the other hand, whilst partly free from this objection, possesses great technical advantages arising from economy in the transport of bullion and from the avoidance of loss of interest. Many countries, as for example Japan, have employed it for many years with great advantage, keeping reserves at more than one foreign centre and varying the proportions at each centre in accordance with circumstances. Germany appears to fluctuate in her attitude towards Exchange Management, with some signs of bias against it on the part of the Reichsbank authorities. The prejudice shown against Exchange Management by some sections of Indian opinion has been partly due, I think, to a confusion between Exchange Management and an Exchange Standard, the element of dependence which is more characteristic of the latter being erroneously attributed to the former in an equal degree.

Sterling during the war, or rather from 1915 to 1919, was an example of Exchange Management. From January 13, 1916, to March 19, 1919, sterling was maintained at about the value of $4·76½ in terms of U.S. dollars, by Messrs. J. P. Morgan and Co., acting as agents of the British Treasury, standing ready in the New York foreign exchange market to buy any quantity of sterling offered at this rate, or, alternatively, to buy dollars for sterling at 4·77.[1]

Exchange Management has been frequently adopted in the case of Fiat Moneys which have no fixed ob-

[1] Exchange management began in August 1915, but the exchange was not "pegged" until January 13, 1916, from which date the rate was kept steady between 4·76½ and 4·77. After May 1916 the fluctuation was kept between 4·76$\frac{7}{16}$ and 4·76$\frac{9}{16}$.

jective standard. The cases of "official support" and of "pegging" of rates of exchange, variable from time to time, during the post-war period of European currency collapse are well-known examples of this.

Finally, just before the war, there came into being the greatest managed system which the world has yet seen—the Federal Reserve System of the United States, a system which was mainly borrowed at its inception from the British system but has since been developing along new and original lines of its own—though what, precisely, these are to be is still a matter of some doubt and controversy.

As regards the British System, in the form in which it has emerged, by virtue of the Currency Act of 1925, out of several years of Fiat Money, it is still too soon to speak. One definite change, however, is embodied in the Act—the British currency is no longer a composite system. Pre-war commodity money, in the shape of the sovereign, has not been restored; Ricardo's proposal of a hundred years previously has been adopted; and sterling is established by law as a pure Managed Money.

The controversy which preceded the restoration of the Gold Standard in Great Britain was believed by many people to concern the question whether sterling should be henceforward a Managed Money or an "automatic" money. But this was a misapprehension. Unless "automatic" money means a money rigidly linked in quantity to the supply of "commodity" money, it means nothing; and of this there was no likelihood or possibility. The misapprehension occurred because the public knew no third alternative between the Fiat Money of the post-war period and the Commodity Money of the pre-modern age. Nevertheless it was precisely this third form which was certain to be adopted, whatever decisions might be made on other matters—

namely a Representative Money managed so as to conform to an objective standard.

The real subjects of the controversy were two. First, was it expedient to change the standard of sterling at such a time or in such a way that the transition would involve a significant alteration in the level of money-incomes? Should not any change of standard be so made that the purchasing power of the new standard is, at the moment of transition, both equal to the purchasing power of the existing money-of-account and in equilibrium with money-incomes, with the result that the change of standard, in itself and at the moment, does not involve any alteration, up or down, in the current level of money-values? The opposition, more impressed than the official party with the objections to a deliberate lowering of money-values, maintained that it was inexpedient to alter the standard in conditions which would necessitate such a lowering. But the official party attached great importance to the *precise number* of Troy ounces of gold which was to answer to the money-of-account. They were willing neither to adapt the number of ounces to the existing purchasing power of the money-of-account nor to wait until the purchasing power of the money-of-account was adapted to the desired number of ounces, but preferred, for a variety of reasons, to run the risks which must attend any forced or sudden disequilibrium in the existing levels of incomes and prices.

This bone of contention was quite distinct from the further subject of controversy concerning the choice of the Standard itself, namely whether or not gold was the most suitable objective standard. Those who came to be known as the Monetary Reformers were not less anxious than others to bring to an end the period of Fiat Money; indeed they laid *more* stress than their opponents on the importance of a stable objective standard. But they argued that gold possesses now, even less than formerly, the qualities of a satisfactory objective standard, and they proposed to substitute for it some composite representative commodity on the general lines of the so-called Tabular Standard which has been long familiar in economic writings.

CHAPTER 2

BANK-MONEY

(i.) The "Creation" of Bank-Money

We have seen in the preceding chapter how the transference of claims to money may be just as serviceable for the settlement of transactions as the transference of money itself. It follows that members of the public, when they have assured themselves that this is so, will often be content with the ownership of transferable claims without seeking to turn them into cash. Moreover there are many conveniences and incidental advantages in handling bank-money over handling cash.

A modern bank is an institution which is made possible by the establishment of habits of this kind. Historically a bank may have been evolved from a business which dealt in the precious metals or in the remittance of money from one country to another, or which offered its services as an intermediary to arrange loans or for the safe custody of valuables, or which borrowed the savings of the public on the security of its reputation and then invested them at its own discretion and at its own risk.[1] But we shall be concerned in what follows with banks of the fully developed modern type existing as going concerns.

Such a bank creates claims against itself for the

[1] For the actual origins in England see R. D. Richards, "The Pioneers of Banking in England" (*Economic Journal History Supplement*, Jan. 1929).

delivery of money, *i.e.* what, hereafter, we shall call Deposits, in two ways. In the first place it creates them in favour of individual depositors against value received in the shape either of cash or of an order (*i.e.* a cheque) authorising the transfer of a deposit in some bank (either another bank or itself). A member of the public comes along with cash in his pocket or with a cheque drawn on a bank, which he hands in on the understanding that he is entitled in return to a claim to cash (*i.e.* a deposit) which he can either exercise or transfer to someone else.

But there is a second way in which a bank may create a claim against itself. It may itself purchase assets, *i.e.* add to its investments, and pay for them, in the first instance at least, by establishing a claim against itself. Or the bank may create a claim against itself in favour of a borrower, in return for his promise of subsequent reimbursement ; *i.e.* it may make loans or advances.[1]

In *both* cases the bank creates the deposit ; for only the bank itself can authorise the creation of a deposit in its books entitling the customer to draw cash or to transfer his claim to the order of someone else ; and there is no difference between the two except in the nature of the inducement offered to the bank to create the deposit.

It follows that a bank in active business will be, on the one hand, continually creating deposits either for value received or against promises, and, on the other hand, cancelling deposits, because claims against it are being exercised in cash or transferred to other banks. Thus it is constantly receiving cash and paying out cash ; and it is constantly receiving claims *against* other banks and having to meet claims *from* other banks.

Now it is evident that the bank must so conduct its business that these opposite processes can be

---

[1] An analogous distinction has been made by Prof. C. A. Phillips (*Bank Credit*, p. 40) between what he terms " primary " and " derivative " deposits.

approximately offset against one another, *i.e.* so that the amount of cash paid out day by day together with the amount of the claims from other banks are not very different from the amount of cash received together with the amount of the claims against other banks. The practical problem of the banker consists, therefore, in so managing his affairs that his daily accruing assets in the shape of cash and claims shall be as nearly as possible equal to his daily accruing liabilities in these forms.

It follows that the rate at which the bank can, with safety, *actively* create deposits by lending and investing has to be in a proper relation to the rate at which it is *passively* creating them against the receipt of liquid resources from its depositors. For the latter increase the bank's reserves even if only a part of them is ultimately retained by the bank, whereas the former diminish the reserves even if only a part of them is paid away to the customers of other banks; indeed we might express our conclusion more strongly than this, since the borrowing customers generally borrow with the intention of paying away at once the deposits thus created in their favour, whereas the depositing customers often have no such intention.

Practical bankers, like Dr. Walter Leaf, have drawn from this the conclusion that for the banking system as a whole the initiative lies with the depositors, and that the banks can lend no more than their depositors have previously entrusted to them. But economists cannot accept this as being the common-sense which it pretends to be. I will, therefore, endeavour to make obvious a matter which need not, surely, be obscure.[1]

Even if we look at the matter from the standpoint of one bank amongst many, it is apparent that the

[1] See F. W. Crick, "The Genesis of Bank Deposits", *Economica*, June 1927, for a good attempt to make the point clear. See also for an able, but somewhat prolix, discussion of the topic of this chapter, Prof. C. A. Phillips' *Bank Credit*.

rate at which a bank passively creates deposits partly depends on the rate at which it is actively creating them. For although the borrowing customers will probably pay away promptly the proceeds of their loans, some of those to whom they pay them may be depositor-customers of the same bank. To the extent that this occurs, so far from the actively-created deposits being the offspring of the passively-created deposits, it is the other way round. This illustrates in little what is happening to the banking system as a whole. For to the extent that the borrowing customers pay away their deposits to customers of other banks, these other banks find themselves strengthened by the growth of their passively-created deposits to the same extent that the first bank has been weakened; and in the same way our own bank finds itself strengthened whenever the other banks are actively creating deposits. So that a part of its passively-created deposits, even when they are not the offspring of its own actively-created deposits, is nevertheless the offspring of the actively-created deposits of the other banks.

If we suppose a closed banking system, which has no relations with the outside world, in a country where all payments are made by cheque and no cash is used, and if we assume further that the banks do not find it necessary in such circumstances to hold any cash reserves but settle inter-bank indebtedness by the transfer of other assets, it is evident that there is no limit to the amount of bank-money which the banks can safely create *provided that they move forward in step*. The words italicised are the clue to the behaviour of the system. Every movement forward by an individual bank weakens it, but every such movement by one of its neighbour banks strengthens it; so that if all move forward together, no one is weakened on balance. Thus the behaviour of each bank, though it cannot afford to move more than a step in advance of the others, will be governed by the average behaviour of the banks as a whole—to which average, however, it is able to contribute its quota small or large. Each Bank Chairman sitting in his parlour may regard himself as the passive instrument of outside forces over which he has no control; yet the " outside forces " may be nothing but himself and his fellow-chairmen, and certainly not his depositors.

A monetary system of this kind would possess an inherent instability; for any event which tended to influence the behaviour of the majority of the banks in the same direction whether backwards or forwards, would meet with no resistance and would be capable of setting up a violent movement of the whole system. We shall see that actual monetary systems are not generally as bad as this and that checks on their inherent instability have been devised. Nevertheless this tendency towards sympathetic movement on the part of the individual elements within a banking system is always present to a certain extent and has to be reckoned with. Moreover, where the conditions for a " closed " system are satisfied, as in the case of a country having an inconvertible paper currency or in the case of the world as a whole, the tendency to instability by reason of sympathetic movement is a characteristic of the utmost practical importance.

In the hypothetical case just considered, we have assumed that all payments are made by cheque and that the member banks are under no obligation or necessity to maintain cash reserves. These limitations we must now remove. If some payments are made by cash, the amount of cash so used will generally bear some proportion, more or less stable, to the amount of bank-money. In this case the creation of more bank-money by the banks as a whole will lead to a drain of cash out of the banks as a whole, which will set a limit to the extent that the banks can afford to create bank-money unless they are in a position to obtain command of an increased quantity of cash.

But any given banker will not only require cash to meet such a contingency. Even when he is moving in step with his neighbours, there will be day-to-day differences between his claims on them and their claims on him, and the magnitude of these daily differences will partly depend on the scale of his business, which may be roughly measured by the volume of his deposits. Accordingly, in order to deal with the inevitable minor discrepancies which are bound to occur over short periods, a banker will always maintain some liquid resources in hand, partly in the form of cash and partly in the form of deposits with some other bank or banks—which resources, called his "reserves", rise and fall with the volume of his deposits and sometimes, by law or custom, are in a rigid ratio to them. To deal with inter-bank claims, the banks have set up an office called the Clearing House, which calculates each day how much is due on balance to (or from) any bank from (or to) other banks. For the purpose of settling the eventual differences cash could, if necessary, be used; but as a matter of convenience the banks generally accept for the purpose of day-to-day settlements a claim on a single selected bank—the Banker's Bank as it is sometimes called—which is usually the Central or State Bank. Moreover a Central Bank deposit is not only available to meet Clearing House differences, but can also be encashed when the cash portion of a bank's reserves need replenishment.

A bank must, therefore, first of all decide what amount of reserves it will be prudent to aim at—or, sometimes, it has this matter decided for it by law. The figure, which we shall discuss in detail in Volume ii., will depend partly on the habits of the depositors, as governed by the practices of the country and of the period and by the class of business conducted by the particular bank's clients, and partly on the scale of the bank's business which for this purpose is generally measured by the amount of its deposits. Thus each bank fixes in its own mind on a certain proportion of its deposits (*e.g.* 10 per cent) which it will aim at keeping in reserve—a proportion which is not necessarily the same for different banks and which a given bank may vary at different seasons or from time to time, unless the law forces uniformity on them. Having fixed on this proportion, the bank will then be as unwilling to see its reserves rise above it, since this generally means that it is doing less profitable business than it might, as to see them fall below it. Consequently it will be actively creating deposits by lending and investing on a smaller or on a larger scale, according as its reserves, apart from day-to-day fluctuations, are showing a tendency to diminish or to increase.

We now perceive that there exists, not only the check on individual banks that they must keep step, but also a check on the banks as a whole. For if the banks as a whole are creating deposits at a rate which will cause the reserves as a whole to fall too low, some bankers will find their reserve-ratios deficient and will, therefore, be compelled to take a step backwards; whilst if the aggregate deposits are below their normal ratio to reserves, some banks will find their reserve-ratios excessive and will be stimulated to take a step forwards. Thus it is the aggregate of the reserve-resources which determines the "pace" which is common to the banking system as a whole.

To pursue the argument to the further point of discovering what determines the aggregate of the reserve-resources of the member banks would be to anticipate subsequent chapters. But the elements of the problem may as well be stated here.

Assuming that the Central Bank is also the note-issuing authority, the aggregate reserve-resources of the member banks will be under the control of the Central Bank, provided the latter can control the aggregate of its note-issue and its deposits. In this case the Central Bank is the conductor of the orchestra and sets the tempo. It may be, however, that the amount of deposits created by the Central Bank itself is placed by law or custom outside its deliberate control, being regulated by some rigid rule, in which case we might describe it as an " automatic " system. Finally, it may be that the Member Banks themselves have some power, perhaps within limits, of increasing at will their deposits with the Central Bank or the amount of the notes which they draw out of its note-issuing departments. In this case, sympathetic movements on the part of the Member Banks will gather strength as they go and provide their own food in the shape of increased reserve-resources, with the result that it will be difficult to restrain the inherent instability of the system.

I have endeavoured to say enough to show that the familiar controversy as to how and by whom bank-deposits are " created " is a somewhat unreal one. There can be no doubt that, in the most convenient use of language, all deposits are " created " by the bank holding them. It is certainly not the case that the banks are limited to that kind of deposit, for the creation of which it is necessary that depositors should come on their own initiative bringing cash or cheques. But it is equally clear that the rate at which an individual bank creates deposits on its own initiative is subject to certain rules and limitations; —it must keep step with the other banks and cannot raise its own deposits relatively to the total deposits out of proportion to its quota of the banking business of the country. Finally, the " pace " common to all the Member Banks is governed by the aggregate of their reserve-resources.

(ii.) Current Money is Predominantly Bank-Money

The proportionate importance of State-Money and of Member Bank-Money, created as above, in making up the aggregate of Current Money varies widely at different periods and in different countries, according to the stage which has been reached in the evolution of monetary practice. But the tendency is towards a preponderant importance for Bank-Money—which in such countries as Great Britain and the United States constitutes perhaps nine-tenths of the aggregate of Current Money—and towards State-Money occupying a definitely subsidiary position.

It will, therefore, simplify the argument, without seriously detracting from its generality, if we assume not only that all the Central Bank-Money is held by the Member Banks, but also that *all the Current Money in the hands of the public is Member Bank-Money, i.e. Bank Deposits*. This simplified version does not, of course, represent the actual facts. But it will save many unnecessary words and is easily adapted to the actual facts. Moreover, the consequences of such an assumption will be nearly identical with the actual facts, in so far as the *proportions*, in which the total stock of State-Money is held by the Public, the Member Banks and the Central Bank, tend to be constant. When the actual facts differ from this simplified scheme in a relevant way, I will do my best to bring them back again into the picture.

In the case of the United States fairly exact estimates are available as to the proportion of demand-deposits, or, as I shall call them, cash-deposits, to notes and coin circulating outside the banks and in the hands of the public, as follows :

[Table

UNITED STATES [1]

	Cash-deposits.	Money.	Percentage of Money to Total.
	$1,000,000	$1,000,000	
1919	18,990	3,825	17
1920	21,080	4,209	17
1921	19,630	3,840	16
1922	20,470	3,583	15
1923	22,110	3,836	15
1924	23,530	3,862	14
1925	25,980	3,810	13
1926	25,570	3,777	13

Thus, even during the eight years following the war, the proportion of actual cash to the total of cash and cash-deposits in the United States fell from about one-sixth to as little as one-eighth. Since, as we shall see subsequently, cash-deposits are turned over much faster than cash, the preponderance of the former in terms of the volume of payments effected would be even greater. If we include time-deposits we find that State-Money held by the Public is less than 10 per cent of Current Money.

In the case of Great Britain we are thrown back on more precarious guesses. But I estimate that in 1926-28 cash-deposits (*i.e.* excluding fixed deposits) in Great Britain may have been £1,075,000,000 and notes circulating in the hands of the public £250,000,000, in which case the latter were 19 per cent of the total or, say, one-fifth. Including fixed deposits, we find that, as in the United States, State-Money held by the Public is about 10 per cent of Current Money.

Thus in Great Britain and the United States—and also increasingly elsewhere—the use of Bank-Money is now so dominant that much less confusion will be

[1] The figures for cash-deposits are taken from Mitchell, *Business Cycles*, p. 126, and those for money in circulation outside the banks from *The Review of Economic Statistics*, July 1927, p. 136.

caused by treating this as typical and the use of other kinds of currency as secondary, than by treating State-Money as typical and bringing in Bank-Money as a subsequent complication. The latter practice, which has outstayed the facts, leads to insufficient emphasis being placed on some of the most typical features of modern money, and to its essential characteristics being treated as anomalous or exceptional.

CHAPTER 3

THE ANALYSIS OF BANK-MONEY

(i.) Income-Deposits, Business-Deposits, and Savings-Deposits

LET us now consider Bank-Money (or any other kind of money) from the standpoint of the depositor (or holder of it). A man holds a stock of money, whether in the form of Bank-Deposits or in any other form, for one or other of three reasons.

He may hold it to cover the interval between the dates when he receives his personal income and the dates when he spends it. If his receipt of income and his expenditure against it were nearly simultaneous, the average amount which he would need to hold for this purpose would be inappreciable. If everyone received all his income on Quarter-Days and paid his bills the same day, all cheques being drawn at the same moment in anticipation that the cheques paid in would be cleared just in time to meet the cheques paid out, the bank-deposits required to finance the normal circle of exchange between earnings and consumption would be next door to nothing; whilst if bills were paid, not simultaneously, but within a few days, the aggregate bank deposits of private individuals, whilst standing at a high figure for a few days, would be very low on the average of the quarter. The money balances of the working classes approximate, indeed, to this situation, in so far as they receive their

THE ANALYSIS OF BANK-MONEY

wages on Saturday and pay them away again the same day or shortly afterwards. But, whether long or short, some interval there generally is between an individual's receipts and his expenditure. Moreover, he cannot always foresee the precise date of either. He must, therefore, hold a stock of money, or a ready command over it in the form of a bank-deposit, both to bridge the intervals of time between receipts and expenditure and to provide against contingencies. Deposits of this kind, replenished by individuals out of their personal incomes and employed by them to meet their personal expenditure and their personal savings, we shall call *Income-deposits*. Cash in the hands of workers and others, who have no bank accounts, are, of course, to be included in the same category.

In the same way a business man, a manufacturer or a speculator, is unable, in general, to arrange his receipts and his outgoings so as to be simultaneous. Sometimes by " clearings ", " settlements ", etc., outside the monetary system—as, for example, the Stock Exchange Fortnightly Settlements—he is able to offset, in part at least, the one against another. But, in general, the match is not perfect, and a proportion of business transactions, varying according to the nature of the business, will lead to the payee finding himself in the possession of temporary balances of cash or bank-deposits. Further, as in the case of personal expenditure, so also in the case of business expenditure, the precise date at which obligations will fall due cannot always be foreseen, so that it is convenient to keep a margin against contingencies. Such deposits as these, held for business purposes, we shall call *Business-deposits*.

The *Income-deposits* and the *Business-deposits* together make up what we shall call the *Cash-deposits*.[1]

---

[1] It is interesting to record that a distinction closely analogous to the above was made by Adam Smith (*Wealth of Nations*, Bk. II. chap. ii.) : " The circulation of every country may be considered as divided into two

But a bank-deposit may also be held, not for the purpose of making payments, but as a means of employing savings, *i.e.*, as an investment. The holder may be attracted by the rate of interest which his banker allows him ; or he may anticipate that other investments are likely to depreciate in money value ; or he may attach importance to the stability of the money-value of his savings and to being able to turn them into cash at short notice ; or he may find this the most convenient way of holding small increments of savings with the intention of transforming them into a specific investment when they have accumulated to a sufficient sum ; or he may be awaiting an opportunity of employing them in his own business ; or other such reasons may influence him. We shall call deposits of this type *Savings-deposits*. It is the criterion of a savings-deposit that it is not required for the purpose of current payments and could, without inconvenience, be dispensed with if, for any reason, some other form of investment were to seem to the depositor to be preferable.

(ii.) Demand-Deposits and Time-Deposits

A Cash-deposit roughly corresponds to what Americans call demand-deposits and we call current-accounts ; and a Savings-deposit to what Americans call time-deposits and we call deposit-accounts. A Savings-deposit also corresponds to what used to be called in theories of Money, which were stated with primary reference to a Commodity Money, the use of money as a " Store of Value ". But the correspond-

---

different branches ; the circulation of the dealers with one another, and the circulation between the dealers and the consumers. Though the same pieces of money, whether paper or metal, may be employed sometimes in the one circulation and sometimes in the other, yet as both are constantly going on at the same time, each requires a certain stock of money of one kind or another, to carry it on."

ence is not exact. In Great Britain the old-fashioned distinction between deposit-accounts and current-accounts, namely that the former earn interest but the latter do not, is fast becoming blurred; for, increasingly, banks allow interest on the average of a customer's current-account in excess of an agreed minimum — with the result that deposit-accounts and current-accounts are tending to correspond to differences of banking custom between different parts of the country and different classes of customers, rather than to the payment or non-payment of interest.[1]

There are also—this again is, in Great Britain, a very common practice — current-accounts which are held, not because they are necessary as cash for the convenient transaction of current business, but as a means of remunerating the banker for his services. Sometimes a customer may remunerate his bank by a commission, which is calculated by reference to the turnover of his account and the trouble he has given in other ways; but very often the remuneration will take the form of an agreement by the customer to maintain a minimum balance on which he will receive no interest. Since the balances, held in virtue of such understandings, are usually allowed to fall below the agreed minimum on payment of interest on the difference, it is difficult to decide whether to regard them as savings-deposits or as cash-deposits. In whichever way they are regarded, however, they constitute a

[1] Broadly speaking, in London the sharpness of the old distinction between current-accounts and deposit-accounts is, as a rule, preserved. In the provinces, however, there is no uniformity of practice, and the competition between the banks leads to a variety of arrangements. One of the commonest is for the bank to allow a rate of interest, somewhat (say ½ per cent) below the advertised deposit rate, on the average amount of the current-account in excess of an agreed minimum. This means that it is often not worth while to transfer what are really savings-deposits from current-account to deposit-account. Thus, short-period savings-deposits are liable to be classified amongst the current-accounts rather than the deposit-accounts. This is also true of small increments of savings-deposits, which are only transferred at intervals and in larger units to deposit-account.

form of deposit which is not easily shifted and is likely to remain fairly constant in normal circumstances.

Apart from difficulties of classification arising out of banking practices, the line between savings-deposits and cash-deposits is often not sharp even in the mind of the depositor himself—especially as regards that part which is held against unforeseen contingencies. For the holder of a substantial savings-deposit may feel himself strong enough to economise in the amount of the cash-deposit which he holds against contingencies. Thus a part of his total deposit serves both purposes, and the depositor himself might find it hard to say exactly what proportion of his total deposit he holds for the one purpose and what proportion for the other. But the broad distinction is clear, and can be expressed as follows: the amount of the savings-deposits depends upon the comparative attractions, in the mind of the depositor, of this and of alternative securities; whilst the amount of the cash-deposits depends upon the volume and the regularity of what he receives and pays by means of cheques and the length of the interval between receipts and expenditure.

There is no opportunity at present to make an accurate statistical estimate of the proportions in which these two categories make up the published aggregate of deposits. In Great Britain the banks do not even publish separate figures for deposit-accounts and current-accounts respectively. And in the United States, where the separate publication of time-deposits and demand-deposits is required by law, this distinction does not, for various reasons, correspond exactly with the distinction made above; in particular, all savings-deposits held at less than thirty days' notice reckon as demand-deposits.

There is, nevertheless, enough information, which will be given in detail in Volume ii., to enable us to make a rough guess at the relative importance of the two types of deposit. In the United States the percentage of Time Deposits to Total Deposits varies widely in different Federal Reserve Districts, being about twice as high in San Francisco as in New York, whilst the average for the whole country has been undergoing a progressive change, rising from 23 per cent in 1918 to about 40 per cent in 1928. In Great Britain it used to be said before the war that the total deposits of the banks were about equally divided between deposit-accounts and current-accounts.[1] During the war investments in government issues, under the stimulus of official propaganda, probably drained away some of the most permanent of the deposit-accounts, with the result that the proportion of deposit-accounts fell to about one-third of the total. During the last ten years, however, the proportion has been gradually returning to the pre-war proportion of about one-half. If, therefore, we allow for interest-bearing current-accounts and for " minimum balances " held to remunerate the bank, it would appear that in Great Britain the true savings-deposits may be somewhat in excess of one-half of the total; though we must on the other side allow for the fact that deposit-account rules (seven days' notice) are not always expected to be adhered to strictly.

Let the reader remember that these percentages are given merely as indications of the order of magnitude of the quantities in question. The proportions of the two types of deposit to the total deposits are by no means constant, and it is precisely this liability to variation which will give importance to the above analysis in our subsequent argument.

The foregoing classification naturally includes Notes

[1] I have also heard the pre-war proportion of deposit-accounts estimated at nearer a third than a half. Leaf (*Banking*, p. 124), writing in 1926, says that current-accounts are as a rule in excess in England, but deposit-accounts considerably in excess in Scotland and Ireland.

as well as Bank-deposits. Since Notes never carry interest, there is a greater presumption in their case than in the case of Bank-deposits that they are held as cash and not as a form of savings. There is also, in a modern economic community, a presumption that they are held as income-deposits rather than as business-deposits, transactions between business men being mainly carried on by means of cheques.

There has been, indeed, during the past hundred years a steady evolution away from the use of Notes to the use of Cheques; and the proportions of Bank-deposits, which in any country we may expect to represent Savings-deposits, Business-deposits and Income-deposits respectively, depends on the stage in this evolution which that country has reached. In the first stage Bank-deposits are mainly in the nature of investments, most payments being made by Notes. In the second stage Bank-deposits are partly used as a means of holding cash, but are generally turned into Notes when it comes to making a payment. In the third stage business transactions are mainly done by cheque, the use of Notes being limited to wage payments and petty cash. In the fourth stage wage payments also are made by cheque, and Notes are employed for little except petty cash and out-of-pocket expenditure. Most continental countries are between the second and third stage. Great Britain is in the third stage, but possibly on the eve of the fourth. The United States is between the third and the fourth stage. The significance of Notes in a monetary system and the appropriate means of regulating their volume must obviously depend (though this is not yet generally recognised) on the stage of evolution which has been reached. The statistical significance of fluctuations in the note-issue must also vary in the same way.[1]

[1] If in Great Britain we had statistics of the active note issue, this might have much value as an index of the wages bill. At present no

(iii.) DEPOSITS AND OVERDRAFTS

We have characterised *cash-deposits* as furnishing the ready command over money which is required for the convenient transaction of current payments. But the analysis is complicated, in a modern community, by the fact that a cash-deposit is not the only means of providing this facility. It is provided, equally well, by the *overdraft, i.e.* by an arrangement with the bank that an account may be in debit at any time up to an amount not exceeding an agreed figure, interest being paid not on the agreed maximum debit, but on the actual average debit. A customer of a bank may draw a cheque against his deposit, thus diminishing his *credit* with the bank; but he may, equally well, draw a cheque against his overdraft, thus increasing his *debit* with the bank.

The settlement of indebtedness by means of book-entries at banks can, indeed, be done just as effectively by transferring debits from one account to another as by transferring credits from one account to another. It is just as effective to pay by increasing the debit balance of the debtor and decreasing the debit balance of the creditor as it is by decreasing the credit balance of the former and increasing the credit balance of the latter. Thus it is not in the least essential to the efficient working of the cheque-money system that any of those who have cheque books should also have deposits. The resources of the bank might consist entirely of its own capital or they might be drawn from a class of customer, namely from those who run fixed savings-accounts with the bank, quite

---

statistics are available for the active circulation, since the Joint Stock Banks give no figures for the amount of notes held by them in their reserves, though there seems no reason why the figures should not be given. In the course of time, however, the totals of bankers' balances published by the Bank of England may, taken in conjunction with the totals of cash and balances published by the banks, allow some approximate inferences to be drawn.

distinct from the customers who run cash-accounts; in which case the cash-accounts would consist entirely of debit-accounts (*i.e.* overdrafts) and not at all of credit-accounts (*i.e.* cash-deposits).

In Great Britain in particular—I do not venture to speak with confidence as to banking practices elsewhere—there has been a growing practice of economising the amount of the cash-deposits by developing the technique of the overdraft.[1] In the case of large and well-organised firms, the tendency is for their cash-accounts to tend on the average (reckoning cash-deposits *plus* and overdrafts *minus*) towards zero, or, at any rate, a very low figure, partly by the use of the overdraft and partly by investing temporary surplus balances in bills or in loans to the money market. If the minimum balances, maintained in pursuance of an agreement for the remuneration of the bank, be subtracted, the average cash-accounts of big business (reckoned as above) bear a very small proportion to the volume of the cheques passing through the accounts. But private individuals also are making an ever-increasing use of overdraft facilities.

The reader must notice that it is not the amount of the customer's used overdraft appearing on the assets side of the bank's balance-sheet, but the amount of his *unused* overdraft, which does not (at present) appear anywhere at all in a bank's statement of its assets and liabilities, which corresponds to a cash-deposit;—so that it is the total of the cash-deposits and the unused overdraft facilities outstanding which together make up the total of *Cash Facilities*. Properly speaking, unused overdraft facilities—since they represent a liability of the bank—ought, in the same way as acceptances, to appear on both sides of the account. But at present this is not so, with the result that there exists in unused overdraft facilities a form

---

[1] The original home of the overdraft was, I think, Scotland. It has never won much favour in the United States.

of Bank-Money of growing importance, of which we have no statistical record whatever, whether as regards the absolute aggregate amount of it or as regards the fluctuations in this amount from time to time.

Thus the Cash Facilities, which are truly cash for the purposes of the Theory of the Value of Money, by no means correspond to the Bank Deposits which are published. The latter include an important proportion of something which is scarcely money at all (not much more than *e.g.* a Treasury Bill is), namely the savings-deposits; whilst, on the other hand, they take no account of something which is a Cash Facility, in the fullest sense of the term, namely unused overdraft facilities. So long as savings-deposits and unused overdraft facilities are both of them a nearly constant proportion of the total deposits, the figures of Bank Deposits as published are a sufficiently satisfactory index of the amount of Cash available. But if, as we shall see subsequently, these proportions are capable of wide fluctuations, then we may be seriously misled, as indeed many people have been misled, by treating Bank Deposits as identical with Cash.

(iv.) THE VOLUME OF DEPOSITS IN RELATION TO THE VOLUME OF TRANSACTIONS

We have seen that the Cash-deposits, whether Income-deposits or Business-deposits, are held for the purpose of making payments—in distinction from Savings-deposits which are held for a different purpose. The next question is, therefore, as to the relationship between the amount of such cash-deposits and the volume of the payments on which they are employed. We shall deal with this question statistically in Volume ii.; but it will be convenient to make some preliminary observations at once.

Let us begin with the Income-deposits. In this case the volume of payments out is easily specified.

For, obviously, it is equal to the money-income of the community, which constitute the payments in, *minus* any increase (or plus any decrease) in the amount of the income-deposits themselves.[1] Put broadly, the annual turnover of the income-deposits will equal one year's salaries *plus* one year's wages *plus* one year's rentier interest *plus* one year's business earnings; or, in other words, one year's earnings of the factors of production. Thus aggregate money-incomes will fluctuate with the money costs of current output, if we include in the latter not only everything newly created which is the subject of exchange including services, but also income from the use of fixed consumption capital (*e.g.* houses).[2]

What will be the relationship between this turnover, *i.e.* the aggregate annual money-income of the community, and the amount of the income-deposits? The latter will be some more or less stable fraction of the former. Let us call this fraction k_1, and its inverse V_1.

Generally speaking, one would expect the average value of k_1 in a given economic society to be a fairly stable quantity from year to year. But this average stability may be accompanied by considerable seasonal fluctuations, if income, though accruing steadily day by day, is not received and disbursed daily but at intervals. Where, as in the case of working-class wages, the payments of income are made weekly, k_1 will have a different value for each day of the week, falling steadily or sharply from pay-day onwards; but its weekly average will be stable. Where, as in the case of many middle-class salaries, the payments are made quarterly, k_1 will be at its maximum on quarter-days and will

[1] To avoid misunderstanding, it should be stated that the non-income transactions of private individuals, arising out of (*e.g.*) loans for building or other purposes or changes of investments are to be reckoned on the above classification as business transactions and the balances connected with such transactions as Business-deposits.

[2] For a more precise definition of income see Chapter 9 below.

show a progressive fall between one quarter-day and the next. But the most important seasonal fluctuation in the value of k_1 is likely to be found in the case of agriculturalists who receive their incomes when they sell their crops. In the case of such a country as India, for example, the seasonal fluctuations in the demand for cash in different districts due to this cause are so great as to be a matter of common observation. In a community made up of weekly wage-earners, quarterly salary-earners and agriculturalists, it is evident, therefore, that the composite value of k_1 (we include—the reader will remember—notes as well as bank-accounts under the designation income-deposits) will describe a complex curve with many peaks and depressions through the year, even though its yearly average is fairly constant.

Its average value, moreover, will depend not only on the average length of the intervals between paydays but also on the habits of the community in the matter of paying its bills *pari passu* with consumption or in arrear; *i.e.* on whether its disbursements are made at a level daily rate or whether they are concentrated in the periods immediately after pay-days. Where certain heavy payments are concentrated at particular seasons, this will be reflected in a corresponding seasonal drop in k_1—as, for example, in the case of the British income-tax which is well known to have the effect of appreciably depressing the level of the income-deposits in the spring.

Changes in such customs and habits affecting the times and seasons of receipts and disbursements—which are, however, likely to be slow—will generally have more influence on the average value of k_1 over the whole year than will fluctuations in trade or in prices. A temporary falling away in real incomes may have some effect in reducing k_1 as a result of the effort to maintain consumption at a time when such incomes are falling. A distrust of the currency, such as existed in Europe during the post-war inflation period, may also reduce k_1 far below its normal value by inducing customers to make their purchases in a hurry. But apart from such exceptional causes, k_1 is unlikely to change its value materially between one year and another.

To make a guess at what this stable average value of k_1 actually is, is made difficult by the absence (at present) of any statistics which would enable us to distinguish between the income-deposits and the business-deposits. Since the matter will be examined more carefully in Volume ii., it will be sufficient to say here that in the case of Great Britain the average value of k_1 is in all probability more than 5 per cent and less than 12 per cent of the community's annual income, and may be put provisionally at somewhere in the neighbourhood of 8 per cent.

Let us turn next to the Business-deposits. Here we are likely to find much less stability and regularity than in the case of the Income-deposits. The volume of transactions, in respect of which the business-deposits are turned over, will consist of the cheques drawn to cover all the exchanges of goods, documentary instruments and titles, etc., passed backwards and forwards between business men, and may be classified as follows :

(i.) Transactions arising out of the division of productive functions, namely :

(a) Payments from entrepreneurs to the income-deposits of the factors of production ;

(b) Transactions between those responsible for the stage of process (of extraction, manufacture, transport or distribution) just completed and those responsible for the next stage or for assembling the different components ;

(ii.) Speculative transactions in capital goods or commodities ;

(iii.) Financial transactions, *e.g.* the redemption

CH. 3   THE ANALYSIS OF BANK-MONEY   47

and renewal of Treasury Bills, or changes of investments.

Now of these (i.), like the transactions in respect of income-deposits, will be a fairly stable function of the money-value of current output; (i.*a*) indeed will be exactly equal to the receipts placed to the credit of the income-deposits, since every cheque paid in to the income-deposits will be a cheque paid out of the business-deposits and *vice versa*—except where there is a direct purchase by a consumer from a producer which is the case with some personal services. Category (i.*b*) will also fluctuate on the whole with the money-value of a year's output, though it will also change gradually with the character and technique of production, and, over short periods, according to whether entrepreneurs are or are not anticipating their requirements. Further, as we shall see subsequently, the price-level appropriate to (i.*b*) will not move precisely with the price-level appropriate to the consumption paid for out of the income-deposits, with the result that the changes in the money-value of transactions (i.*b*) may not correspond accurately to the money-value of expenditure by consumers at the same time. In the language of Chapter 15 below, business-deposits held for the purposes of transactions (i.*a*) and (i.*b*) make up, together with the income-deposits, what we shall call the *Industrial Circulation*.

Transactions in categories (ii.) and (iii.), on the other hand, need not be, and are not, governed by the volume of current output. The pace at which a circle of financiers, speculators and investors hand round one to another particular pieces of wealth, or titles to such, which they are neither producing nor consuming but merely exchanging, bears no definite relation to the rate of current production. The volume of such transactions is subject to very wide and incalculable fluctuations, easily double at one time what it is at another, depending on such factors as the state of speculative sentiment; and, whilst it is possibly stimulated by the activity and depressed by the inactivity of production, its fluctuations are quite different in degree from those of production. Moreover the price-level of the capital goods thus exchanged may vary quite differently from that of consumption goods. Business-deposits held for the purposes of transactions (ii.) and (iii.) make up, together with the savings-deposits, what in Chapter 15 we shall call the *Financial Circulation*.

Unfortunately these transactions are not only highly variable, and varying differently from transactions arising out of production and consumption; they are also large enough compared with the latter transactions to confuse the statistics. For example in Great Britain the total cheque transactions of all kinds in 1927 probably approached £64,000,000,000, to which must be added the transactions for which notes are used, making a total of more than sixteen times the annual income. Since each item of current output cannot change hands on the average so many as sixteen times, it is evident that transactions arising out of current production and consumption are swamped by business transactions of other kinds. This confusion of production and income statistics by the large and variable factor of financial transactions is a serious obstacle to reaching reliable inductive results concerning modern monetary problems.

The corresponding figures for the United States in 1926 were about 700 billion dollars for cheque transactions, which was about ten times the annual income.

It is evident from the above that the proportion, k_2, of the average level of the business-deposits to the volume of the business transactions may be quite different from k_1, the proportion of the income-deposits to the income transactions. Also it is likely both to vary differently and to be much more variable. Some

CH. 3   THE ANALYSIS OF BANK-MONEY   49

estimates as to the magnitude and variability of k_2, or rather of its inverse V_2, will be given in Volume ii.

Now, whilst k_1, in any given economic community, can reasonably be thought of as a steady fraction of the national income in terms of money, this is not the case with k_2. For both the volume and the price-level of the transactions which govern k_2 are capable of wide variations which do not correspond to variations of the national money-income. Thus it is misleading to represent the *total* cash-deposits (*i.e.* income-deposits *plus* business-deposits) as bearing any stable or normal relationship to the national money-income.

The reader will have noticed that k_1 and k_2 are the inverse of what are generally called the " velocities of circulation " of the income-deposits and of the business-deposits respectively.

We must now embark on a very long argument as to the manner in which the creation of deposits by the banking system is related to the price-level. To begin with, the Second Book of this Treatise—constituting an inevitable digression from the central theme—will be devoted to an analysis of the meaning, and to the problem of the measurement, of the Value of Money.

BOOK II

THE VALUE OF MONEY

CHAPTER 4

THE PURCHASING POWER OF MONEY

(i.) THE MEANING OF PURCHASING POWER

A MAN does not hold money for its own sake, but for its Purchasing Power—that is to say, for what it will buy. Therefore his demand is not for units of money as such, but for units of purchasing power. Since, however, there is no means of holding general purchasing power except in the form of money, his demand for purchasing power translates itself into a demand for an " equivalent " quantity of money. What is the measure of " equivalence " between units of money and units of purchasing power ?

Since the Purchasing Power of Money in a given context depends on the quantity of goods and services which a unit of money will purchase, it follows that it can be measured by the price of a *composite commodity*, made up of the various individual goods and services in proportions corresponding to their importance as objects of expenditure. Moreover, there are many types and purposes of expenditure, in which we may be interested at one time or another, corresponding to each of which there is an appropriate composite commodity. The price of a composite commodity which is representative of some type of expenditure, we shall call a *Price-level*; and the series of numbers indicative of changes in a given price-level we shall call *Index-numbers*. It follows that the number of units of money which is " equivalent " in a given context to a unit of purchasing power, depends on the corresponding Price-level and is given by the appropriate Index-number.

Is there any one of these Price-levels, and if so which, corresponding *par excellence* to what we mean by the Purchasing Power of Money ? We need not hesitate over the answer to this question. However great the theoretical and practical difficulties of measuring *changes* in the Purchasing Power of Money, there need not be any doubt as to what we mean by it. We mean by the Purchasing Power of Money the power of money to buy the goods and services on the purchase of which for purposes of consumption a given community of individuals expend their money income.[1] That is to say, it is measured by the quantity of such goods and services, weighted according to their importance as objects of consumption, which a unit of money will buy ; and the appropriate index-number is of the type sometimes designated as the Consumption Index. It follows that Purchasing Power must always be defined with reference to a particular set of individuals in a given situation, namely those whose actual consumption furnishes us with our standard, and has no clear meaning unless this reference has been given.

This does not mean that there are not other types of composite commodities, price-levels, and price index-numbers of great interest and importance for various purposes and inquiries. Indeed the notion of there being a variety of price-levels, which fluctuate relatively to one another just as the prices of individual commodities fluctuate relatively to one another, is very helpful to an understanding of Monetary Theory.

---

[1] Cf. Marshall, *Money Credit and Commerce*, p. 21 : " The term ' the general purchasing power of money ' is usually and reasonably taken to mean the power which money has of purchasing commodities in a country (or other place) in those proportions in which they are in fact consumed there." And again p. 30 : " The general purchasing power of money should properly be measured by reference to the retail prices paid by the ultimate consumers of finished commodities."

But the existence of a plurality of other and, as they may fairly be called, secondary price-levels appropriate to different purposes and different contexts is not a reason for admitting any ambiguity as to the meaning of the Purchasing Power of Money itself.

The money-of-account—with which we began Chapter 1—was devised long ago in order to satisfy the need for a term in which to *express* general purchasing power. A definite *measure* of purchasing power by means of index-numbers of prices is, however, a conception of modern times. A short summary of the History of Index-Numbers is given in Appendix IV. of Professor Irving Fisher's *The Making of Index-Numbers*; to which I need only add a mention of Bishop Fleetwood's *Chronicon Preciosum*, 1706 (particularly the first part of chap. iv. and chap. vi.), described by Edgeworth as " the earliest treatise on index-numbers and one of the best ", where the conception of purchasing power and the measures of the changing purchasing power of money are first treated after the modern manner. The following quotation indicates the Bishop's line of approach : " Since money is of no other use, than as it is the thing with which we purchase the necessaries and conveniences of life, 'tis evident, that if £5 in H. VI. days would purchase 5 Quarters of Wheat, 4 Hogsheads of Beer, and 6 Yards of Cloth, he who then had £5 in his pocket was full as rich a man as he who has now £20 if with that £20 he can purchase no more Wheat, Beer, or Cloth than the other." But for practical purposes Price Index-Numbers date from the 1860's.[1]

Thus the Money-of-Account is the term in which units of Purchasing Power are *expressed*. Money is

[1] The important literature of the subject is comprised within a small compass, namely :
    1. Jevons, Papers reprinted in *Investigations in Currency and Finance*.
    2. Edgeworth, Papers reprinted in *Papers relating to Political Economy*, vol. i.

[Continued on the next page.

the form in which units of Purchasing Power are *held*. The Index Number of the price of the composite commodity representative of consumption is the standard by which units of Purchasing Power are *measured*.

The problems which arise in the Theory of Price-Levels (or Index-numbers) will be discussed in the following order:

1. The Purchasing Power of Money or Consumption Standard will be discussed in this chapter, along with the Labour Power of Money or Earnings Standard which measures the power of money to command units of human effort.

2. Certain secondary standards will be examined in Chapter 5.

3. Some peculiar standards, which are appropriate to certain equations arising in the Theory of Money or to doctrines, such as the alleged Intrinsic Value of Money, which have been held about it, will be considered in Chapter 6 under the heading of " Currency Standards ".

4. The relationships between different price-levels and the tendencies, real or alleged, for them to move together will be briefly considered in Chapter 7 under the heading of " The Diffusion of Price-Levels ".

5. Finally in Chapter 8 we must attack the very difficult problems involved in measuring changes in the Purchasing Power of Money and the best means of solving them.

---

3. C. M. Walsh, *The Measurement of General Exchange-Value*.

4. Irving Fisher, *The Purchasing Power of Money* and *The Making of Index-Numbers*.

5. Wesley Mitchell, *Index-Numbers of Wholesale Prices* (U.S. Bureau of Labour Statistics Bulletins 173 and 284).

6. A. C. Pigou, *The Economics of Welfare*, part i. chap. v.

7. G. Haberler, *Der Sinn der Indexzahlen*, 1927.

8. M. Olivier, *Les Nombres Indices de la variation des prix*, 1927 (an excellent and learned *résumé* and criticism of the existing literature).

Professor Fisher has in preparation a dictionary of existing Price Index-Numbers.

(ii.) The Purchasing Power of Money or Consumption Standard

There is at present a most serious lack of satisfactory index-numbers of Purchasing Power. Hitherto no official authority has compiled an index-number which could fairly be called an Index-Number of Purchasing Power. They generally deal with one or other of the secondary price-levels, such as the wholesale, or cost-of-living price-levels, which we shall examine below. Apart from this, all the Index-Numbers at present available are much too crude to take account of the subtleties and serious difficulties of the problem of measuring changes between one position and another, which we are postponing to Chapter 8.

An Index-Number of the Purchasing Power of Money should include, directly or indirectly, once and once only, all the items which enter into final consumption (as distinct from an intermediate productive process) weighted in proportion to the amount of their money-income which the consuming public devote to them. Since it would be a matter of great complexity to compile a completely comprehensive index on these lines, we should be satisfied in practice with an index which covered a large and representative part of total consumption. But we have not at present even this.

The failure to compile a complete or adequate index-number of consumption is partly to be explained by the great practical difficulties; but it is also due to the excessive prestige attaching to a particular type of secondary index-number, namely the index-number of wholesale prices. When we are considering short-period phenomena, as in the Credit-Cycle, this Index-Number has the defect that its movements do not occur at the same time or in the same degree as the correlated movements in the Purchasing Power of Money. And when we are considering long-period phenomena, it is open to the objection that it omits altogether or weights inadequately certain important objects of consumption—in particular, personal services and complex manufactured goods (*e.g.* motorcars). The first omission (though sometimes partly balanced by the second omission) is a serious source of confusion in a community which is technically progressive and increasing in wealth, inasmuch as technical progress tends to lower the cost of commodities in terms of services, whilst at the same time the community spends an increasing proportion of its income on services as its average wealth increases. In most countries the nearest thing to a Consumption Index-Number is the Index-Number of the Cost of Living of the Working Classes. This Index-Number has the same defect, however, as the wholesale index-number, though in a less degree, particularly if it is extended to apply to other classes in the community, namely that it under-weights expenditure on personal services in comparison with expenditure on commodities.

Nevertheless, with the growth of statistical material, the resources of an energetic Government department ought to be equal to the compilation of a reasonably accurate index of the purchasing power of money within a few years' time. Meanwhile we must be content to do the best we can by combining some of the existing series of secondary index-numbers.

Some valuable pioneer work along these lines has been carried out by Mr. Carl Snyder, the statistician of the Federal Reserve Bank of New York.[1] His index-number, which he calls "the index of the general price level", is arrived at by combining the four following secondary index-numbers with weights in proportions as stated:

Wholesale prices	. 2	Cost of living	.	$3\frac{1}{2}$
Wages	. $3\frac{1}{2}$	Rent	.	1

[1] See his *Business Cycles and Business Measurements*, chap. vi., and the current Monthly Bulletins of the Federal Reserve Bank of New York for more precise particulars as to his methods.

CH. 4   THE PURCHASING POWER OF MONEY   59

I shall use this index as providing a tolerable approximation to a consumption standard. But it must be remembered that it was devised by Mr. Snyder for a different purpose, namely, as (what I shall designate below, p. 78) a Cash Transactions standard.

It will be noticed that certain items of expenditure appear, directly or indirectly, in more than one of Mr. Snyder's component indexes; but there is no harm in this, provided the weight given to them in the aggregate is not disproportionate. The chief superiority of Mr. Snyder's index over others, regarded as an index-number of consumption, lies in the fact that by bringing in the composite of Wage Payments it gets nearer to making a due provision for the cost of personal services.

Mr. Snyder has carried his index for the United States back to 1875. In the following table [1] the earlier years are given in terms of quinquennial averages. The index of wholesale prices, which, except in the early years, is the U.S. Bureau of Labour wholesale index, is placed beside it for comparison; and a third column gives the ratio between the two.

This table is of the highest interest to those of us who have been brought up (and who has not?) to look on index-numbers of the wholesale type, such as Sauerbeck's or the *Economist's*, as representing " the value of money ". It is evident that in an age of technical progress these index-numbers have tended, except during such an exceptional period

[1] Mr. Snyder has published subsequently (*Review of Economic Statistics*, Feb. 1928) a revised " Index of the General Price Level " for the years 1913–1927 compiled on somewhat different lines from the above. This new version, however, is much less serviceable as a Consumption Index than the version given above, because—in pursuit of Mr. Snyder's object which is to produce, not a Consumption Index, but, as stated above, a Cash-Transaction Index—it takes account not only of consumption goods and services but also of Realty Values and Security Prices. Thus, whilst Mr. Snyder's new index may be more suitable for his purpose, his old index is certainly much more suitable for mine.

Snyder's "Index of General Price-Level" for the United States compared with the Wholesale Index (1913 = 100)

	Consumption Index (Snyder).	Wholesale Index.	Ratio of the Two.
1875–79	78	96	81
1880–84	78	101	77
1885–89	73	82	89
1890–94	74	77	95
1895–99	72	69	104
1900–4	79	83	95
1905–9	88	92	96
1910	96	97	99
1911	96	95	101
1912	99	99	100
1913	100	100	100
1914	101	98	103
1915	103	101	102
1916	116	127	91
1917	140	177	79
1918	164	195	84
1919	186	207	90
1920	213	227	94
1921	178	147	121
1922	170	149	114
1923	181	154	117
1924	181	150	121
1925	186	159	117
1926	186	151	123

as the War, progressively to over-estimate the value of money-income for the general purposes of consumption. It may be that Mr. Snyder's index errs in the opposite direction, and that its method of compilation has the effect of over-weighting the cost of services. The determination of this must await that further investigation of the relevant facts to which practical statisticians may be expected to give more attention in the future than they have in the past.

A further source of error—the correction of which might bring an accurate Consumption Index nearer

CH. 4   THE PURCHASING POWER OF MONEY   61

to the Wholesale Index than the above—is to be found in the inadequate weighting of manufactured goods, the price of which has tended to fall relatively to services. The Snyder Index makes some allowance for such goods both in its Wholesale Index component and in its cost of living component. But it is questionable whether the allowance is adequate.[1]

Taking the Snyder index, however, at its face value if only for the sake of illustration, it appears that a policy which had aimed at stabilising the wholesale index-number over the past fifty years would nevertheless have caused the Snyder index to rise by 50 per cent; whilst *vice versa* a policy aimed at stabilising the Snyder index would have caused the wholesale index to fall by one-third. It is at least evident that the practice of employing the usual wholesale index-numbers as an approximate guide to the purchasing power of money is not *prima facie* justifiable.

Mr. Snyder has suggested the compilation of a similar index-number for Great Britain, the weights and components proposed being as follows:

Board of Trade Wholesale Prices . . .	2
Ministry of Labour Cost of Living . .	3¼
Bowley's Wages Index	3½
Rent	½

It is probable that this weighting could be improved upon. But for the time being this composite probably provides as good a Consumption Index for Great Britain as is practicable in the present state of our statistical knowledge. Carried back to 1913 this index works out as follows:

---

[1] I believe that Marshall used to justify the use of the Wholesale Standard as a working substitute for a non-existent Consumption Standard on the ground that the omission of services tended to be balanced in its effect by the omission of manufactured goods. But the assumption of any exact balance between these two sources of error is, of course, highly precarious and unsatisfactory.

THE PURCHASING POWER OF MONEY OR CONSUMPTION INDEX
FOR GREAT BRITAIN (1913 = 100)

	Consumption Index.	Wholesale Index.	Ratio of the Two.
1913	100	100	100
1919	215	258	83
1920	257	308	83
1921	223	198	113
1922	181	159	114
1923	170	159	107
1924	172	165	104
1925	172	159	108
1926	169	148	114
1927	166	142	117
1928	164	140	117
1929	162	126	119

As in the case of the United States, it is seen that the wholesale index, whilst it exaggerated the fall and rise in the purchasing power of money in the post-war boom and slump, tends over the whole period since 1913 progressively to under-estimate its fall.

It would be of great advantage to a clear understanding of the social consequences of changes in the purchasing power of money if the Board of Trade were to compile a really good general Consumption Index and carry it back, if possible, for some fifty years. An index which deliberately aimed at representing consumption would obviously be preferable to any of the "mixed" index-numbers, such as Mr. Snyder's index just discussed, or Professor Wesley Mitchell's "general-purpose" index-number, which is the average of several index-numbers of distinct types; though such index-numbers [1] may be serviceable as a sub-

[1] Characteristically described by Edgeworth in his British Association Memorandum as "a compromise between all the modes and purposes—*the* method, if practical exigencies impose the condition that we must employ one method, not many methods . . . recommended by a jumble of heterogeneous and incommensurable considerations, like the celebrated

stitute for an adequate Index of Purchasing Power, failing anything better.

(iii.) THE LABOUR POWER OF MONEY OR EARNINGS STANDARD

This Standard aims at measuring the purchasing power of money over units of human effort as contrasted with units of commodity, so that the Purchasing Power of Money divided by its Labour Power furnishes an index of real earning power and hence of the Standard of Life.

The chief obstacle in the way of computing this Standard is to be found in the difficulty of finding a common unit in which to compare different kinds of human effort. For even if we agree—as we must—that it is proper to ignore degrees of skill in this connection and to mean the rate of earnings per unit of effort averaged over all the grades of skill actually prevailing in the community, we ought still, theoretically at least, to take account of variations in the intensity, distastefulness and regularity of work. In practice the best we can achieve—even if we can achieve that—is to take as our index of the Labour Power of Money or Earnings Standard the average hourly money-earnings of the whole body of workers of every grade.

Some writers would present the Earnings Standard as a rival claimant of the Consumption Standard for the position of the ideal objective standard in terms of which the monetary unit should be stabilised. This is a question of convenience and expediency which we shall discuss subsequently. It might be, of course, that in certain types of social organism there was a strong case on grounds of expediency for stabilising the Labour Power of Money rather than its Purchasing Power, just as there might be

---

resolution declaring the throne vacant after the flight of James II." (*op. cit.* p. 256).

grounds for stabilising the price of wheat or the price of electrical power or the price of gold. In this case the answer must depend on whether, in the given circumstances of a particular economic society, it is better that changes in the efficiency of human effort should be reflected in changed money-earnings or in changed money-prices.

(iv.) WORKING CLASS INDEX-NUMBERS

Corresponding to the Consumption Standard and the Earnings Standard for the community as a whole, we have the (so-called) Cost-of-Living Index-Number and the Wages Index-Number for the Working Class, the ratio between the two furnishing an index of Real Wages. These Working Class Index-Numbers are practically important, because the necessary statistics are more easily obtained than the corresponding figures for the community as a whole, with the result that it is these index-numbers which have been actually compiled.

For this reason it is sometimes convenient to use the working class cost-of-living index-number as a first approximation to the Consumption Standard, to which it generally lies much nearer than does the Wholesale Standard—provided we remember that it is limited, not merely to the consumption of the working class, but to a part only of the consumption of that class, namely to the necessaries pertaining to the established standard of life. It would be natural to employ it as a component part of any Consumption Standard. It is now currently compiled for most countries and, while its basis is not revised frequently enough, there is a considerable accumulated experience of the statistical and practical difficulties involved and the best means of overcoming them. It is, however, so familiar and well understood as to need no further comment.

CHAPTER 5

THE PLURALITY OF SECONDARY PRICE-LEVELS

THE pioneer in distinguishing the different types of price-levels from one another was Edgeworth. The first thorough Classification of Index-Numbers of Prices was that prepared by him in his Memoranda for the British Association (1887 to 1889), which still remain the most important discussions of this matter. He there distinguishes six leading types—the Capital Standard, the Consumption Standard, the Currency Standard, the Income Standard, the Indefinite Standard and the Production Standard. Nearly forty years later (*Economic Journal*, vol. xxxv. (1925) p. 379) Edgeworth classified index-numbers into *three* leading types—Index-Numbers representing Welfare, Unweighted Index-Numbers and the Labour Standard. Of these three categories the first and third correspond to variants of the Consumption and Earnings Standards as defined above; and the second, in respect of which I have a fundamental difference of opinion with Edgeworth, will be dealt with in the second section of Chapter 6.

But in addition to these fundamental price-levels, we have a plurality of secondary price-levels corresponding, not to the general purchasing power of money over consumption as a whole or over effort as a whole, but to its purchasing power for special purposes; as, for example, the purchasing power of money over staple commodities at wholesale, or over bonds and shares, and so forth. Further, in addition to these partial but more or less generalised price-levels, there are also a number of subsidiary price-levels, useful for particular purposes or as component parts in building up the more generalised price-levels. Amongst the most valuable of these for practical purposes are those which are now being compiled with increasing accuracy and completeness for particular trades and services ; as, for example, the indexes of sea-freights, of railway charges, of cotton textiles, of woollen textiles, of building materials, of iron and steel goods, of chemicals, of electric power, of cereals, of poultry and dairy produce, and so forth. It may be by the appropriate combination of sub-indexes of this type that there will be built up the Consumption Standard of the future for the measurement of General Purchasing Power, rather than by combining, as Mr. Snyder has done in default of better material, other existing indexes of a more general type, such as the Wholesale Index and the Wages Index.

Amongst the standards other than the Consumption Standard dealt with in Chapter 4, and the Currency Standards which we shall treat in Chapter 6, two stand out as being of sufficient importance to deserve separate mention, namely:

(i.) The Wholesale Standard ; and
(ii.) The International Standard.

(i.) The Wholesale Standard

This price-level is made up of the prices of basic commodities at wholesale. Sometimes they are divided into the two groups, foods and materials ; sometimes into the groups, agricultural and non-agricultural. It is based, almost entirely, on the prices of raw materials, in various stages of completion, either of manufacture or position, on their journey through the productive process to the consumer ; that

CH. 5 PLURALITY OF SECONDARY PRICE-LEVELS 67

is to say, it roughly corresponds to the price-level of what in subsequent chapters we shall call working capital, *i.e.* of unfinished goods.

The older wholesale index-numbers were either unweighted, all the principal basic commodities being treated as of equal importance, or at best roughly weighted, wheat for example being reckoned two or three times as important as tin, whereas its real relative importance is perhaps ten times or more. More recently, however, the best official index-numbers have been elaborately and scientifically weighted, on the basis of the relative importance of different articles in the national economy as indicated by the Census of Production. The culmination of these improvements up to the present is to be found in the excellent wholesale index of the United States Bureau of Labour, which, since its latest revision (September 1927), is based on 550 individual commodities scientifically weighted.

Nearly all the early index-numbers—such as Jevons's, Soetbeer's, Sauerbeck's and the *Economist's* —were of the wholesale type; mainly because this was, formerly, the only type for the compilation of which adequate statistics were forthcoming over a series of years. Since no other index-numbers were available, these were accepted without much qualification, both in popular and in learned discussions of Monetary Problems, as indicative of "the value of money". Most of us were brought up to employ such index-numbers as Sauerbeck's or the *Economist's* much too light-heartedly, and without sufficient warning that, while there might be nothing better available, nevertheless the actual divergences between these indexes and the Purchasing Power of Money might prove to be, if we could calculate them, of very great significance both theoretical and practical. This light-heartedness was much encouraged by the doctrine, fallacious in my opinion, put into currency under distinguished authority, to the effect that, for reasons of theoretical statistics, *any* index-number, which embraced a fairly wide range of independent price quotations, would work out in practice to much the same results as any other, and that it was, therefore, unnecessary to trouble with a variety of price-levels. This attitude has sunk so deep into popular economics that it still prevails widely and is the source of a good deal of misunderstanding. I deal with what I believe to be its errors in the second section of Chapter 6.

The reasons for possible discrepancies between the Wholesale Standard and the Consumption Standard are of two quite distinct kinds, which—in the interests of a much later stage of our argument—it will be useful to disentangle here. These two standards may fluctuate differently either because the goods of which the former takes account in an unfinished state are different, or are accounted for in different proportions, from the goods of which the latter takes account in a finished state; or because the unfinished goods considered by the former correspond in price by anticipation to finished goods existing at a different *date* from the finished goods considered by the latter.

As regards the varying importance of different objects of expenditure for the Wholesale and Consumption Standards respectively, it is evident—apart from other discrepancies in weighting — that the former ignores personal services and most of the costs of marketing and all that part of consumption which is derived from the enjoyment of fixed consumption capital (as, for example, house-room) into the cost of which the rate of interest enters as an important constituent; whereas these items account between them for a large proportion of the consumer's expenditure. There is, therefore, no reason in the world why, over long periods, we should expect them to move together.

Moreover, there is a good reason for expecting a Wholesale Index to fluctuate more violently than a Consumption Index, inasmuch as the former is more influenced by the prices of highly specialised items, whereas the latter takes more account of relatively unspecialised services, such as transport and marketing. For example, the prices of agricultural products to the farmer vary much more widely than the prices of the same products, which include transport and marketing charges, to the consumer.[1]

Over short periods there is the additional reason for discrepancies between the fluctuations of the Wholesale Standard and the Consumption Standard, that unfinished goods, which are not available for consumption, have no value except what is derived from their prospective value as constituents of finished goods, and therefore reflect, not to-day's value for finished goods, but their anticipated value at the date when there will have been time to complete the process of finishing the goods which are now unfinished. That the wholesale index-number is governed by the anticipated level of the consumption index-number of some *subsequent* date will be found to have practical importance when we reach the discussion of the credit cycle.

(ii.) INTERNATIONAL STANDARDS

There are in the modern economic world a number of articles of international trade which flow freely between one country and another, freight charges, tariffs and other obstacles being not sufficient to prevent this flow. For each country there is an index, which we may call its International Index, made up in practice of the principal standardised commodities, mainly raw materials, in which there is an inter-

[1] Cf. my review of "Inter-relationships of Supply and Prices" by G. F. Warren and F. A. Pearson, in the *Economic Journal* (1929), p. 92.

national market, weighted by reference to their importance in the trade of the country in question. A complete version of this index-number would, of course, also include manufactured articles such as cotton piece-goods, which are the subject of international trade on an important scale. This Index corresponds, in the case of any given country, to what it is now usual to call the Unsheltered Price-Level.

Now, after allowances for tariffs and costs of transport, the price of every constituent of an International Index must be the same for all countries if they are reduced to terms of the same currency. Subject, therefore, to corrections for changes in tariffs and costs of transport, fluctuations in the ratio of any international index expressed in terms of the prices of one country to the same index expressed in terms of the prices of another country must correspond closely to fluctuations in the rates of exchange between the currencies of the two countries. That is to say, the rates of foreign exchange between currencies must be at a parity with the comparative purchasing powers of those currencies over the staple commodities of International Trade.

We must not, however, overlook the fact that the corrections required for tariffs and costs of transport may be very substantial over a period of time, even in the case of articles which we think of as having, beyond question, an international market. The following table for the seventeen years 1896–1913, based on statistics collected by Mr. F. C. Mills (*The Behaviour of Prices*, Section II.), exhibits this very clearly:

[TABLE

CH. 5 PLURALITY OF SECONDARY PRICE-LEVELS 71

CHANGE IN PRICES IN 1913 AS COMPARED WITH 1896 RELATIVELY TO THE CHANGE IN GREAT BRITAIN [1]

	Great Britain.	United States.	Germany.	France.
Wheat	100	112	104	97
Potatoes	100	186	157	188
Raw Sugar	100	86	89	..
Raw Cotton	100	101	100	101
Pig-iron	100	91	75	..
Bituminous Coal	100	97	108	111
Petroleum	100	164	..	141
Wool	100	102	..	..
Hides	100	103	..	..
Coffee	100	248	..	172

A few of these figures are probably erroneous and not strictly comparable. In the case of potatoes, which enter dubiously into international trade, the British figure may have been heavily influenced by transient circumstances of crop or season. But the broad lessons of the table are evident. Raw materials, such as cotton, wool and hides, which are not subjected to tariffs, and travel easily, maintain their international parities very accurately. But the prices of many other important commodities, such as wheat and pig-iron, are capable of sustaining a markedly discrepant trend in different countries.

Nevertheless, when there are marked differences between the movements of the Purchasing Power of Money within a country and those of its International Price-Level, this is likely to be a matter of importance for the interpretation of the monetary equilibrium and price movements of the locality. At the date at which I write this chapter (1927), one of the most interesting monetary phenomena of the day is the general tendency for the International Price-Levels to

[1] *I.e.* if the price of a commodity has risen 10 per cent in Great Britain within this period and 20 per cent in the United States, our index above shows 109 for the U.S., *i.e.* 120/110.

fall relatively to the Index of the local Purchasing Power of Money in a great many countries.

A further phenomenon of considerable significance for economic interpretation is the movement for any country of that part of its International Price-Level which enters into its trade as imports relatively to that part which enters as exports. The ratio between these movements yields a derivative index of the relative prices of Exports and Imports or, as we may express it, of the Terms of Trade. It measures the quantity of home goods which have to be offered in order to obtain a unit of foreign goods. This Index is peculiarly exposed, as Professor Bowley has shown, to the difficulties of changing composition due to the frequent and rapid fluctuations in the proportions in which given classes of goods are exported or imported. It was first introduced in Giffen's calculations for the Board of Trade (Parl. Papers, 1878–79, 2247, and subsequent years).[1]

The Purchasing Power Parity Theory of the Foreign Exchanges, which has been much discussed in recent years, is in its purest form no more than a re-statement of the proposition given above to the effect that the rates of foreign exchange between two currencies move in the same way as the ratio of an International Index expressed in the prices of one country to the same Index expressed in the prices of the other country.

This is, indeed, little more than a truism, which might not have received so much attention as it has, even supported by Professor Cassel's authority, if it had not been extended—illegitimately in my opinion —to the Purchasing Power of Money itself. Since the prices of imports and exports react on other prices,

[1] For discussions of this Index in the case of Great Britain vide Bowley, *Economic Journal*, vol. xiii. p. 628; Keynes, *Economic Journal*, vol. xxii. p. 630, vol. xxxiii. p. 476; Beveridge, *Economica*, Feb. 1924, p. 1; Robertson, *Economic Journal*, vol. xxxiv. p. 286; Taussig, *Economic Journal*, vol. xxxv. p. 1.

CH. 5 PLURALITY OF SECONDARY PRICE-LEVELS 73

there will generally be some correlation between large changes in a country's International Standard and changes in its Consumption Standard. But there is no justification, even in the long run, for any precise, necessary or immediate relationship between changes in the rate of exchange of the currencies of two countries and the changes in their Consumption Standards relatively to one another. To suppose that there is overlooks the possibility of a change in the Terms of Trade.

The prestige of the Purchasing Power Parity Theory, as being something more than a truism, has depended, not so much on the somewhat crude theory underlying it, as on the supposed verifications which have followed from applying it to some of the most familiar national index-numbers.[1] But these apparent verifications are explicable by the fact that many of the most old-established wholesale index-numbers are mainly composed of the staple commodities of international trade, for the intelligible reason that it is precisely for these commodities that satisfactory price quotations are most easily obtainable over a long series of years. If they were entirely composed of such articles, and if the systems of weighting were the same in each case,[2] the verifications would be as nearly as possible perfect. For the Purchasing Power Parity Theory is true, not only of an *index* of the articles which enter into international trade, but also if it is applied to the price of each one of these articles taken separately, provided allowance be made for changes in the costs of transport, etc. Since, however, these index-numbers generally include

[1] I have given some examples in my *Tract on Monetary Reform*, pp. 99-106.
[2] The amount of the error introduced by different systems of weighting, where local wholesale indexes are employed, has been discussed by Professor Bowley in his *International Comparison of Price Changes* and his *Comparative Price Index-Numbers for Eleven Principal Countries* (London and Cambridge Economic Service, Special Memoranda, No. 19, July 1926, and No. 24, July 1927).

two or three commodities which do not enter freely into international trade, and since the systems of weighting and the grades and qualities of the selected articles are various, there has been just that degree of discrepancy in the "verifications" to make the Theory seem *prima facie* interesting.

Where, on the other hand, the comparison is really made on the basis of the Purchasing Power of Money in different countries, then the Purchasing Power Parity Theory of the Foreign Exchanges is not borne out by the recorded facts. I used to think this Theory [1] more interesting than I think it now. It now seems to me that the really significant matter for discussion in this connection is the much more complicated problem of the International Diffusion of Price-Levels between one country and another. Professor Cassel's most recent applications of his theory to current events seem to me to be vitiated by his underlying assumption that the terms of trade do not change; whereas the fact that they can do so— as the result, for example, of variations in the rate of foreign investment—is, as we shall see in Chapter 21, one of the greatest difficulties in the way of the maintenance of a country's external equilibrium.

It is evident that the common practice of publishing various versions of Index-Numbers which are popularly described as Index-Numbers of Prices without sufficient further qualification may be dangerously misleading. Professor Cassel himself has come near to being misled, in my opinion, by applying conclusions true of a particular type of price-level, namely, what I have called International Price-Levels, beyond their appropriate field. At the

[1] For a fuller discussion of this Theory *vide* my *Tract on Monetary Reform*, pp. 87 *et seq*. See also Cassel's *Money and Foreign Exchange after 1914*, and Dr. Keilhau, *Economic Journal*, vol. xxxv. (1925) p. 221.

time of Great Britain's return to the Gold Standard the Treasury and the Bank of England were led to the false conclusion that, because the Wholesale Index, which was almost the same thing as the British International Index, was moving rapidly into adjustment—as an International Index necessarily must—with the movement of the gold exchanges, therefore the same thing was true of "prices generally". Moreover, students of the Theory of the Credit Cycle, and, indeed, of all those parts of Economic Theory which deal with short-period phenomena, have sometimes, by overlooking the temporary divergences between price-levels which in the long run are likely to move together, assumed away the very facts which it is the task of such a theory to investigate.

Nevertheless the enormous increase since the War in the variety of price-levels for which index-numbers are being compiled, and the greater adequacy of the statistical data on which they are based, are gradually destroying the popular conception that an Index-Number of Prices, such as Sauerbeck's Index or the *Economist's* Index, can be used to furnish more or less satisfactorily an index of the value of money in all sorts of contexts, different from that for which it was expressly compiled. The duty of official Statistical Departments should be, I think, firstly to prepare a really good Index of the Purchasing Power of Money, and secondly to multiply the number and variety of the specialised secondary and sub-Indexes which they compile and publish (preferably with the assistance of trade bodies and trade experts), so as to render it as easy as possible to build up by various combinations of these sub-indexes more complex indexes appropriate to the particular purpose or inquiry on hand.

CHAPTER 6

CURRENCY STANDARDS

(i.) THE CASH-TRANSACTIONS STANDARD AND THE CASH-BALANCES STANDARD

THE new Fundamental Equation, which I shall propound in Chapter 10, leads up, as it should, to the Purchasing Power of Money. The Quantity Equations which have been in use hitherto do not, however, do so. They refer, as we shall see in Chapter 14, to Price-Levels which weight different articles, not in proportion to their importance to consumers, but in proportion to their importance in connection with the volume either of cash-transactions or of cash-balances—two types of Currency Standard, as they may be termed, which we shall call respectively the Cash-Transactions Standard and the Cash-Balances Standard.

These Currency Standards must necessarily differ from the Purchasing Power of Money, because the relative importance of different articles as objects of monetary transactions is not the same as their relative importance as objects of consumption. It is evident that the systems of weighting appropriate to a Consumption Standard and to a Currency Standard respectively can differ materially from one another. An object of expenditure which passes straight from the original producer to the ultimate consumer, such as personal services for example, gives rise to a less volume of monetary transactions than an object of equal value which passes through many hands and through many stages of production, each of which involves a monetary transaction, before it reaches the consumer. These two objects of expenditure would, therefore, be weighted equally for the purposes of the Consumption Standard, but unequally for the purposes of a Currency Standard. Moreover there are many types of financial business which give rise to a large volume of transactions but are of little or no importance for the Consumption Standard; as, for example, Stock Exchange business or three-month Treasury Bills which in each three-monthly period give rise to a large volume of cheque transactions, and may be the subject of several more by reason of their changing hands during the period of their three-month currency.

Nevertheless Currency Standards have been not infrequently confused with the Purchasing Power of Money itself; and even the very few writers who have got so far as to distinguish the Currency Standards from the Purchasing Power of Money, have often overlooked the fact that there are two distinct types of this standard. In the first type of Currency Standard the different objects of expenditure are weighted in proportion to the amount of the cash-transactions (payment by cheque as well as by cash, being, of course, included in this expression) to which they give rise. But in the second type the objects of expenditure are weighted by reference to the demand for bank-balances or stock of money which they occasion. The two are distinct because some transactions require a greater holding of anticipatory money-balances to meet them than others of equal money-value, according to their regularity and the certainty with which their date and amount can be anticipated. It follows that a rise or fall in the price of certain articles causes a greater fluctuation in the amount of the cash-balances of the community than a similar movement in the price of other articles which give rise to an equal volume of cash-transactions.

I propose to call the first type of Currency Standard the *Cash-Transactions Standard* and the second type the *Cash-Balances Standard*. The significance of the distinction will be developed in Chapter 14, where we shall see that the " Fisher " Quantity Equation leads up to the former, whilst the " Cambridge " Quantity Equation leads up to the latter.

Writers on the Currency Standard have generally meant by it, I think, the Cash-Transactions Standard rather than the Cash-Balances Standard. The designation *Currency Standard*, defined as a Cash-Transactions Standard, was in fact first introduced by Professor Foxwell, who regarded it as " *par excellence* the measure of appreciation or depreciation " in such contexts as discussions relating to Bimetallism, choice of standards, etc. The leading exposition of it, however, is not by Professor Foxwell himself but by Professor Edgeworth, on the basis of conversations with the former, in his Third Memorandum for the British Association, 1889 (reprinted *op. cit.* p. 261). Edgeworth's concluding comment is as follows: " Upon the whole, it appears that the Currency Standard deserves more attention than it has received. The stone unaccountably set aside by former builders of index-numbers may become the corner-stone of future constructions." The Cash-Transactions Standard is also important because—as mentioned above—it is the price-level appropriate to Professor Irving Fisher's widely celebrated formula $PT = MV$.[1]

It is the Cash-Balances Standard, on the other hand, which is characterised *par excellence* by the

---

[1] M. Divisia (" L'Indice monétaire et la théorie de la monnaie," *Revue d'Économie politique*, 1925, p. 1001) has defined the value of money by reference to the Cash-Transactions Standard calculated from year to year by the Chain Method.

fact that a change in it *ceteris paribus* alters *in the same proportion* the quantity of money required by the public.

In practice the most important differences between the Currency Standards and the Consumption Standard are that the former weight goods much higher and services much lower than does the latter, and that the former includes, whilst the latter excludes, the objects of financial transactions; with the result that when the value of transactions in capital goods is moving relatively to that of consumption goods, or when the price of commodities is moving relatively to the price of services, the fluctuations of the two types of Standard may be materially different. This, as we shall find, is of particular importance for the short-period economic theory of trade and credit fluctuations. It also means that the relation of the Purchasing Power of Money to its quantity can vary without loss (or gain) of convenience even though there is no change in banking habits and practices. But this is to anticipate the subject-matter of later chapters.

In some contexts the fluctuations of the Wholesale Standard may be nearer to those of the Currency Standards than are those of the Consumption Standard; but the fact that the Currency Standards are influenced by capital transactions whilst the Wholesale Standard is not, makes it impossible to place any reliance on such correspondence.

(ii.) Is there such a Thing as an " Objective Mean Variation of General Prices " ?

There is, however, a kind of Currency Standard different from the above, which has played an important part in the history of the subject and has exercised a very great influence on the prevailing conceptions of the nature of index-numbers of prices.

The first economist effectively to introduce index-numbers of prices into Monetary Science (though like other original geniuses not without precursors), namely Jevons, did not contemplate his idea from any of the angles from which it has been viewed above —neither from that of the Purchasing Power of Money nor from that of the Currency Standards as just defined. Nor did Edgeworth exclusively, either in his earliest or in his latest contributions to the problem over a space of forty years. Nor has Dr. Bowley— at least not unequivocally in his theoretical treatment. The name of Cournot, the great parent of so many brilliant errors based on false analogies between the moral and the physical sciences, should also be mentioned here, inasmuch as he illustrated the variation in prices due to a change on the part of money by that change in the position of the earth with respect to the stars which is due to the motion of the earth. Some of these eminent authorities have been, of course, as familiar as any one else with the conception of the Index-Number of Prices as being the price of a composite commodity, and with the appropriateness of different composite commodities to different times, places and purposes. Nor would they necessarily differ on any substantial point from what I have written above. Nevertheless, Jevons certainly, and Edgeworth and Dr. Bowley to the best of my understanding, have also pursued something distinct from the Purchasing Power of Money, something reached in quite a different way, something which has to do with what they might describe as the value of *money as such* or, as Cournot called it, the " intrinsic value of money ".[1] I have long believed that this is a will-o'-the-wisp, a circle-squaring expedition which has given an elusive taint, difficult to touch or catch, to the treatment of the Theory of Price Index-

---

[1] As distinguished from what he called the " power of money " or, in modern terminology, the " purchasing power of money ".

Numbers traditional in England. This is not equally true of America. The methods of approach characteristic of C. M. Walsh, Irving Fisher and Wesley Mitchell are virtually free from the " taint " which I attribute to Jevons, Edgeworth and Dr. Bowley. Nevertheless, whilst the Americans have not worshipped the mythical creature, they have not (with the exception, perhaps, of Mr. Walsh) actively combated him or dragged him out of the twilit cave where Edgeworth judiciously kept him.[1] At any rate it is necessary for the completeness of this discussion that I should endeavour to make my point explicit, and to bring the difference, if there is one, to a head.[2]

According to the Jevons-Edgeworth conception, the fluctuations in the prices of individual things are subject to two distinct sets of influences—one set due to " changes on the side of money " which (subject to friction in the dimension of time) affect *all* prices *equally* in direction and in degree, the other set due to " changes on the side of the things " which affect prices relatively to one another. Now as regards the second set, changes in the prices of things relatively to one another can involve no absolute change in the value of money itself. Changes in relative prices may, of course, affect partial index-numbers which represent price changes in particular classes of things, *e.g.* the index of the cost of living of the

[1] In the long controversy waged between Mr. Walsh and Edgeworth, in the pages of the *Economic Journal* and elsewhere, on the appropriateness of the application to Price Index-Numbers of certain ideas drawn from the Calculus of Probabilities, I am, in main substance, on the side of the former. Prof. Allyn Young, who was previously inclined to lean slightly to the " tainted " British School, subsequently (1923) went over to the other side (*vide* his *Economic Problems*, pp. 294-296). On the Continent, in Italy Professor Gini (*Metron*, 1925) and in Austria Dr. Haberler (*op. cit.*, 1927) are taint-free; whilst in France Lucien March (*Metron*, 1921) is " tainted ", but Divisia (*op. cit.* pp. 847-858) notably free. From certain allusions I believe Marshall to have been free; but he never discussed the matter in explicit terms.

[2] I first endeavoured to deal with this point, though inadequately, in an Essay on Index-Numbers which gained the Adam Smith Prize in the University of Cambridge in the year 1907.

working classes. But such changes cannot affect the price-level "as a whole" or the value of money in itself. By a change in the value of money in itself or in the price-level as a whole, they mean the amount of the uniform residual movement due to "changes on the side of money" after we have "averaged out" the chaotic but compensatory movements in individual prices due to their movements relatively to one another and to the price-level. For the purpose of isolating "changes on the side of money" they employ the Doctrine of Averages based on the Theory of Probability. If we take enough unbiassed observations of individual prices, their relative movements will, it is argued, cancel out in accordance with the law of error, and we shall be left—subject to a probable error calculated in the usual way—with a reasonably satisfactory index of the residual movement of the price-level itself which is our *quaesitum*.[1]

Three quotations from Jevons, Dr. Bowley[2] and Edgeworth respectively will indicate the line of thought which I am trying to describe.

Jevons, *Investigations in Currency and Finance*, p. 181:

The geometric mean seems likely to give in the most accurate manner such general change in prices as is due to a change on the part of gold. For any change in gold will affect all prices in an equal ratio ; and if other disturbing causes may be considered proportional to the ratio of change

[1] This *quaesitum* is the same as Edgeworth's *Indefinite Standard* in Sections VIII. and IX. of his Memorandum prepared for the British Association in 1887 (reprinted in his *Papers relating to Political Economy*, vol. i. pp. 233 *et seq*.). His Section VIII. seeks the "Determination of an index irrespective of the quantities of commodities : upon the hypothesis that there is a numerous group of articles whose prices vary after the manner of a perfect market, with changes affecting the supply of money ". Section IX. seeks the "Determination of an index utilising quantities of commodities : upon the hypothesis that a common cause has produced a general variation of prices ".

[2] Cf. also the first part of Dr. Bowley's "Notes on Index Numbers" (*Economic Journal*, June 1928).

of price they produce in one or more commodities, then all the individual variations of prices will be correctly balanced off against each other in the geometric mean, and the true variation of the value of gold will be detected.

Bowley, *Elements of Statistics* (5th ed.), p. 198 :

Thus if we start out to measure prices in general . . . in order that the resulting index-number should be subject to the analysis of the law of error, the samples should be random and independent in their fluctuations from the general movement; dependence increases the number of samples necessary for an assigned precision. . . . If the number of independent quantities is at all considerable, any reasonable system of weights is likely to give as good a result as the conditions of the problem allow.

Edgeworth, *Papers relating to Political Economy*, vol. i. p. 247 :

We have seen that, upon the supposition of a change in the supply of money, Jevons' method of combining the variations of prices without regard to the corresponding volumes of transactions is by no means so absurd as has been thought by some. The case is, as if we wanted to discover the change in the length of shadows, due to the advance of day. If the objects casting shadows were unsteady—waving trees, for instance—a single measurement might be insufficient. We might have to take the mean of several shadows. Now for our purpose the *breadth* of the upright object casting the shadow would be unimportant. The " wide-spreading beech " and the mast-like pine would serve equally well as a rude chronometer.

Again, p. 256 :

There seem to be combined in popular thought two elements which we have sought to distinguish in analysis, namely, the conception of an objective mean variation of general prices, and the change in the power of money to purchase advantages.

We have, in short, to this way of thinking, a typical problem in the combination of observations, where each individual observation is subject to a disturbing factor which it is our business to eliminate.

We mean by the rise or fall " in the value of money " the hypothetical movement which would have been brought about if the " changes on the side of money ", *i.e.* the changes which tend to affect all prices equally, had been the only changes operating and there had been no forces present " on the side of the things " tending to change their prices relatively to one another.

The problem being of this character, it is supposed that what we need as a sound scientific basis for our calculations are *numerous* observations of individual prices, particularly of prices which are subject to " independent " influences, though we may, if we like, indulge in some rough weighting, to counterbalance a possible want of a full measure of independence. Such weighting can do no harm, but will, on the other hand, if our observations are a numerous and random selection, make but little difference to the final result, and is therefore, on the whole, more trouble than it is worth. Having obtained a numerous and random selection of individual prices, our next task is to determine the most appropriate method of combining them. What is the law according to which the relative movements are most likely to distribute themselves round the bull's eye ? Will it be such that the geometrical average of the individual prices will be nearest to the mark, as Jevons believed ? Or is the arithmetical average good enough, as most computers have supposed, for no better reason, perhaps, than that it is easier to add than to multiply ? Or is the mode on the whole preferable, as Edgeworth inclined to think ? Or are there good arguments for " fancy " formulae like the harmonic average, or the root of the mean square, or another ?[1]

[1] Some authors have tried to settle this question by observing whether the dispersions of individual prices which actually occur distribute themselves along the Gaussian curve corresponding to the arithmetic mean or along the curve corresponding to the geometric mean, and so forth. For a good account of the results of this method see Olivier, *Les Nombres*

CH. 6   CURRENCY STANDARDS   85

Now, whilst the conception of a price index as being the price of a composite commodity (Edgeworth's "power of money to purchase advantages") has been becoming increasingly prevalent (all the old-fashioned index-numbers were almost entirely unweighted, whilst the best new ones, as for example the U.S. Bureau of Labour Index, are carefully and elaborately weighted), yet this other conception has not been rooted out and still maintains a demi-sway, a traditional influence over the statistical world. The conclusion of the British Association Committee of 1888 (in spite of their recommending a weighted index-number for practical purposes as " commanding more confidence "), that " the scientific evidence is in favour of the kind of index-number used by Prof. Jevons, provided there is a large number of articles ", has never been expressly repudiated by the economic world.

Nevertheless I venture to maintain that such ideas, which I have endeavoured to expound above as fairly and as plausibly as I can, are root-and-branch erroneous. The " errors of observation ", the "faulty shots aimed at a single bull's-eye" conception of the index-number of prices, Edgeworth's " objective mean variation of general prices ", is the result of a confusion of thought. There is no bull's-eye. There is no moving but unique centre, to be called the general price-level or the objective mean variation of general

---

Indices, chap. 4 ; see also Bowley, " Notes on Index Numbers " (*Economic Journal*, June 1928, pp. 217-220). But the method seems to me to be misconceived, except for negative purposes, *i.e.* to show that there is no regularity in the shape of the dispersion, unless it were to be applied to a great number of cases. To apply it in a few cases, as its exponents have done, proves nothing, except as a corroboration of something we have reason to expect *a priori*. If it were to be shown that the curve of dispersion is of the same type in a great number of different contexts, then one would take notice ; but the investigations, so far as they have gone, show nothing of the kind. It is worth mentioning, however, that M. Olivier and Prof. Bowley both conclude that, as a matter of curve-fitting, the geometric curve fits better, in the cases which they have examined, than the arithmetic.

prices, round which are scattered the moving price-levels of individual things. There are all the various, quite definite, conceptions of price-levels of composite commodities appropriate for various purposes and inquiries which have been scheduled above, and many others too. There is nothing else. Jevons was pursuing a mirage.

What is the flaw in the argument? In the first place it is assumed that the fluctuations of individual prices round the " mean " are " random " in the sense required by the Theory of the Combination of Independent Observations. In this theory the divergence of one " observation " from the true position is assumed to have no influence on the divergences of other " observations ". But in the case of prices a movement in the price of one commodity necessarily influences the movement in the prices of other commodities,[1] whilst the magnitudes of these compensatory movements depend on the magnitude of the change in expenditure on the first commodity as compared with the importance of the expenditure on the commodities secondarily affected. Thus, instead of "independence", there is between the "errors" in the successive " observations " what some writers on Probability have called " connexity ", or, as Lexis expressed it, there is " sub-normal dispersion ".

We cannot, therefore, proceed further until we have enunciated the appropriate law of connexity. But the law of connexity cannot be enunciated without reference to the relative *importance* of the commodities affected—which brings us back to the problem that we have been trying to avoid, of weighting the

---

[1] Divisia ("L'Indice monétaire", *Revue d'Économie politique*, 1925, p. 858) has been one of the very few writers to point this out quite clearly. See also Olivier, *Les Nombres Indices*, pp. 106, 107. M. Divisia shows, not only that the non-independence of relative price changes is conclusive against the applicability of the Gaussian Law of Error, but also that it is a gratuitous assumption that a so-called " monetary " cause, however defined, will affect all prices equally.

items of a composite commodity. If we mean by "influences on the side of money being unchanged" that the total volume of monetary transactions remains the same, then the Index-Number in question is the one which I have catalogued above under the name of the Cash-Transactions Standard. Or if we mean that the total stock of money remains the same, then the Index-Number is the Cash-Balances Standard. Thus our *quaesitum*, namely a measure of the "intrinsic value" of money, has no separate existence, but is merely one of the Currency Index-Numbers over again.

The point of view under criticism makes the mistake of assuming that there is a meaning of price-level, as a measure in some sense or another of the value of money, which retains its value unaltered when only *relative* prices have changed. The abstraction between the two sets of forces, which seemed momentarily plausible when we made it, is a false abstraction, because the thing under observation, namely the price-level, is itself a function of relative prices and liable to change its value whenever, and merely because, relative prices have changed. The hypothetical change in the price-level, which would have occurred *if* there had been no changes in relative prices, is no longer relevant if relative prices have in fact changed—for the change in relative prices has in itself affected the price-level.

I conclude, therefore, that the unweighted (or rather the randomly weighted) Index-Number of Prices—Edgeworth's "Indefinite" Index-Number—which shall in some way measure the value of money "as such" or the amount of influence on general prices exerted by "changes on the side of money" or the "objective mean variation of general prices" as distinguished from the "change in the power of money to purchase advantages", has no place whatever in a rightly conceived discussion of the problems of Price-Levels. There is nothing left of the conception under criticism over and above one of the Currency Index-Numbers already defined, which is, like all other Price Indexes, the price of a composite commodity.

The Jevonian conception would have been intellectually delightful and of great scientific convenience if it had been based on a true analysis. It is one of several quasi-mathematical economic conceptions, borrowed by analogy from the physical sciences, which seemed likely to be so fruitful when they were first devised fifty or sixty years ago, but which have had to be discarded on further reflection, in whole or in part.

CHAPTER 7

THE DIFFUSION OF PRICE-LEVELS

CURRENT economic theory is permeated by the notion that the Purchasing Power of Money or Consumption Standard, the Wholesale Standard, the International Standard, etc., etc., whilst doubtless theoretically distinct, all come to much the same thing in practice. It is the prevalence of this belief which explains the common habit of using such index-numbers as Sauerbeck's and the *Economist's* to measure the movements of price-levels generally, and, in recent times, the illegitimate extension of the Purchasing-Power-Parity Theory of the Foreign Exchanges to the Purchasing Power of Money from its legitimate application to the International Standard. I do not believe that Great Britain would have returned in 1925 to the Gold Standard at the pre-war parity if it had not been for the habit of regarding the Wholesale Standard as a satisfactory indicator of general purchasing power.

This notion has flourished under a combination of influences. In the first place the influence of the "normal" theory of value has encouraged a readiness to ascribe to actual conditions the attributes of "a perfect market". It is argued that in stable conditions different price-levels stand in defined relationships to one another, and that, if these relationships are temporarily disturbed, nevertheless forces will be set up tending to restore the former relationships rapidly. This restoration of the previous equilibrium can, it is thought, be assumed with particular confidence when the initial impulse towards change is obviously " on the side of money ", such as an inflation of the currency, whilst nothing new has occurred " on the side of things " calculated to affect relative real costs of production to any material extent; for in such a case all individual prices tend to be affected *equally*—the initial price-changes, that is to say, *diffuse* themselves equally after a certain time through all price-levels alike. Money, being a mere counter, cannot, it is argued, have any permanent influence on the relative value of the things which are transiently related to it. We must allow for friction and an interval of time for diffusion, as in all other processes of economic adjustment. But subject to this the theory of price diffusion in a perfect market is reasonably near to the facts.

This way of thinking has been reinforced by the influence of the unweighted Index-Numbers, which we have just discussed above. The Jevons-Edgeworth " objective mean variation of general prices ", or " Indefinite " Standard, has generally been identified, by those who were not as alive as Edgeworth himself was to the subtleties of the case, with the purchasing power of money—if only for the excellent reason that it was difficult to visualise it as anything else. And since any respectable Index-Number, however weighted, which covered a fairly large number of commodities could, in accordance with the argument, be regarded as a fair approximation to the Indefinite Standard, it seemed natural to regard any such Index as a fair approximation to the Purchasing Power of Money also.

Finally, the conclusion that all the standards " come to much the same thing in the end " has been reinforced " inductively " by the fact that rival index-numbers (all of them, however, of the wholesale type) have shown a considerable measure of agreement with one another in spite of their different compositions. Furthermore, most of the traditional index-numbers have not only been of the wholesale type but have also, by chance, approximated pretty closely in their composition to that of International Standards. This has supplied another batch of inductive " verifications ", tending to the conclusion that all index-numbers " come to the same thing in the end ", since index-numbers of international type have, as they ought, tended to agree with one another not only inside a given country but as between different countries also. Apart, however, from the fact that the measure of agreement has not really been anything remarkable considering how many of the commodities are the same in all of them, it is obviously illogical to conclude that, because different indexes of the Wholesale Standard or of International Standards agree with one another, therefore they are good indicators of the Consumption Standard. On the contrary, the tables given above (pp. 60, 62) supply strong presumptive evidence that over long periods as well as over short periods the movements of the Wholesale and of the Consumption Standards respectively are capable of being widely divergent.

The prevalence of these ideas has been particularly unfortunate in its effect on the study of short-period fluctuations ; for the failure of different price-levels to move in the same way is the essence of such fluctuations, so that to take a wholesale index as measuring all of them alike has been to assume away the very problem under investigation.

In the notion that a change in any one price-level tends to be diffused, there is, of course, an important element of truth, especially when the initial disturbance has been of a monetary character. There is a pressure on other price-levels in the same direction. Given sufficient time, and assuming that no non-monetary influence has come into operation meanwhile to affect relative prices, various distinct price-levels may settle down in the end to much the same position as before relatively to one another. Nevertheless we must not argue for these reasons that an expansion of the currency influences relative prices in the same way as the translation of the earth through space affects the relative position of the objects on its surface. The effect of moving a kaleidoscope on the coloured pieces of glass within is almost a better metaphor for the influence of monetary changes on price-levels. For the way of thinking which I have criticised overlooks, or under-values, the importance of two other factors, neither of which is conveniently included in " economic friction ".

In the first place, when increased or decreased purchasing power in the form of money, seeking to realise itself in actual purchases, comes into, or is withdrawn from, the market, the increase or decrease (as the case may be) is not spread evenly and proportionately over the various buyers. It will, in general, be concentrated in the hands of particular classes of purchasers: in the case of war inflation, for example, in the hands of the Government; in the case of a credit boom, probably in the hands of those who borrow from banks; and so on. Thus the immediate effect is on the goods in which the purchasers primarily affected are most interested. Undoubtedly this will set up a diffusion of price-changes. But the working-out of the social and economic consequences of the new distribution of purchasing power will end up in establishing a new equilibrium which will be different, in greater or less degree, from the old equilibrium. Thus a change in the available " counters ", which does not affect everyone's holding equally (and in practice such changes never do), may have a fairly large lasting effect on relative price-levels. It is evident that there are two types of influences which can change relative prices—(1) a technical change in the costs or processes of production by which something is produced at a changed real cost, and (2) a change in the direction of demand from a changed taste on the part of consumers, or more often from a changed distribution of the available purchasing power. Since, therefore, a change in the quantity of money generally involves a changed distribution of purchasing power, it follows that relative prices can be affected, not only by a change on the side of things, but also by a change on the side of money.

In the second place, there is the familiar fact, which needs, all the same, to be frequently recalled to mind, that there are many kinds of money-contracts, money-customs and money-understandings fixed over periods of time, which is a further cause why relative values (*i.e.* prices) under a monetary régime do not move freely, even in the fairly long run.[1] The most important factor of this type for short-period investigations is of course Wages. The failure of wages to move quickly with the Wholesale Standard or with the International Standard over short periods and the ability of wages to have a trend of their own over long periods is, indeed, probably the largest part of the actual explanation of the failure of different price-levels to move together.

For these reasons it is much safer to keep our minds alive to the Plurality of Secondary Price-Levels and the separate influences which determine their movements in relation to General Purchasing Power, rather than to regard any divergence of particular Price-Levels

[1] I need not repeat in this familiar connection what I have already written at greater length in my *Tract on Monetary Reform*, chap. i., on " The Consequences to Society of Changes in the Value of Money ", from the text : " A change in the monetary unit, which is uniform in its operation and affects all transactions equally, has no consequences. Such changes have produced in the past, and are producing now, the vastest social consequences, because, as we all know, when the value of money changes, it does *not* change equally for all persons and for all purposes." See also my *Economic Consequences of Mr. Churchill*.

from uniformity of movement as a temporary abnormality which will soon cure itself.

Even if the ultimate effect of monetary changes on different prices were to be, at long last, uniform, this would still be less important for many purposes than the initial variability. It may, indeed, be conceded that relative price-levels in England and France may not be appreciably different now from what they would have been if the disturbances of the Wars of Napoleon had never occurred — though this may only be an example of the general proposition that the influences of even the most catastrophic episodes of history evaporate away in time or at least lose themselves as unidentifiable drops in the ocean of subsequent events. But however this may be, it is above all with short-period consequences that we are concerned in some of our most practically important inquiries into monetary phenomena—in the case of all those, for example, connected with the fluctuations of credit and of business activity. To act in such cases on the assumption that all classes of prices are affected more or less in the same way by a change " on the side of money " is, as we have said above, to assume away the very phenomenon which we are out to investigate. The fact that monetary changes do not affect all prices in the same way, in the same degree, or at the same time, is what makes them significant. It is the divergences between the movements of different price-levels which are at once the test and the measure of the social disturbances which are occurring.

When we are concerned with the Diffusion of Price-Levels, not within a single country, but internationally, there are still greater obstacles to the assumption of a rapid and unimpeded action. This topic belongs to the Theory of International Trade rather than to the Theory of Money. But Chapter 21 below will contain some observations bearing on it.

CHAPTER 8 [1]

THE THEORY OF COMPARISONS OF PURCHASING POWER

(i.) THE MEANING OF COMPARISONS OF PURCHASING POWER

WHEN the composite commodity representative of expenditure is stable in its constitution for different classes and different situations, and tastes are unchanged, comparisons of Purchasing Power raise no theoretical difficulty. To prepare a series of index-numbers of the price of a specified composite commodity over a series of positions in time or place involves no problem beyond the practical one of obtaining a series of reliable price quotations for individual commodities.

In fact, however, the composite commodities representative of the actual expenditure of money incomes are not stable in their constitution as between different places, times or groups. They are unstable for three reasons—either (1) because the need which the object of expenditure is intended to satisfy, *i.e.* the purpose of the expenditure, varies, or (2) because the efficiency of the object of expenditure to attain its purpose varies, or (3) because there is a change in what distribution of expenditure between different

[1] This chapter deals with a special problem of some technical difficulty. It could be omitted by readers who are in haste to reach monetary problems proper.

objects is the most economical means of attaining the purpose. The first of these reasons we may classify as a change in tastes, the second as a change in environment, and the third as a change in relative prices. For these reasons every change in the distribution of real incomes or in habits and education, every change in climate and national customs, and every change in relative prices and in the character and qualities of the goods offering for purchase, will affect in some degree the character of average expenditure.

The problem of how we are to compare purchasing powers when the character of consumption has changed is one of great difficulty. It has proved a stumbling-block in the way of a clear treatment of the whole subject of Purchasing Power. But the confusion which has enveloped its discussion hitherto has been mainly due, I think, to a failure to be clear as to exactly what we *mean* by a comparison of the Purchasing Power of Money for communities differently situated in time or place, the character of whose expenditure is not identical.

In the first place, we do *not* mean by Purchasing Power the command of money over quantities of utility. If two men both spend their incomes on bread and both pay the same price for it, the purchasing power of money is not greater to the one than to the other merely because the former is hungrier or poorer than the latter. The purchasing power of money is not different to two individuals with equal incomes because one has greater powers of enjoyment than the other. A redistribution of money-incomes which has the effect of increasing the aggregate of utility does not in itself affect the purchasing power of money. In short, comparisons of Purchasing Power mean comparisons of the command of money over two collections of commodities which are in some sense " equivalent " to one another, and not over quantities of utility. The problem, therefore, is to find the criterion of "equivalence" for this purpose.

Our task in such a case is, not to prove something, but to elucidate by means of reflection a precise definition which shall correspond as closely as possible to what we really mean by a term in common use. On reflection it seems to me—and I hope the reader will agree—that the criterion of equivalence is to be found as follows. Two collections of commodities are "equivalent" if they represent the commodity-incomes, *i.e.* the things which are purchased by the money-incomes, of two persons of equal sensitiveness [1] and possessed of equal real-incomes of utility.[2] Let us call such persons *similar* persons. If, then, we say that the purchasing power of money in position A is r times what it is for similar persons in position B, we mean that similar persons will have r times the money-income in B that they have in A. Thus comparisons of the purchasing power of money are the same thing as comparisons of the amounts of the money-incomes of similar persons.

There remains, however, a further serious difficulty. On the above definition it is fundamental to the meaning of a comparison between the purchasing powers of money in two positions that it should be related to individuals who have equal real-incomes. It does not enable us to make the comparison for communities as a whole, which are comprised of individuals having various levels of real-income, unless the change in the purchasing power of money, as given by the above definition, is uniform for all the different levels of real-income. Yet, conceivably, it might have doubled for the working-classes, trebled for the middle-classes, and quadrupled for the very wealthy. By how much, in

[1] In what follows I shall, to avoid unnecessary complications, assume that the condition of equal sensitiveness is fulfilled.

[2] The importance for the Theory of Price Index-Numbers of the triple distinction between money-incomes, commodity-incomes, and real-incomes, is well brought out by Haberler in his *Der Sinn der Indexzahlen*, p. 81.

such a case, has it changed for the community as a whole?

There is, in my opinion, no satisfactory answer to this question — for the reason that we can give no meaning to a numerical comparison between the purchasing power of money to a poor man and its purchasing power to a rich man, the two things being, so to speak, in different dimensions. Any attempt to strike an average for the amount by which purchasing power has changed for a community as a whole necessarily involves equating the purchasing power of money for one class to its purchasing power for a different class, which cannot be done except by an arbitrary assumption. For example, let us suppose that the income of the community is equally divided between three classes, and that purchasing power doubles in position B as compared with position A for the lower class, trebles for the middle class, and quadruples for the upper class. Then, if we assume that the purchasing power of money was equal for all three classes in position A, we find that the average rise in position B is 3 times; but if we assume that it was equal for the three classes in position B, then we find that the average rise in position B is $2\frac{9}{13}$ times.[1] Not only is there no means of reconciling these conclusions, but I see no *meaning* in an assumption to the effect that the purchasing power of money is *equal* for different classes of the community.

When, therefore, the change in the purchasing power of money is different for different ranges of real-income, the best we can do is to neglect those ranges in which comparatively few persons are to be found, and to say that the change in purchasing power for the community as a whole lies *between* the largest and the smallest change shown when the changes for those ranges of real-income, which include the bulk

[1] In effect we are taking the arithmetic mean of 1, 2, 3 in the first case and the inverse of their harmonic mean in the second case.

of the population, are arranged in order of magnitude. In the numerical example given above, that is to say, we can only conclude that the increase in purchasing power lies between 2 and 4.

This difficulty in making precise quantitative comparisons is the same as arises in the case of many other famous concepts, namely of all those which are complex or manifold in the sense that they are capable of variations of degree in more than one mutually incommensurable direction at the same time. The concept of Purchasing Power, averaged over populations which are not homogeneous in respect of their real-incomes, is complex in this sense. The same difficulty arises whenever we ask whether one thing is superior in degree to another *on the whole*, the superiority depending on the resultant of several attributes which are each variable in degree but in ways not commensurable with one another.[1]

In what follows we shall assume, for the sake of simplicity and precision, that we are dealing with the non-complex cases where the purchasing power of money has changed equally for all relevant levels of real-incomes.

(ii.) Methods of Approximation

We have seen that the right way to compare the purchasing powers of money in two positions is to compare the total money-incomes of two " similar " persons in the two positions. But there is a difficulty in applying this method of comparison in practice owing to the want of an objective test by which we can select our " similar " pair for comparison. Consequently, the general practice hitherto has been, not to make any attempt to find a pair of similar persons and then compare their money-incomes, but to find

[1] The difficulty is the same as that which I have discussed in my *Treatise on Probability*, chap. iii., especially §§ 7-16.

two schedules of expenditure which we consider representative of the consumption of similar persons in the respective positions and then compare the prices of the two "equivalent" composite commodities which correspond to the two schedules.

It is unlikely that complete accuracy will be obtainable either by the direct method of comparing the money-incomes of "similar" persons or by the indirect method of comparing the prices of "equivalent" composite commodities. We are faced, therefore, with a problem of approximation. The methods of approximation in current use suffer, I think, from those who employ them not being sufficiently clear exactly what they are trying to compare. In the following discussion I try to analyse what the different methods of approximation amount to and what they assume—both those which seem to me to be valid and those which seem to be invalid.

A. *The Direct Method of comparing Incomes of Similar Persons*

This method, which has been entirely discarded by statisticians, is, in fact, the method which is most often employed by common sense. It depends on a common-sense judgment of degrees of well-being by persons who have a general acquaintance with the conditions of life in both of the two positions under comparison. When a Scotsman is offered an appointment in London, or an Englishman is offered one in Australia or the United States or Germany, and is wondering what the money-income he will get is going to be "worth" compared with the income he is now getting at home, *i.e.* what the comparative purchasing power of money will be in the new place, he does not usually consult any of the official index-numbers, and he would not get a very useful answer if he did. He asks a friend who is acquainted with the conditions of life in the two places. The friend thinks in his mind's eye of a pair of persons, one in each of the places, who seem to him to be enjoying roughly the same general standard of life, compares their money-incomes, and makes his answer on the basis of this comparison. He may tell him that he will have to get £1200 a year to be as well off in New York as with £700 a year in London or £500 a year in Edinburgh. That is to say, the purchasing powers of money for this income-range come out in the proportions 12 to 7 to 5; for a working man the ratio would not be necessarily the same.

The same method is used to compare purchasing power at different dates, where the judgments of memory are available. We often ask how purchasing power for a given class compares now with what it was before the war, and decide on the basis of our general memories of comparative well-being what the ratio is for the middle-class or the agricultural labourer, and so forth.

If comparisons of this kind were to be made on the basis of inquiries expressly carried out for the purpose by trained inquirers and checked by statistics of prices and consumption, they might be very valuable indeed. But there are two sets of circumstances in which even comparisons, having the inevitable vagueness and inaccuracy of mere memory and general impression, may still give a better answer than we get from index-numbers—namely, those where the character of expenditure has greatly changed, and those where a substantial proportion of the expenditure is of the non-standardised sort which an index cannot cover.

For example, the comparison between the purchasing power of money for an Englishman here and in the East may be better made by general impression of the costs of equivalent standards of life than in any other way, since the things on which a man spends his money are so different in the two cases.

And the comparison of purchasing power for a middle-class parent before and after the war may also be better made by general impression, because so substantial a part of the expenditure in question—as rent, servants, education and travelling—is of a kind which inevitably escapes inclusion in an index-number.

It is in such cases as these that the direct method may yield a result materially different from the indirect method and yet be nearer the truth. When, on the other hand, we are dealing with standardised expenditure which has not much changed in character, as for example with that of the working classes now and five years ago, the indirect method will probably be much more accurate.

Whether it is a merit or a defect of comparison by general impression that it will usually make full allowance for conventional expenditure which yields little utility but is required by local custom if one is to avoid disutility, raises a subtle question of just what one means by purchasing power which I will not allow to detain me.

B. *The Indirect Method of comparing Prices of Equivalent Composite Commodities*

This is the usual method. In the form in which the problem of establishing index-numbers of purchasing power is generally set, we know, at best, the prices of different commodities and the distribution of expenditure between them, and we have little or no information about what pairs of persons are " similar ", wherewith to supplement these figures.

We generally do know, however, that some part of the expenditure—and sometimes a larger part—is in both positions identical in character and in power to yield satisfaction to pairs of similar consumers. Let us represent that part of the composite commodities representative of average expenditure in the two positions, which is thus common to both, by a, and those parts which are different by b_1 and b_2. Where a relatively greater quantity of something is purchased in one position than in the other, the quantity common to both positions is, of course, included in a, and only the excesses, peculiar to each position, in b_1 or b_2 as the case may be. On the other hand, consumption, which is physically similar but not similar in real-income yielding capacity, owing to change of tastes or environment, must be included not in a but in b_1 and b_2. Further, the unit of quantity for b_1 must be such that the expenditure in the first position on a unit of b_1 is in the same ratio to the expenditure on a unit of a as the total expenditure on b_1 is to that on a; and similarly with b_2.

Sometimes, moreover, we can get a little further than this by establishing an equivalence between a pair of commodities which are substitutes for one another. If, for example, 1 lb. of tea and 2 lb. of coffee are alternative means of serving the same purpose or nearly similar purposes with approximately equal efficiency, so that in *both* positions under comparison it would be almost a matter of indifference to most consumers whether they purchased 1 lb. of tea or 2 lb. of coffee, provided the prices were the same; but 1 lb. of tea is cheaper than 2 lb. of coffee in the first position and dearer in the second position, so that tea enters into the composite commodity appropriate to the first and coffee into that appropriate to the second; then we can fairly regard 1 lb. of tea and 2 lb. of coffee as approximately equivalent, without entering into any further complications. Similarly if the national diet is different in the different positions, wheat or oatmeal or rye or potatoes being substituted for one another, we can probably establish reasonably satisfactory ratios of equivalence. To the extent that we can employ this method of equivalent substitution[1]—as we shall call it—we are in effect increasing the field of a, *i.e.* that part of the consumption that is common to, or strictly comparable in, both positions, and diminishing the fields of b_1 and b_2. Let us, therefore, in what follows include in a those items of consumption for which we are in a position to establish ratios of equivalence when one is substituted for another.

There will generally remain, nevertheless, a number of intractable articles comprised in b_1 and b_2, for which it is beyond our power to apply the method of equivalent substitution. We are not in a position to weigh the satisfactions for similar persons of Pharaoh's slaves against Fifth Avenue's motor-cars, or dear fuel and cheap ice to Laplanders against cheap fuel and dear ice to Hottentots.

We are left, therefore, with $a+b_1$ and $a+b_2$ as representative of average consumption in the two positions respectively. Now since a has been assumed to be identical in its power of yielding satisfaction to any pair of similar persons in the two positions, we could, if a represented the whole of consumption, compare purchasing powers in the two positions merely by comparing the prices of a. But the residuals b_1 and b_2, which we cannot equate in this way or otherwise compare, cut us off from so simple a method. We have no right to assume that b_1 and b_2 are equiva-

[1] I think that Edgeworth probably had this method in mind in the following somewhat confusing passage, *Economic Journal*, vol. xxxv. p. 380: "We may indeed construct a 'cargo' of goods definite in quantity and quality, the varying values of which from time to time shall constitute a series of index-numbers. But even in starting with such a cargo we are no longer on the *terra firma* of perfectly objective quantity. For in the selection of the assortment forming the cargo there must be some regard to utility. At any rate, to continue the metaphor, when we have put out to sea, the composition of the cargo suffering a sea-change, we have to abandon the *prima facie* exact method of comparing prices and to substitute the more indefinite procedure of comparing amounts of satisfaction. So Professor Bowley, with reference to a period in which there had occurred considerable changes in the prices and quantities of commodities, would then compare the 'satisfaction' obtainable from different combinations of commodities at given prices."

lent, *i.e.* that average consumers in the two positions are similar; and we do not know how many units of $a+b_2$ in the second position are equivalent for similar consumers to a given number of units of $a+b_1$ in the first position. The problem before us, therefore, is to discover a valid method of approximation applicable in such cases. To this problem we must now address ourselves. I shall argue that two methods, and only two, are legitimate, the first of which is the more generally applicable, and the second of which provides limits between which the correct solution lies in cases where we can assume that nothing has changed between the two positions except relative prices.

1. *The " Highest Common Factor " Method*

Let p_1 be the price of a in the first position and p_2 its price in the second position. The first method of approximation consists in neglecting b_1 and b_2 and employing $\frac{p_2}{p_1}$ as an index of the change in the price-level as between these two positions. There are two conditions, the satisfaction of either of which will render this a legitimate approximation. We are assuming—it will be remembered—that the satisfaction derived from the consumption of a per unit of a is approximately the same in the two positions for any pair of similar persons.

The first condition is that the expenditures of every individual consumer on a should in both positions be large compared with his expenditure on b_1 or b_2.

The second condition is that the real-incomes derived by any consumer from the consumption of a and b_1 in the first position should be approximately in the same proportion as his expenditures on them, and similarly with a and b_2 in the second position.

The sufficiency of each of these conditions can be established as follows. Let persons of real-incomes E consume n_1 units of $a + b_1$ in the first position at prices p_1 for a and q_1 for b_1, with a similar notation for the second position. The ratio of the purchasing power of money in the first position to its purchasing power in the second position is then $\frac{n_2(p_2 + q_2)}{n_1(p_1 + q_1)}$. It follows from this:

(i.) If q_2, q_1 are small compared with p_2 and p_1, n_1 and n_2 must be nearly equal for persons of equal real-incomes; in which case $\frac{p_2}{p_1}$ is a satisfactory approximation for the above expression. This is the same as our first condition above.

(ii.) If the real-incomes derived from consumption of a and b_1 in the first position are approximately in the same proportions as the expenditures on them for persons whose total real-incomes are E, satisfaction from $n_1 a$ is $\frac{p_1}{p_1 + q_1}$ E, and, given similar conditions in the second position, satisfaction from $n_2 a$ is $\frac{p_2}{p_2 + q_2}$ E. If, therefore, satisfaction from consumption of a is approximately the same per unit in the two positions, we have $\frac{p_1}{n_1(p_1 + q_1)} = \frac{p_2}{n_2(p_2 + q_2)}$; so that $\frac{n_2(p_2 + q_2)}{n_1(p_1 + q_1)} = \frac{p_2}{p_1}$ approximately. This is the same as our second condition above.

One or other of these conditions is quite likely to be satisfied to a fair degree of approximation in the case of many of the comparisons of purchasing power which we want to make. The second of them is, however, somewhat precarious, since—unless the first condition is satisfied—it breaks down whenever the second position offers many opportunities for useful expenditure owing to the supply of new commodities which were not available in the first position; for in this event average satisfaction per unit from b_2 is likely to be higher in proportion to average satisfaction per unit from a than is average satisfaction per unit from b_1, so that we need some further hypothesis if we are to compare the purchasing powers successfully.

The method of approximation by taking as the basis of our comparison that part of expenditure a which is common to all the positions under consideration and neglecting the rest has the great advantage over more complicated formulae that we are dealing with the same composite commodity throughout, and have, therefore, no need to resort to the Chain Method (which will be considered later). Moreover, it would seem to be obviously preferable to, and not less simple than, the method nearly always adopted by practical statisticians, namely, to take either $a + b_1$ or $a + b_2$ as though it were appropriate throughout. For this procedure must, as a rule, involve a greater error than to take a throughout; inasmuch as its effect is always to overestimate purchasing power in the position to which our composite is strictly appropriate as compared with the position to which it is less appropriate, whenever the change in the character of the expenditure is due to a change in relative prices and represents a move on the part of the consumer to take advantage of what is relatively cheaper.

In those cases, therefore, where we are not entitled to assume that nothing has changed except relative prices, this " highest common factor " method—as it may be called—will probably give us as good a result as is obtainable in the circumstances. For example, the best index of Purchasing Power over a period of ten years may be obtained by taking as our compromise composite the highest common factor of general expenditure in the successive yearly periods, and—as a check on the closeness of the approximation —setting alongside this index-number a statement showing the proportion of total expenditure in each year which is common to all the years. At any rate I see no advantage, but on the other hand much disadvantage, in the usual procedure of using $a + b_1$ throughout as compared with the method, not adopted hitherto, of using a throughout.

The value as an approximation of using a throughout generally diminishes as the proportion of common expenditure becomes smaller. But if we want something better than this, we must seek it by developing our opportunities to make more use of the method of the substitution of equivalents, thereby increasing the proportion of the field covered by a, rather than by employing some intermediate formula such as $a + \dfrac{b_1 + b_2}{2}$ or any other. In practice, however, the substitution of equivalents has not been applied hitherto on scientific lines except in the case of certain inquiries into the comparative cost of living of the working classes in different centres. In these inquiries an attempt has sometimes been made to deal with the problem of changes in the conventional diet of the working man by working out a system of assumed equivalents.[1]

In certain historical inquiries the "highest common factor" method may be better than any feasible alternative, even though a is no longer large compared with b_1 and b_2. If, for example, we are trying to make a very rough comparison between widely separated epochs—so widely separated that the substitution of equivalents is impracticable—there is nothing to be done except to take some small number of important commodities for which comparable price quotations are obtainable which are common to both positions. If we want to compile a Consumption Index-Number

---

[1] According to Edgeworth (*op. cit.* p. 213) Drobisch was the first to propose a formula of equivalent substitution, though based on a very unsatisfactory, indeed an absurd, criterion (namely *avoirdupois*).

for the value of gold or silver money over the past 3000 years, I doubt if we can do better than to base our composite on the price of wheat and on the price of a day's labour throughout that period.[1] We cannot hope to find a ratio of equivalent substitution for gladiators against cinemas, or for the conveniences of being able to buy motor-cars against the conveniences of being able to buy slaves.

2. *The Method of Limits*

Let us now confine ourselves to the cases where we can assume that tastes, etc., are substantially the same in the two positions under comparison and that nothing has changed except relative prices. In these circumstances it is legitimate to argue that a given income in terms of commodities would yield the same real-income in both positions. Although, therefore, the character of consumption in the second position has changed as a result of changes in relative prices, we can nevertheless be sure that the corresponding real-income is the same as would have been yielded by a similar distribution of consumption in the first position.

These considerations permit a method of establish-

[1] Cf. Marshall, *Money Credit and Commerce*, pp. 21, 22: " Records of prices of staple grain have a double significance. For in every age except our own, by far the greater part of the wages of ordinary labour has been generally taken out in these grains; and by far the greater part of that produce of the fields, which the actual cultivators in past times have retained for themselves, has consisted of them. Further, the methods of raising grain have remained nearly constant throughout the ages. . . . Hence it arises that the wages of ordinary labour and the price of the standard grain in the country, or district, under observation were commonly taken as representatives of value in general. Such a course would be wholly unreasonable now in regard to any country of the western world. But it was reasonable in the times of Adam Smith and Ricardo; and it is necessary to interpret ' classical ' doctrines as to value by reference to it. Locke, writing two generations earlier, had said ' that grain which is the constant general food of any country is the fittest measure to judge of the altered value of things in any long tract of time.' See *Works*, vol. v. p. 47." This traditional method for dealing with the value of money is, it will be seen, an example of the Highest Common Factor Method. Cf., also, Adam Smith, *The Wealth of Nations*, Bk. I. chap. xi.

ing limits within which the true comparison must lie, as follows :

Let P and Q be the composite commodities representative of expenditure in the first and second positions respectively.

Let the amount of P which can be purchased for £1 in the first position be chosen as our unit of P, and the amount of Q which can be purchased for £1 in the second position be chosen as our unit of Q ; and let p be the price of a unit of P in the second position, and $\frac{1}{q}$ the price of a unit of Q in the first position. Let similar persons having a real-income E buy n_1 units of P in the first position and n_2 units of Q in the second position.

Then, since the money-incomes of similar persons are £n_1 in the first position and £n_2 in the second position, the index-number comparing purchasing powers in the two positions $= \frac{n_2}{n_1}$. It can be shown that this must lie between p and q.

For since the consumer has a choice in the first position between buying n_1 units of P or $n_1 q$ units of Q and prefers the former, and since by hypothesis the satisfaction of the former purchase is equal to that of buying n_2 units of Q, it follows that $n_2 > n_1 q$; and similarly, since in the second position he has a choice between buying n_2 units of Q, equal in satisfaction by hypothesis to n_1 units of P, or buying $\frac{n_2}{p}$ units of P, and prefers the former, it follows that $n_1 > \frac{n_2}{p}$; hence $\frac{n_2}{n_1}$ is greater than q and less than p.

Thus if q is greater than 1, the value of money has certainly fallen ; and if p is less than 1, its value has certainly risen ; and in any case the measure of the change in the value of money lies *between* p and q.

This conclusion is not unfamiliar—though the above

formula is simpler than those previously given, and the proof is more rigorous. It is reached, for example, by Professor Pigou (*Economics of Welfare*, part i. chap. vi.). The matter is also very well treated by Haberler (*Der Sinn der Indexzahlen*, pp. 83-94). The dependence of the argument, however, on the assumption of uniformity of tastes, etc., is not always sufficiently emphasised.[1] Moreover, it must be noticed that, in the class of case where p is less than q, this condition proves that tastes *must* have changed, and that an assumption to the contrary must be invalid, since it infringes the condition that $\frac{n_2}{n_1}$ is less than p and greater than q.

In certain circumstances a combination of the Highest Common Factor Method with the Method of Limits may be practicable. We may know that tastes are unchanged over a considerable part of the field of consumption, measured in terms of expenditure, and also that the real-incomes derived from this part of the field are either a considerable part or a constant part of the total real-incomes. In this case our method of approximation may consist first of all in using the Highest Common Factor Method to reduce the field of comparison to that part of the expenditure over the series of positions for which it is legitimate to assume unchanged tastes, and then applying the Method of Limits to this part of the field.

3. *The " Crossing of Formulae "*

The method of procedure, to which Professor Irving Fisher has devoted much attention [2] and to which he has given the name of " Crossing the Formulae ",[3] is,

[1] Dr. Bowley in his " Notes on Index Numbers " published in the *Economic Journal*, June 1928, may be mentioned amongst those who have expressly introduced this necessary condition.
[2] *Vide* especially his *The Making of Index Numbers*.
[3] *Op. cit.* chap. vii.

in effect, an attempt to carry the Method of Limits somewhat further—further, in my opinion, than is legitimate.

The reasoning employed is of the following character. As before, let P be the composite commodity appropriate to the first position (of time, place or class), and p the price in the second position of a unit of P which costs £1 in the first position; and let Q be the composite appropriate to the second position, and $\frac{1}{q}$ the price in the first position of a unit of Q which costs £1 in the second position. Then, as we have seen above, the true measure of comparison—assuming that tastes, etc., are constant and that only relative prices are changed—between the price-levels in the two positions necessarily lies somewhere *between p* and *q*. Professor Fisher (amongst others) concludes from this that there must be some mathematical function of p and q which will afford us the best possible estimate of whereabouts between p and q the true value lies. Setting out on these lines, he has proposed and examined a great variety of formulae with the object of getting the best possible approximation to the true intermediate position.

Now, to my way of thinking, the proportion between the price-levels under comparison is not, in general, *any* definite algebraic function of these two expressions. We can concoct all sorts of algebraic functions of p and q as determining the point's position, and there will not be a penny to choose between them. We are faced with a problem in probability, for which in any particular case we may have relevant data, but which, in the absence of such data, is simply indeterminate.

For this reason I see no real substance in Professor Fisher's long discussion, by which, after examining a vast number of formulae, he arrives at the conclusion that $\sqrt{pq}$ (in my notation) is theoretically ideal—if, that is to say, he means by this that it is likely to be arithmetically nearer to the truth than other formulae. This conclusion is the result of applying a number of tests, as for example that the formula must be symmetrically placed in respect of the two extremes between which it is to lie. All these tests, however, are directed to showing, not that it is correct in itself, but that it is open to fewer objections than alternative *a priori* formulae. They do not prove that any one of the formulae has a leg to stand on, regarded as a probable approximation.

If, however, we regard formulae intermediate between p and q, not as probable approximations, but merely as conveniences for the purpose of rapid narration, then we may legitimately be influenced by considerations of algebraical elegance, of arithmetical simplicity, of labour-saving, and of internal consistency between different occasions of using a particular system of short-hand. If p and q are widely discrepant, any form of short-hand may be seriously misleading; but if p and q are nearly equal, it may be a nuisance to use the expression "between p and q", and much more convenient, without being seriously misleading, to name some intermediate figure, even if the choice of this figure is quite arbitrary. Provided, therefore, it is understood that such formulae as $\sqrt{pq}$ are no more than a convenient self-consistent short-hand for "between p and q", I see no objection to them.

In practice, therefore, Professor Fisher's formula may often do no harm. The objection to the formula is that it leads just as easily to a comparison when no such comparison is legitimate, and that it does not bring home to the computer, as the previous methods inevitably do, the nature and degree of the error which is involved. Professor Fisher's formula is condemned by the fact that it appears on the face of it to permit with equal facility a numerical comparison between *any* two price-levels whatever—regardless of whether tastes have changed and of everything else. It leads to just as good a result where it is obvious to common sense that no intelligible comparison is possible at all, as in cases where the strictly appropriate composites are so nearly similar that any compromise intermediate between them will yield a very tolerable approximation.

The oldest formula of this type—though this is a case of what Professor Fisher calls "crossing the weights", not "crossing the formulae"—which was proposed independently many years ago both by Marshall and by Edgeworth (see Edgeworth, *Papers relating to Political Economy*, vol. i. p. 213), is not less objectionable. This method of approximation compares the prices in the two positions of $\frac{P+Q}{2}$, *i.e.* it assumes that a third composite intermediate between the two composites strictly appropriate to the two positions is approximately appropriate to both of them. This amounts (in the above notation) to taking $\frac{p+1}{q+1} \cdot q$ as the measure of the change in the price-level.[1]

It may be of interest, before we conclude this discussion, to show by an example that, when tastes and environment are not constant, p and q are not reliable guides to the change in the value of money, even when $p = q$.

Suppose that in the first position Beef and Whisky (one unit of each) are the predominant objects of expenditure, and in the second position Rice and Coffee (one unit of each); suppose further that units of beef and coffee are 50 per cent cheaper in the second position than in the first, whilst units of whisky

---

[1] Dr. Bowley has given ingenious reasons, in his "Notes on Index Numbers" (*Economic Journal*, June 1928), for preferring this formula to any other, subject to certain assumptions as to continuity and as to what quantities can be regarded as small enough to be neglected.

and rice are 50 per cent cheaper in the first than in the second ; then

$$\frac{\text{price of a unit of beef and a unit of whisky in 1st position}}{\text{price of ditto in 2nd position}}$$
$$= \frac{\text{price of a unit of rice and a unit of coffee in 1st position}}{\text{price of ditto in 2nd position}}$$

(our units being chosen so that expenditure is equally divided between beef and whisky in the first position and between rice and coffee in the second position). The assumption that coffee and rice are not consumed at all in the first position, nor beef and whisky in the second, is not essential to the argument and is only introduced for simplicity of statement. Substantially the same equation would hold if we were to give relatively small weights to coffee and rice in the first position, and to beef and whisky in the second position. Now, if we were to neglect the conditions required for the Method of Limits or were to suppose that the ideas underlying Professor Fisher's ideal formula were universally valid, we could conclude from the above with complete precision that the purchasing power of money in the position where people mainly consume Beef and Whisky is exactly the same as in the position where they mainly consume Rice and Coffee. Yet this conclusion might be quite wrong. Suppose, for example, that in the second position rice is consumed in preference to beef, in spite of rice being relatively dearer than in the first position, because the climate requires it, so that consumers prefer rice ; whereas coffee is consumed in the second position in preference to whisky merely because it is cheaper, so that whisky would be consumed if it was as cheap compared with coffee as it was in the first position. If we knew the money-incomes of "similar" persons in the two positions, we might find that the purchasing power of money was much lower in the second position than in the first.

4. *The Chain Method*

The "Chain Method" of compiling a series of Index-Numbers, which was first introduced by Marshall, is an attempt to deal with the problem of changes in the character of consumption by assuming that the differences are small between any two consecutive positions in the series of positions to be compared. It also assumes—though this is not generally stated—that the successive small errors involved are non-cumulative. A series of comparisons are made, the first of which assumes that the composite appropriate to the first position is virtually equivalent to the composite appropriate to the second position, and the next of which assumes that the composite appropriate to the second position is virtually equivalent to the composite appropriate to the third.

The method is as follows :

Let p_1 p_2 be the prices in the first and second positions of the composite appropriate to the first position ;

q_2 q_3 the prices in the second and third positions of the composite appropriate to the second position ;

r_3 r_4 the prices in the third and fourth positions of the composite appropriate to the third position ; and so on.

Let n_1 n_2 n_3 be the series of Index-Numbers comparing the price-levels in the successive positions.

Then the Chain Method computes n_2, n_3 in terms of n_1 thus :

$$n_2 = \frac{p_2}{p_1} \cdot n_1,$$

$$n_3 = \frac{q_3}{q_2} \cdot n_2 = \frac{q_3}{q_2} \cdot \frac{p_2}{p_1} \cdot n_1,$$

$$n_4 = \frac{r_4}{r_3} \cdot n_3 = \frac{r_4}{r_3} \cdot \frac{q_3}{q_2} \cdot \frac{p_2}{p_1} \cdot n_1 \text{ ; and so on.}$$

Thus the final result is reached by comparing each position with its neighbours in two ways, and then assuming that these two alternative measurements of the same thing are approximately equal. In other words:

if n_1 is the price-level strictly appropriate to the first position;
if n_2 is the price-level strictly appropriate to the second position;
if n'_2 is the price-level in the second position obtained by assuming that the composite appropriate to the first position is also appropriate to the second;
if n'_3 is the price-level in the third position measured by assuming that the composite appropriate to the second position is also appropriate to the third,

then
$$n'_3 = \frac{q_3}{q_2} n_2,$$
$$n'_2 = \frac{p_2}{p_1} n_1,$$
so that, assuming $n_2 = n'_2$, we have
$$n'_3 = \frac{q_3}{q_2} \cdot \frac{p_2}{p_1} n_1 \text{; and so on.}$$

Let us analyse the validity of the above procedure in the light of the preceding argument. In the first place it is clear that it assumes constancy of tastes, etc.; on the other hand, it permits not only changes in relative prices but also the introduction in the later positions of new objects of expenditure which were not available to the consumer in the earlier positions (whilst assuming, however, that any objects of expenditure on the market in one position are still on the market and have not dropped out in the next position). In the second place it is assumed that $n_2 = n'_2$ approximately; which is only justifiable if we have applied the method of limits to the comparison between the two positions and have found (in the notation of p. 110 above) that $p=q$ approximately. In the third place we assume that the successive small errors of approximation—and this is the most serious assumption—are not cumulative so as to add up to a substantial error, when the procedure is repeated a number of times over a succession of positions.

If each pair of successive positions are closely similar to one another, the second of these assumptions may be justified. But the third one is more dangerous, especially in the type of case for which the Chain Method is commonly recommended, namely, for the comparison of a chronological series. For example, the Chain Method will show a cumulative error if each substitution which we assume as approximately equivalent is progressively a slight improvement, *i.e.* if each new composite is slightly better for the purpose in view than its predecessor, and is not just as likely to be slightly worse. For this reason it will mislead us when it is employed over a period of time during which habits are gradually changing as a result of progressively improving opportunities; that is to say, it will in such conditions underestimate the purchasing power of money at the later dates as compared with the former. The Chain Method assumes in effect that, when margarine first comes in, the advantage is trifling, and that the margarine consumed is practically the equivalent in advantage of the butter (or other consumable goods) displaced by it, and so on with each gradual transference of consumption to the new or improved or relatively cheaper product.

It is a further serious objection to the Chain Method that the comparison between two positions is dependent on the path which prices and the character of consumption have pursued over the intervening positions. For example, it might be that prices and consumption are such and such, that a serious disturbance—such as a war—intervenes which materially changes relative prices and the character of consumption, but that after an interval equilibrium is restored and both prices and consumption return to exactly what they were before. Now it is obvious that in such circumstances the purchasing power of money at the end is exactly the same as it was at the beginning. But if the Chain Method has been employed, there is no guarantee that the index-number will return to its original position—indeed one may be pretty sure that it will not.[1]

Finally, the Chain Method is statistically laborious and inconvenient to apply in practice—so much so that it has been very seldom employed, in spite of the many years which have passed by since it was first recommended and the general approval (more than it deserves in my opinion) which it has received from theorists.

I conclude, therefore, that it would be better in comparing, let us say, the purchasing power of money to-day and fifty years ago to compare the price of that part of expenditure (say 50-70 per cent —I have no idea as to the true proportion) which is more or less unchanged in character, supplementing this by a list of the expenditures discarded and added (so as to enable a general judgment to be made as to the extent of the improved opportunities), rather than to compare the price-levels by means of the Chain Method applied year by year over the intervening period.

We are left, therefore, with the Highest Common Factor Method supplemented by the Method of

[1] An interesting analysis bearing on the above, though primarily directed to an examination of the conditions in which a Chain Index diverges from the corresponding Fixed Base Index, has been published by Professor Persons (*Review of Economic Statistics*, May 1928, " The Effect of Correlation between Weights and Relatives in the Construction of Index Numbers," pp. 100-105).

Equivalent Substitution and the Method of Limits as the only valid methods of approximation—other than the direct estimation of the money-incomes of persons who are on general grounds deemed similar.

That, in spite of so many practical and theoretical difficulties, useful comparisons of purchasing power can often be made in actual practice is due to the fact that, even when the relative, as well as the absolute, prices of individual commodities are fluctuating, the average character of typical expenditure and of typical tastes and the average level of real-incomes do not shift, as a rule, rapidly or widely as between communities not much removed from one another in time or place; so that the problem, arising out of the shifting composition of consumption and out of changes in taste and environment, is not acute. For example, the evidence indicates, according to Dr. Bowley, that the changes in taste and habit in England between 1904 and 1927 as tested by general statistics of working-class consumption were comparatively slight.

BOOK III
THE FUNDAMENTAL EQUATIONS

CHAPTER 9

CERTAIN DEFINITIONS

BEFORE we can formulate our Fundamental Equations, we must first make precise our use of certain terms.

(i.) INCOME, PROFITS, SAVINGS AND INVESTMENT

(1) *Income.*—We propose to mean identically the same thing by the three expressions: (1) *the community's money-income*; (2) *the earnings of the factors of production*; and (3) *the cost of production*; and we reserve the term *profits* for the difference between the cost of production of the current output and its actual sale-proceeds, so that profits are not part of the community's income as thus defined.

More particularly we include in Income:

(a) Salaries and wages paid to employees, including any payments made to unemployed or partially employed or pensioned employees —these being in the long run a charge on industry just as much as other outgoings to remunerate the factors of production;
(b) The normal remuneration of entrepreneurs;
(c) Interest on capital (including interest from foreign investments);
(d) Regular monopoly gains, rents and the like.

The entrepreneurs being themselves amongst the factors of production, their normal remuneration—the definition of which for the present purpose will be given in (2) below—is included in income, and, therefore, in the costs of production, under heading (*b*). But we exclude their windfall profits or losses represented by the difference (positive or negative) between the earnings, thus defined, of the factors of production and the actual sale proceeds. The income of holders of ordinary shares will usually include elements of each of the items (*b*), (*c*) and (*d*), and they will also be recipients of windfall profits and losses.

(2) *Profits.*—Thus the difference between the actual remuneration of the entrepreneurs, arrived at by deducting from the sale proceeds their outgoings (*a*), (*c*), and (*d*) above and their normal remuneration (*b*), is, whether positive or negative, the Profits.

Accordingly, whilst the amount of the entrepreneurs' normal remuneration must be reckoned, whether their actual remuneration exceeds it or falls short, as belonging to the income of the individuals who perform entrepreneur functions, the profits must be regarded, not as part of the earnings of the community (any more than an increment in the value of existing capital is part of current income), but as increasing (or, if negative, as diminishing) the value of the accumulated wealth of the entrepeneurs. If an entrepreneur spends part of his profits on current consumption, then this is equivalent to negative saving; and if he restricts his normal consumption because he is suffering windfall losses, this, on the other hand, is equivalent to positive saving.

To make this precise, however, we need to give a definition of entrepreneurs' " normal " remuneration, which will enable us to divide their total receipts (positive or negative) between income on the one hand and profits (positive or negative) on the other. What is the most appropriate and convenient definition partly depends on the nature of the inquiry on hand. For my present purpose I propose to define the "normal" remuneration of entrepreneurs at any time as that rate of remuneration which, if they were open to make new bargains with all the factors of production at the currently prevailing rates of earnings, would leave them under no motive either to increase or to decrease their scale of operations.

Thus when the actual rate of entrepreneurs' remuneration exceeds (or falls short of) the normal as thus defined, so that profits are positive (or negative), entrepreneurs will—in so far as their freedom of action is not fettered by existing bargains with the factors of production which are for the time being irrevocable—seek to expand (or curtail) their scale of operations at the existing costs of production. When, however, an entrepreneur has entered into commitments which cannot be revised immediately—when, for example, he has sunk part of the resources over which he has obtained command in the form of fixed capital—then in certain easily conceivable circumstances it may not be worth his while, even though his profits are negative, to reduce his output until after the expiry of a period of time, the length of which depends on the character of the commitments which he has entered into; so that there may be a time-lag between profits turning negative and the full reaction of this on output.

It has been suggested to me that, owing to the variety of ways in which the term *Profits* has been employed, both by economists and in business usage, it might be better to employ the term *Windfalls* for what I here call *Profits*. It may help some readers mentally to substitute this term; but for my own part I prefer the term *Profits* as carrying with it on the whole the most helpful penumbra of suggestion.

The fact that entrepreneurs have generally entered into long-time contracts with the factors of production, particularly in respect of fixed capital, is indeed of great importance. For it is the explanation—taken in conjunction with the costs of shutting-down production and opening up again, so that results have often to be averaged over a period,—of how there can be losses, *i.e.* of why entrepreneurs continue to produce though at a loss. And, just in the same way, the period which must elapse before the supply of specialised factors of production can be increased, and the long-time contracts (partly conditioned by the length of life of these specialised factors) into which entrepreneurs must enter to induce this increase of supply, are the explanations why, for a time, profits can exist.

(3) *Savings.*—We shall mean by Savings the sum of the differences between the money-incomes of individuals and their money-expenditure on current consumption.

Thus profits, not being part of the income of the community, are not part of its savings either—even when they are not spent on current consumption. They are not only the balancing figure which accounts for the difference between the value of the national output (or national dividend) and its cost of production, both in terms of money; but they also account, as we shall see, for the difference between the value of the increment of the national wealth in any period and the aggregate of individual savings as defined above.

That is to say, the value of the increment of the wealth of the community is measured by Savings *plus* Profits.

(4) *Investment.*—We shall mean by the rate of Investment the net increment during a period of time of the capital of the community (as defined in the next section of this Chapter); and by the value of Investment, not the increment of value of the total capital, but the value of the increment of capital during any period. We shall find, therefore, that the value of current investment, as thus defined, will be equal to the aggregate of Savings and Profits, as thus defined.

(ii.) AVAILABLE AND NON-AVAILABLE OUTPUT

The current output[1] of the community, as distinguished from its money-income, is a flow of goods and services, which consists of two parts—(a) the flow of liquid goods and services which are in a form available for immediate consumption, and (b) the net flow of increments (after allowing for wastage) to capital-goods and to loan capital (to be defined more particularly in the next section) which are not in a form available for consumption. We shall call the former "liquid" or "available" output; the latter "non-available" output; and the two together total output. It will be observed that the available output may either exceed or fall short of the total output, according as the non-available output is positive or negative.

The liquid or available output is made up of two streams, namely, (a) the flow of use accruing from fixed consumers' (or final) capital, and (b) the flow of consumers' (or final) goods emerging from the productive process in a liquid form.[2]

The non-available output is made up of (a) the excess of the flow of increment to unfinished goods in process over the flow of finished goods (whether fixed or liquid) emerging from the productive process, and (b) the excess of the flow of fixed capital goods emerging from the productive process over the current wastage of old fixed capital, together with the net increase in loan capital.

It follows that current consumption must be equal

[1] Meaning by this all output for which the factors of production are remunerated, including amongst the factors of production the owners of capital, and therefore including in output the current use of fixed consumption capital and income from foreign investments.

[2] Including in these, for the sake of convenience, not only goods the production of which occupies an appreciable time, but also goods the consumption and production of which are capable of proceeding almost *pari passu*, *e.g.* personal services; for there is no sharp line between the two.

to the available output, *plus* subtractions from, or *minus* additions to, stocks of liquid consumers' goods which we shall call "hoards"; and current investment must be equal to the non-available output *plus* additions to, or *minus* subtractions from, hoards. Thus consumption is governed by the amount of the *available* output (*plus* any drafts on hoards), not by that of the *total* output; whereas—so long as the money-rates of remuneration of the factors of production are unchanged—the money-income of the community tends to move with the *total* output.

(iii.) THE CLASSIFICATION OF CAPITAL

The stock of Real Capital or material wealth existing at any time is embodied in one or other of three forms :

(1) Goods in use, which are only capable of giving up gradually their full yield of use or enjoyment.

(2) Goods in process, *i.e.* in course of preparation by cultivation or manufacture for use or consumption, or in transport, or with merchants, dealers and retailers, or awaiting the rotation of the seasons.

(3) Goods in stock, which are yielding nothing but are capable of being used or consumed at any time.

We shall call goods in use *Fixed Capital*, goods in process *Working Capital*,[1] and goods in stock *Liquid Capital*.

Working Capital is necessary because some goods take time to produce ; and Fixed Capital is necessary because some goods take time to use or consume. Liquid Capital is only possible when goods will "keep".

There is, of course, no sharp line of division between fixed and liquid goods ; we have a continuous series,

---

[1] A more detailed definition of Working Capital will be given in Volume ii., Chapter 28.

each member of which has more duration of use or consumption than its predecessor—services, food, clothing, ships, furniture, houses, and so on. But the broad distinction is clear enough.

The goods existing at any time can also be classified into *Finished Goods* and *Unfinished Goods*. The finished goods consist of *Final Goods* which are for the enjoyment of the ultimate consumer, and *Instrumental Goods*, which are for use in process.

In the case of unfinished goods there is sometimes an ambiguity as to whether raw materials are best regarded as liquid or in process. In Vol. ii. Chap. 28 we shall complete our definition to the effect that normal stocks required for efficient business are part of Working Capital and therefore in process, whilst surplus stocks are to be regarded as liquid. Thus the unfinished goods existing at any time consist partly of Working Capital and partly of Liquid Capital.

It is convenient to reserve the term " Hoards " to mean the stock of Liquid Final Goods, and the term " Stocks " to mean other forms of Liquid Capital.

Thus Finished Goods = Final Goods *plus* Instrumental Goods = Fixed Capital *plus* Hoards. Unfinished Goods = Working Capital *plus* Stocks. Liquid Capital = Stocks *plus* Hoards. Finished Goods *plus* Unfinished Goods = Fixed Capital *plus* Working Capital *plus* Liquid Capital = Aggregate Real Capital.

If we are considering the wealth of individuals, or of a particular community, as distinct from the wealth of the world as a whole, we have to include —in addition to the ownership of Real Capital as defined above—claims on money, for payment on demand or over a series of dates in the future, as positive and the corresponding debts or obligations as negative. When we are dealing with a closed system as a whole, these items can be neglected, since they cancel out. But when we are dealing with a single country which is part of an international system, this is not so, and there will be a positive or negative balance of wealth in the form of monetary claims for or against the country. Thus when we are concerned with the wealth of a part of the total system under consideration, whether the part is an individual or a country, we have a fourth category, namely, the net balance of claims on money, which we will call *Loan Capital*.

The aggregate of the Real Capital and the Loan Capital we shall call the amount of Investment—which, for a Closed System, is the same thing as the amount of the Real Capital; and the value of the aggregate of Real and Loan Capital is the Value of the Investment. The increment of investment in any period is the net increase of the items belonging to the various categories which make up the aggregate of Real and Loan Capital; and the value of the increment of investment is the sum of the values of the additional items (minus, of course, the value of the items by which, in any particular case, the stock has been diminished).[1]

There is, however, still a further distinction, namely that between the production of Capital-goods and the production of Consumption-goods, of which we shall make more frequent use than of the above in the ensuing pages. We define the output or production of *Capital-goods* during any period as being the increment of Fixed Capital *plus* the increment of Working Capital which will emerge from the productive process as Fixed Capital; whilst that of *Consumption-goods* during any period is defined as the flow of available output *plus* the increment of Working Capital which will emerge as available output. Finally, the output or production of *Investment-goods* during any

[1] This enables us to clear up a point of definition which seems to me to have been unsatisfactorily handled by Prof. Pigou in the *Economics of Welfare* (3rd Edition), part i. chap. iv. The value of the National Dividend during any period is the value of the current consumption *plus* the value of the increment of investment as defined above.

period is equal to the non-available output *plus* the increment of hoards.

(iv.) Foreign Lending and the Foreign Balance

When we are dealing with an international, and not with a closed, system, we must, first of all, adjust our definition of the national output. That part of current output which belongs to foreigners (*e.g.* because they have a claim on the factors of production which have gone to produce it) we exclude from the national output; and similarly we must add to it the current output produced abroad which belongs to our own nationals. Further, where home-owned output of goods or services is exchanged for foreign-owned output of goods or services, we must—when we are dealing with real output as distinct from its value—substitute the foreign items thus received for the home items exchanged for them in our aggregate of national output.

Next, we propose to distinguish by definition between a country's " foreign lending " and its " foreign balance," in a manner partly corresponding to the distinction made above between " saving " and " investment ". The balance of trade on *income* account, resulting from the excess of the value of home-owned output of goods and services (other than gold), whether produced at home or abroad, placed at the use and disposal of foreigners, over the value of the corresponding foreign-owned output placed at our use and disposal, we shall call the country's *Foreign Balance*, which may, of course, be positive or negative.

By *Foreign Lending*, on the other hand, we propose to mean what might, perhaps, be called the unfavourable balance of transactions on *capital* account, *i.e.* the excess of the amount of our own money put at the disposal of foreigners through the net purchase by our nationals of investments situated abroad, over the corresponding amount expended by foreigners on the purchase of our investments situated at home.[1]

The reader will notice that there is a further item entering into the international balance-sheet, namely, movements of gold, which we have excluded from the Foreign Balance. Since the international balance-sheet must always balance, this item must account for any difference between the value of current Foreign Lending and that of the current Foreign Balance; *i.e.* the former is equal to the latter *plus* the current exports of gold.[2]

Thus we use the term "foreign lending" to describe the financial transactions of placing our own domestic money or claims to it at the disposal of a foreigner in return for some kind of bond or title to property or future profits, and correspondingly with "foreign borrowing". The "foreign balance", on the other hand, arises out of the material transactions which take place when a part of the community's current output, as defined above, is transferred into the hands of foreigners, instead of being utilised at home.

By *Home Investment* we shall mean the increment of total capital situated at home, exclusive of gold; by *Foreign Lending* the increment of home-owned capital situated abroad, also exclusive of gold; and by *Total Investment* the sum of Home Investment, Foreign Lending and Imports of Gold. Since the Foreign Balance is equal to the sum of the Foreign Lending and the Imports of Gold, it is the amount of the Foreign Balance, rather than that of the Foreign Lending, which it is convenient to call *Foreign Investment*. For with this definition the Total Investment is equal, as it ought to be, to the sum of the Home Investment and of the Foreign Investment.

---

[1] Loan Capital must be regarded as situated in the country of the debtor (whatever currency it may be expressed in).

[2] "Ear-marked" gold must be regarded as having been exported and being, therefore, situated abroad.

CHAPTER 10

THE FUNDAMENTAL EQUATIONS FOR THE VALUE OF MONEY

THE Fundamental Problem of Monetary Theory is not merely to establish identities or statical equations relating (*e.g.*) the turnover of monetary instruments to the turnover of things traded for money. The real task of such a Theory is to treat the problem dynamically, analysing the different elements involved, in such a manner as to exhibit the causal process by which the price-level is determined, and the method of transition from one position of equilibrium to another.

The forms of the Quantity Theory, however, on which we have all been brought up—I shall give an account of them in detail in Chapter 14—are but ill adapted for this purpose. They are particular examples of the numerous identities which can be formulated connecting different monetary factors. But they do not, any of them, have the advantage of separating out those factors through which, in a modern economic system, the causal process actually operates during a period of change.

Moreover, they have a further fault, in that the standard, to which they apply, is neither the Labour Standard nor the Purchasing Power Standard, but some other, more or less artificial, standard, namely, either the Cash-Transactions Standard or the Cash-Balances Standard, as defined in Chapter 6 above. This is a serious fault, because it must be the two former standards which are our true *quaesita*. For the Labour Power of Money and the Purchasing Power of Money are fundamental in a sense in which price-levels based on other types of expenditure are not. Human effort and human consumption are the ultimate matters from which alone economic transactions are capable of deriving any significance ; and all other forms of expenditure only acquire importance from their having some relationship, sooner or later, to the effort of producers or to the expenditure of consumers.

I propose, therefore, to break away from the traditional method of setting out from the total quantity of money irrespective of the purposes on which it is employed, and to start instead—for reasons which will become clear as we proceed—with the flow of the community's earnings or money-income, and with its twofold division (1) into the parts which have been *earned* by the production of consumption-goods and of investment-goods respectively, and (2) into the parts which are *expended* on consumption-goods and on savings respectively.

We shall find that, if the first of these divisions of the community's income is in the same proportion as the second, *i.e.* if the output measured in cost of production is divided between consumption-goods and investment-goods in the same proportion as expenditure is divided between current consumption and savings, then the price-level of consumption-goods will be in equilibrium with their cost of production. But if the proportionate divisions are not the same in the two cases, then the price-level of consumption-goods will differ from their cost of production.

The price-level of investment-goods, on the other hand, depends on a different set of considerations, which we shall come to later.

(i.) The Fundamental Equations for the Value of Money

Let E be the total money-income or Earnings of the community in a unit of time, and I′ the part of it which has been earned by the production of investment-goods, so that I′ measures the cost of production of new investment and E − I′ the cost of production of the current output of consumption-goods.

Further, let S be the amount of Savings as defined above, so that E − S measures the current expenditure of income on consumption-goods.

Let us choose our units of quantities of goods in such a way that a unit of each has the same cost of production at the base date; and let O be the total output of goods in terms of these units in a unit of time, R the volume of liquid Consumption-goods and Services flowing on to the market and purchased by consumers, and C the net increment of Investment, in the sense that O = R + C.

Let P be the price-level of liquid Consumption-goods, so that P . R represents the current expenditure on consumption-goods and $E \cdot \frac{C}{O}(= I')$ is the cost of production of new investment.

Then, since the expenditure of the community on consumption goods is equal to the difference between its income and its savings, we have

$$P \cdot R = E - S = \frac{E}{O}(R + C) - S = \frac{E}{O} \cdot R + I' - S;$$

or
$$P = \frac{E}{O} + \frac{I' - S}{R}, \qquad . \qquad . \qquad . \quad \text{(i.)}$$

which is the first of our Fundamental Equations.

Let W be the rate of earnings per unit of human effort (so that the inverse of W measures the Labour Power of Money), W_1 the rate of earnings per unit of output, *i.e.* the rate of efficiency-earnings, and e the coefficient of efficiency (so that $W = e \cdot W_1$).

We can then re-write Equation (i.) in the forms:

$$P = W_1 + \frac{I' - S}{R} \qquad \ldots \qquad \text{(ii.)}$$

$$= \frac{1}{e} \cdot W + \frac{I' - S}{R} \qquad \ldots \qquad \text{(iii.)}$$

The price-level of consumption-goods (*i.e.* the inverse of the purchasing power of money) is made up, therefore, of two terms, the first of which represents the level of efficiency-earnings, *i.e.* the cost of production, and the second of which is positive, zero or negative, according as the cost of new investment exceeds, equals or falls short of the volume of current savings. It follows that the stability of the purchasing power of money involves the two conditions—that efficiency-earnings should be constant and that the cost of new investment should be equal to the volume of current savings.

Thus the price-level, as determined by the first term, is upset by the fact that the division of the output between investment and goods for consumption is not necessarily the same as the division of the income between savings and expenditure on consumption. For workers are paid just as much when they are producing for investment as when they are producing for consumption; but having earned their wages, it is they who please themselves whether they spend or refrain from spending them on consumption. Meanwhile, the entrepreneurs have been deciding quite independently in what proportions they shall produce the two categories of output.

The reader will observe that the price-level of consumption-goods is entirely independent of the price-level of investment-goods. Given the level of efficiency wages and the difference between the cost of new investment-goods (as distinguished from their selling price) and the volume of saving, the price-level of consumption-goods is unequivocally determined, quite irrespective of the price-level of investment-goods.

This latter price-level depends, as we have stated above, on a different set of considerations, which we will examine in Section (iii.) of this Chapter. Meanwhile, if we may be allowed to assume the price-level of new investment-goods as given, we can obtain a formula as follows for the price-level of output as a whole.

Let P' be the price-level of new investment-goods,

Π the price-level of output as a whole,

and $I\ (=P'\ .\ C)$ the value (as distinguished from I', the cost of production) of the increment of new investment goods.

Then
$$\Pi = \frac{P\ .\ R + P'\ .\ C}{O}$$
$$= \frac{(E-S)+I}{O}$$
$$= \frac{E}{O} + \frac{I-S}{O}, \quad . \quad . \quad . \quad \text{(iv.)}$$

which is the second of our Fundamental Equations. As before, we can re-write Equation (iv.):

$$\Pi = W_1 + \frac{I-S}{O} \quad . \quad . \quad . \quad \text{(v.)}$$
$$= \frac{1}{e}\ .\ W + \frac{I-S}{O}. \quad . \quad . \quad \text{(vi.)}$$

(ii.) The Characteristics of Profit

Next, let Q_1 be the amount of the profit (defined as above) on the production and sale of consumption-goods, and Q_2 the corresponding profit on investment-goods, and Q the total profit.

Then
$$Q_1 = P \cdot R - \frac{E}{O} \cdot R$$
$$= E - S - (E - I')$$
$$= I' - S ; \quad \quad \quad \text{(vii.)}$$
and, since
$$Q_2 = I - I',$$
$$Q = Q_1 + Q_2$$
$$= I - S. \quad \quad \quad \text{(viii.)}$$

Thus the profits on the production and sale of consumption-goods are equal to the difference between the *cost* of new investment and savings, being negative when savings exceed the cost of new investment; and the total profits on output as a whole are equal to the difference between the *value* of new investment and savings, being negative when savings exceed the value of new investment.

It follows from the above that we can re-write Equations (ii.) and (v.):

$$P = W_1 + \frac{Q_1}{R}, \quad \quad \quad \text{(ix.)}$$

$$\Pi = W_1 + \frac{Q}{O}. \quad \quad \quad \text{(x.)}$$

These equations tell us that the price of consumption-goods is equal to the rate of earnings of the factors of production *plus* the rate of profits per unit of output of consumption-goods; and correspondingly with output as a whole.

These conclusions are, of course, obvious and may serve to remind us that all these equations are purely formal; they are mere identities; truisms which tell us nothing in themselves. In this respect they resemble all other versions of the Quantity Theory of Money. Their only point is to analyse and arrange our material in what will turn out to be a useful way for tracing cause and effect, when we have vitalised them by the introduction of extraneous facts from the actual world.

There is one peculiarity of profits (or losses) which we may note in passing, because it is one of the reasons why it is necessary to segregate them from income proper, as a category apart. If entrepreneurs choose to spend a portion of their profits on consumption (and there is, of course, nothing to prevent them from doing this), the effect is to *increase* the profit on the sale of liquid consumption-goods by an amount exactly equal to the amount of profits which have been thus expended. This follows from our definitions, because such expenditure constitutes a diminution of saving, and therefore an increase in the difference between I' and S. Thus, however much of their profits entrepreneurs spend on consumption, the increment of wealth belonging to entrepreneurs remains the same as before. Thus profits, as a source of capital increment for entrepreneurs, are a widow's cruse which remains undepleted however much of them may be devoted to riotous living. When, on the other hand, entrepreneurs are making losses, and seek to recoup these losses by curtailing their normal expenditure on consumption, *i.e.* by saving more, the cruse becomes a Danaid jar which can never be filled up; for the effect of this reduced expenditure is to inflict on the producers of consumption-goods a loss of an equal amount. Thus the diminution of their wealth, as a class, is as great, in spite of their savings, as it was before.

Since the volume of the public's savings, *plus* the profits (or *minus* the losses) of entrepreneurs turning out liquid consumption-goods, is always exactly equal to the cost of production of investment-goods, does it follow that investment-goods must always sell at a price equal to their cost of production?

No—for the reason that if investment-goods sell at a price above (or below) their cost of production, the resulting profit (or loss) to entrepreneurs producing investment-goods necessarily provides the difference between the selling price of the investment-goods, whatever this may be, and their actual cost of production.[1] Thus whatever the price-level of investment-goods, the amount forthcoming for their purchase, out of current savings augmented by the profits or diminished by the losses on current production, will be exactly equal to their value.

The question, what *does* determine the price of new investment-goods, we shall consider in a moment. Our present conclusion is, in the first place, that profits (or losses) are an effect of the rest of the situation rather than a cause of it. For this reason it would be anomalous to add profits to (or subtract losses from) income; for, in that case, savings could never fall off, however great the expenditure of the public on current consumption, and equally savings could never be increased by a reduced expenditure on consumption; provided merely that entrepreneurs were continuing to produce the same output of investment-goods as before.

But, in the second place, profits (or losses) having once come into existence become, as we shall see (for this will be the main topic of several succeeding chapters), a cause of what subsequently ensues; indeed, the mainspring of change in the existing economic system. This is the essential reason why it is useful to segregate them in our Fundamental Equation.

(iii.) THE PRICE-LEVEL OF NEW INVESTMENT-GOODS

When a man is deciding what proportion of his money-income to save, he is choosing between present

[1] If entrepreneurs producing investment-goods are spending part of their profits on consumption, this must necessarily mean that entrepreneurs producing liquid consumption-goods will have an extra profit accruing to them available for the purchase of investment-goods; so that the net result is the same as if the entrepreneurs producing investment-goods were spending these profits on the purchase of investment-goods.

consumption and the ownership of wealth. In so far as he decides in favour of consumption, he must necessarily purchase goods—for he cannot consume money. But in so far as he decides in favour of saving, there still remains a further decision for him to make. For he can own wealth by holding it either in the form of money (or the liquid equivalent of money) or in other forms of loan or real capital. This second decision might be conveniently described as the choice between " hoarding " and " investing ", or, alternatively, as the choice between " bank-deposits " and " securities ".[1]

There is also a further significant difference between the two types of decision. The decision as to the volume of saving, and also the decision relating to the volume of new investment, relate wholly to current activities. But the decision as to holding bank-deposits or securities relates, not only to the current increment to the wealth of individuals, but also to the whole block of their existing capital. Indeed, since the current increment is but a trifling proportion of the block of existing wealth, it is but a minor element in the matter.

Now when an individual is more disposed than before to hold his wealth in the form of savings-deposits and less disposed to hold it in other forms, this does not mean that he is determined to hold it in the form of savings-deposits *at all costs*. It means that he favours savings-deposits (for whatever reason) more than before at the existing price-level of other securities. But his distaste for other securities is not absolute and depends on his expectations of the future

---

[1] It is difficult to decide what is the most convenient exploitation of existing non-technical language for exact technical meanings. Unfortunately I have already had to use the terms " hoarding " and " investing " with meanings different from the above; for I have defined " hoards " (pp. 128-9) to mean stocks of liquid consumption-goods, and " investing " (p. 126) to mean, not the purchase of securities by members of the public, but the act of the entrepreneur when he makes an addition to the capital of the community. I shall, therefore, use the second set of terms in what follows.

return to be obtained from savings-deposits and from other securities respectively, which is obviously affected by the price of the latter—and also by the rate of interest allowed on the former. If, therefore, the price-level of other securities falls sufficiently, he can be tempted back into them. If, however, the banking system operates in the opposite direction to that of the public and meets the preference of the latter for savings-deposits by buying the securities which the public is *less* anxious to hold and creating against them the additional savings-deposits which the public is *more* anxious to hold, then there is no need for the price-level of investments to fall at all. Thus the change in the relative attractions of savings-deposits and securities respectively has to be met either by a fall in the price of securities or by an increase in the supply of savings-deposits, or partly by the one and partly by the other. A fall in the price-level of securities is therefore an indication that the " bearishness " of the public—as we may conveniently designate, in anticipation of later chapters, an increased preference for savings-deposits as against other forms of wealth and a decreased preference for carrying securities with money borrowed from the banks—has been insufficiently offset by the creation of savings-deposits by the banking system—or that the " bullishness " of the public has been more than offset by the contraction of savings-deposits by the banking system.

It follows that the actual price-level of investments is the resultant of the sentiment of the public and the behaviour of the banking system. This does not mean that there is any definite numerical relationship between the price-level of investments and the additional quantity of savings-deposits created. The amount by which the creation of a given quantity of deposits will raise the price of other securities above what their price would otherwise have been depends on the shape of the public's demand curve for savings-deposits at different price-levels of other securities.[1]

There may also be the case, as we shall see in Chapter 15, where "two opinions" develop between different schools of the public, the one favouring bank-deposits more than before and the other favouring securities. In this case the result depends on the willingness of the banking system to act as an intermediary between the two by creating bank-deposits, not against securities, but against liquid short-term advances.

Without forgetting that we are dealing with a case of multiple equilibrium in which each element affects every other element more or less, and, without anticipating unduly the subject-matter of Chapter 15, we may sum up the matter thus.

The price-level of investments as a whole, and hence of new investments, is that price-level at which the desire of the public to hold savings-deposits is equal to the amount of savings-deposits which the banking system is willing and able to create.[2]

On the other hand—as we have already seen—the price-level of consumption-goods, relatively to the cost of production, depends *solely* on the resultant of the decisions of the public as to the proportion of their incomes which they save and the decisions of the entrepreneurs as to the proportion of their production which they devote to the output of investment-goods—though both of these decisions, and particularly the latter, may be partly influenced by the price-level of investment-goods.

It follows that the price-level of output as a whole and the amount of total profit depend on all four factors—(1) the rate of saving, (2) the cost of new

[1] The rate of interest offered by the banking system on savings-deposits also comes in, of course, as a factor influencing their relative attractiveness.

[2] I am ignoring here the complications, which do not affect the essence of the argument, arising out of the possibility of transferences between the savings-deposits and the cash-deposits. We shall come to these later.

investment, (3) the "bearishness" of the public, (4) the volume of savings-deposits; or, if you like, on the two factors—(1) the excess of saving over cost of investment, and (2) such excess of bearishness on the part of the public as is unsatisfied by the creation of deposits by the banking system.

Thus given the rate of new investment and the cost of production, the price-level of consumption-goods is solely determined by the disposition of the public towards " saving ". And given the volume of savings-deposits created by the banking system, the price-level of investment-goods (whether new or old) is solely determined by the disposition of the public towards "hoarding "[1] money.

I hope I have made clear the distinction between the two types of decision which the earning and wealth-owning public is being constantly called on to make. But however clear we may be about the distinction, it is nevertheless difficult to keep the causes and the results of the two types of decision disentangled, since they act and react on one another in a most perplexing way. For the amount of saving and the amount of investment, and consequently the difference between them, partly depend on the price-level of investment-goods relatively to their cost of production; and at the same time the attitude of the public towards savings-deposits and other securities respectively may be partly influenced by expectations as to the price-level of consumption-goods relatively to their cost of production. In particular, a change in the disposition of the public towards securities other than savings-deposits, uncompensated by action on the part of the banking system, will be a most potent factor affecting the rate of investment relatively to saving and a cause of disturbance, therefore, to the purchasing power of money.

[1] Using this term, for once, to mean their scale of preference for savings-deposits and other securities at different price-levels of the latter.

Nevertheless, although these factors react on one another, the excess-saving factor and the excess-bearish factor [1] (as perhaps we may call them) are independent in the sense that any degree, positive or negative, of the one is compatible in appropriate attendant circumstances with any degree, positive or negative, of the other.

Before leaving this section it may be well to illustrate further the conclusion stated above, that a fall in the price of consumption-goods due to an excess of saving over investment does not in itself—if it is unaccompanied by any change in the bearishness or bullishness of the public or in the volume of savings-deposits, or if there are compensating changes in these two factors—require any opposite change in the price of new investment-goods. For I believe that this conclusion may be accepted by some readers with difficulty.

It follows from the fact that, on the above assumptions, the total value of the investment-goods (new and old) coming on to the market for purchase out of current savings is *always* exactly equal to the amount of such savings and is irrespective of the current output of *new* investment-goods. For if the value of the new investment-goods is less than the volume of current savings, entrepreneurs as a whole must be making losses exactly equal to the difference. These losses, which represent a failure to receive cash up to expectations from sales of current output, must be financed, and the non-receipt of the expected cash receipts must be somehow made good. The entrepreneurs can only make them good either by reducing their own bank-deposits or by selling some of their other capital assets. The bank-deposits thus released and the securities thus sold are available for, and are exactly equal to, the excess of current savings over the value of new investment.

---

[1] *I.e.* bearishness on the part of members of the public which is not balanced by increased credit creation by the banking system.

In the more general case where the public sentiment towards securities or the volume of savings-deposits is changing, then if the extent to which the entrepreneurs have recourse to the expedient of releasing bank-deposits *plus* the increase in savings-deposits allowed by the banking system just balances the increase in the desire of the public to employ their resources in bank-deposits, there is no reason for any change in the price of securities. If the former is in excess of the latter, the price of securities will tend to rise; and if the latter is in excess of the former, the price of securities will tend to fall.

(iv.) The Relation of the Price-level to the Quantity of Money

The reader will have perceived by now that the relationship of the purchasing power of money (or price-level of consumption-goods) and of the price-level of output as a whole to the quantity of money and the velocity of circulation is not of that direct character which the old-fashioned quantity equations, however carefully guarded, might lead one to suppose.

If we assume that banking habits and practices are unchanged, the requirements of the Cash-Deposits are mainly determined by the magnitude of the earnings bill, *i.e.* by the product of the rate of earnings and the volume of output; and the requirements of the Savings-Deposits are mainly determined by the bearishness of the public's disposition taken in conjunction with the price-level of securities. Or putting it the other way round, given the total quantity of money, only those combinations of the rate of earnings, the volume of output and the price-level of securities are feasible which lead to the aggregate requirements of money being equal to the given total.

This means, indeed, that in equilibrium—*i.e.* when the factors of production are fully employed, when the public is neither bullish nor bearish of securities and is maintaining in the form of savings-deposits neither more nor less than the "normal" proportion of its total wealth, and when the volume of saving is equal both to the cost and to the value of new investments —there is a unique relationship between the quantity of money and the price-levels of consumption-goods and of output as a whole, of such a character that if the quantity of money were double the price-levels would be double also.

But this simple and direct quantitative relationship is a phenomenon only of equilibrium as defined above. If the volume of saving becomes unequal to the cost of new investment, or if the public disposition towards securities takes a turn, even for good reasons, in the bullish or in the bearish direction, then the fundamental price-levels can depart from their equilibrium values without any change having occurred in the quantity of money or in the velocities of circulation. It is even conceivable that the cash-deposits may remain the same, the savings-deposits may remain the same, the velocities of circulation may remain the same, the volume of monetary transactions may remain the same, and the volume of output may remain the same; and yet the fundamental price-levels may change.

Such an exact balance is, of course, only a theoretical possibility. In the actual world a change in anything is likely to be accompanied by some change in everything else. But even so the degrees of change in the quantity of money, the velocities of circulation, and the volume of output will not be related in any definite or predictable ratio to the degrees of change in the fundamental price-levels. Indeed this is notoriously the case at the acute phases of a credit cycle.

There are, of course, various possible assumptions as to the effect of profits and losses on the amount of the Business-deposits maintained by entrepreneurs, on which a change in the fundamental price-levels could not occur without some change in the monetary factors. The theoretical possibility mentioned above —and given, avowedly, as an extreme case for the sake of emphasising the essence of the argument— only holds good if entrepreneurs are solely influenced by their costs of production in deciding what amount of Business-deposits to maintain.

If, for example, entrepreneurs were to treat their windfall profits or losses exactly in the same way as though they were regular personal income, when they are deciding what influence the receipt of profits or the incurring of losses ought to have on the volume of their bank-deposits, a rise in the price-level due to an increase in the second term of the Fundamental Equation would require as great an increase in the quantity of money (or equivalent change in other monetary factors) as would a rise due to an increase in the first term. In fact this is not likely to be the case. In fact, the receipt and disbursal of profits will be likely—if it involves *any* material change in the balances held—to involve a less holding of balances than would an equal increase in the receipt and disbursal of incomes—at any rate, over the short period.

Moreover, even though the ultimate recipients of profits, *e.g.* the individual shareholders, may treat their receipt like income in spite of their not belonging to true income-deposits, yet now that the great bulk of business and industry is organised in the form of joint-stock companies (and the same thing was probably true to a large extent even in the days of partnerships), windfall profits are not disbursed to individual accounts, as most incomes are, at weekly, monthly, or quarterly periods, but at much longer intervals and with a much greater time-lag after they have been gained. Not only will an interval of at least half a year usually elapse, but a large part of exceptional profits will often or generally be placed to reserve or withheld from the individual shareholder in one way or another—especially, for example, in the United States. Meanwhile profits are more likely to be used to pay off bank loans than to be held as current cash, and the volume of business-deposits will be primarily determined, as we began by assuming, by the business costs of production.

One other matter we may note in passing. We shall see in later chapters that a change in the price-level, due to the second term of the Fundamental Equation, sets up tendencies towards a *subsequent* increase in the first term. As these tendencies develop, a given rise in the price-level will require a larger volume of cash-balances to support it than when the rise was wholly due to an increase in the second term. The fact that a change in the price-level, due to the first term of the Fundamental Equation, involves a larger change in monetary factors than an equal change due to the second term, accompanied by the fact that change generally begins with the second term and then spreads to the first term, will be found to be a part of the explanation why certain types of price-changes tend to kill themselves as they proceed and to set up a reaction in the opposite direction.

In the case of equilibrium, where $I = I' = S$, we can express our conclusions in terms of the usual monetary factors as follows.

If M_1 is the total of the Income-deposits and V_1 their velocity of circulation, we have $E = M_1 V_1$; for V_1 is, by definition (see p. 44 above), the ratio of the money-income (E) of the community per unit of time to M_1, the amount of the income-deposits.

When $I = I' = S$, we can, therefore, re-write our equations:
$$\Pi = P = \frac{M_1 V_1}{O}.$$

If we wish to relate P to M, the total quantity of

money, we can proceed as follows : Let M_1, M_2, and M_3 be the totals of the income-deposits, the business-deposits, and the savings-deposits respectively, and M that of the total deposits, so that $M = M_1 + M_2 + M_3$. Therefore
$$P = \frac{V_1(M - M_2 - M_3)}{O}.$$

Let w be the proportion of the cash-deposits to the total deposits and V the average velocity of the cash-deposits where V_1 and V_2 are the velocities of the income-deposits and of the business-deposits respectively, so that
$$M_1 + M_2 = wM,$$
$$M_1 V_1 + M_2 V_2 = w \cdot M \cdot V\ ;$$
then
$$M_1 = M \frac{w(V_2 - V)}{V_2 - V_1},$$
and
$$M_1 V_1 = M \frac{w V_1 (V_2 - V)}{V_2 - V_1},$$
so that
$$P = \frac{M}{O} \cdot \frac{w V_1 (V_2 - V)}{V_2 - V_1}.$$

The equation
$$P \cdot O = M_1 V_1$$
evidently bears a family relationship to Professor Irving Fisher's familiar equation
$$P \cdot T = M \cdot V,$$
except that O represents current output whereas T is the volume, not of output, but of transactions, and that M_1, V_1 represent the income-deposits and their velocity, whereas M, V are the cash-deposits and their velocity.[1]

[1] We shall consider further Professor Fisher's type of Quantity Equation in Chapter 14.

CHAPTER 11

THE CONDITIONS OF EQUILIBRIUM

(i.) The Condition of Zero-profits

We have seen in the previous chapter that, since the Profits (Q) are the difference between the value of current output and E, its cost of production, we have

$$Q = I - S;$$

so that entrepreneurs make a profit or a loss according as the money-value of current Investment exceeds or falls short of current Savings.

Thus we have Profits = Value of Output − Cost of Production = Value of Investment − Savings; Profits being the balancing figure not only between Cost of Production and Value of Output, but also between Savings and the Value of Net Investment, both in terms of money.

These Profits (whether positive or negative) are made up of two elements, which we have called (p. 137) Q_1 and Q_2, namely, $Q_1(= I' - S)$, which is the profit on the output of consumption-goods, and $Q_2(= I - I')$, which is the profit on the output of investment-goods.

Now equilibrium requires that Q_1, Q_2 and Q should all be zero. For if either Q_1 or Q_2 is not zero one class of entrepreneurs will have an incentive to expand their output; and if the total profits Q are not zero, the entrepreneurs will tend, so far as they can, to alter the total volume of employment which they offer to the Factors of Production at a given rate of remuneration—upwards or downwards, according as such profits are positive or negative. Thus W_1 and therefore P will be in a condition of disequilibrium, which will continue so long as profits (whether Q_1 or Q_2) have not returned to zero.

Thus the conditions for the equilibrium of the purchasing power of money require that the Banking System should so regulate its rate of lending that the value of Investment is equal to Savings; for otherwise entrepreneurs will, under the influence of positive or negative profits, be both willing in themselves and at the same time influenced by the abundance or scarcity of the bank-credit at their disposal, to increase or diminish (as the case may be) the average rate of remuneration W_1 which they offer to the factors of production. But the conditions for equilibrium also require that the *cost* of new Investment should be equal to savings; for otherwise producers of consumption-goods will be endeavouring, under the influence of profits or losses, to alter their scale of output.

In equilibrium, therefore, both the value and the cost of current investment must be equal to the amount of current savings, and profits must be zero; and in such circumstances the Purchasing Power of Money and the price-level of output as a whole will both correspond to the money-rate of efficiency earnings of the Factors of Production (*i.e.* $P = \Pi = W_1$).

The reader will appreciate that the condition of zero-profits means that *aggregate* profits are zero. For a stability of the price-level as a whole is perfectly compatible with the profits of particular entrepreneurs or particular classes of entrepreneurs being positive or negative, just as it is compatible with the prices of particular commodities rising or falling.

Thus, the long-period or equilibrium norm of the Purchasing Power of Money is given by the money-rate

CH. II   THE CONDITIONS OF EQUILIBRIUM   153

of efficiency earnings of the Factors of Production; whilst the actual Purchasing Power oscillates below or above this equilibrium level according as the cost of current investment is running ahead of, or falling behind, savings.

A principal object of this Treatise is to show that we have here the clue to the way in which the fluctuations of the price-level actually come to pass, whether they are due to oscillations about a steady equilibrium level or to a transition from one equilibrium to another.

By the scale and the terms on which it is prepared to grant loans, the banking system is in a position, under a regime of Representative Money, to determine —broadly speaking—the rate of investment by the business world. At the same time the aggregate result of the decisions of the members of the community, as to how much of their money-incomes they shall expend on consumption and how much they shall save, is determining the rate of saving. According, therefore, as the banking system is allowing the rate of investment to exceed or fall behind the rate of saving, the price-level (assuming that there is no spontaneous change in the rate of efficiency-earnings) will rise or fall. If, however, the prevailing type of contract between the entrepreneurs and the factors of production is in terms of effort-earnings W and not in terms of efficiency-earnings W_1 (existing arrangements probably lie as a rule somewhere between the two), then it would be $\frac{1}{e} \cdot P$, which would tend to rise or fall, where, as before, e is the coefficient of efficiency.

But this disparity between investment and saving sets up a disequilibrium in the rate of profit. The next stage of the argument (to be developed in Book IV.) proceeds, therefore, to show how this profit-disequilibrium reacts—unless the banking system takes steps to counteract it—on the *first* term of the Fundamental Equation, eventually causing the money-rate of efficiency-earnings (or effort-earnings) to rise or fall, as the case may be, to a point which allows the banking system to establish a new position of equilibrium compatible with the criteria by which this system is governed.

(ii.) THE RATE OF INTEREST, OR BANK-RATE

It is now evident in what manner changes in the Bank-rate, or—more strictly—changes in the rate of interest, are capable of influencing the purchasing power of money.

The attractiveness of investment depends on the prospective income which the entrepreneur anticipates from current investment relatively to the rate of interest which he has to pay in order to be able to finance its production;—or, putting it the other way round, the value of capital-goods depends on the rate of interest at which the prospective income from them is capitalised. That is to say, the higher (*e.g.*) the rate of interest, the lower, other things being equal, will be the value of capital-goods. Therefore, if the rate of interest rises, P' will tend to fall, which will lower the rate of profit on the production of capital-goods, which will be deterrent to new investment. Thus a high rate of interest will tend to diminish both P' and C, which stand respectively for the price-level and the volume of output of capital-goods. The rate of saving, on the other hand, is stimulated by a high rate of interest and discouraged by a low rate. It follows that an increase in the rate of interest tends—other things being equal—to make the rate of investment (whether measured by its value or by its cost) to decline relatively to the rate of saving, *i.e.* to move the second term of both Fundamental Equations in the negative direction, so that the price-levels tend to fall.

Following Wicksell, it will be convenient to call the rate of interest which would cause the second term of our second Fundamental Equation to be zero the *natural-rate* of interest, and the rate which actually prevails the *market-rate* of interest. Thus the natural-rate of interest is the rate at which saving and the value of investment are exactly balanced, so that the price-level of output as a whole (Π) exactly corresponds to the money-rate of the efficiency-earnings of the Factors of Production. Every departure of the market-rate from the natural-rate tends, on the other hand, to set up a disturbance of the price-level by causing the second term of the second Fundamental Equation to depart from zero.

We have, therefore, something with which the ordinary Quantity Equation does not furnish us, namely, a simple and direct explanation why a rise in the Bank-rate tends, in so far as it modifies the effective rates of interest, to depress price-levels. To a more complete explanation of the theory of Bank-rate we shall return in Chapters 13 and 37.

(iii.) Inflation and Deflation

We have seen that there are two main types of fluctuation, which can influence price-levels, corresponding to the two terms of our first Fundamental Equation, of which the second can be divided into two parts. We may have a rise or fall in W_1, the rate of efficiency-earnings. We shall call this *Income Inflation* (or *Deflation*), corresponding to changes in the first term of the Fundamental Equation. We may have a rise or fall of Q, the total profits above or below zero, due to an inequality between saving and the value of investment. We shall call this *Profit Inflation* (or *Deflation*).

Further, since $Q = Q_1 + Q_2$, where Q_1 and Q_2 are as defined on p. 137 above, Profit Inflation (or Deflation) is the sum of two terms, Q_1 and Q_2, which we may call *Commodity Inflation* (or *Deflation*) and *Capital Infla-*

tion (or *Deflation*) respectively. Thus (referring back to the definitions of Q_1 and Q_2) Commodity Inflation measures the change in price of liquid consumption-goods, and Capital Inflation the change in the price of capital-goods, relatively to their cost of production. In what ensues, however, we shall be mainly concerned with Income Inflation and Profit Inflation, and we shall seldom require to split up the latter into its component parts of Commodity Inflation and Capital Inflation.

It follows that changes in Π, the price-level of output as a whole, are measured by the sum of the Income Inflation and the Profit Inflation; whilst those in P, the purchasing power of money, are measured by the sum of the Income Inflation and the Commodity Inflation. It will be noticed that Capital Inflation or Deflation does not *as such* affect the purchasing power of money, since I', the cost of investment, is unaffected by it. The significance of Capital Inflation or Deflation in its influence on the purchasing power of money lies in the fact that its presence is almost certain, sooner or later, to affect the output of capital-goods, and hence to produce Commodity Inflation or Deflation.

(iv.) The Causal Direction of Change

It is important for the reader to appreciate that the definition of *Profits* given above, and the division of the total value of the product between what we call *Income* or *Earnings* and what we call *Profits*, are not arbitrary. The essential characteristic of the entity which we call *Profits* is that its having a zero value is the usual condition in the actual economic world of to-day for the equilibrium of the purchasing power of money. It is the introduction of this *fact* from the real world which gives significance to the particular Fundamental Equations which we have selected and saves them from the character of being mere identities.

Under a Socialist system the money-rate of efficiency-earnings of the Factors of Production might be suddenly altered by *fiat*. Theoretically, I suppose, it might change under a system of competitive individualism by an act of collective foresight on the part of entrepreneurs in anticipation of impending monetary changes, or by a *coup de main* on the part of Trade Unions. Practically, as we shall see in a later section of this chapter, prices may be modified as the result of a spontaneous change in the actual rate of earnings relatively to efficiency, on account of a change either in the method of fixing wages or in the coefficient of efficiency. In existing circumstances, however, the most usual and important occasion of change will be the action of the entrepreneurs, under the influence of the actual enjoyment of positive or negative profits, in increasing or diminishing the volume of employment which they offer at the existing rates of remuneration of the Factors of Production, and so bringing about a raising or a lowering of these rates. For the departure of profits from zero is the mainspring of change in the industrial countries of the modern world outside Russia. It is by altering the rate of profits in particular directions that entrepreneurs can be induced to produce this rather than that, and it is by altering the rate of profits in general that they can be induced to modify the average of their offers of remuneration to the factors of production.

Moreover there is a further reason why, in the actual world of to-day, it is appropriate to regard the above as the normal mechanism of change. For when the Central Currency Authority of a country wishes to change the level of money-incomes in the country and thereby the quantity of circulating money which they require, it has no power to order that the money-incomes of individuals shall be reduced;—the only alteration which it has a power to order relates to the terms of lending. It is, therefore, *viâ* the alteration of the terms of lending that the change in the situation is initiated;—this alteration affects the attractiveness of producing capital-goods, which disturbs the rate of investment relatively to that of saving, which upsets the rate of profits for producers of consumption-goods, thus causing entrepreneurs to modify the average level of their offers to the factors of production, and so finally achieving the ultimate objective of changing the level of money-incomes. This is not the only conceivable way of bringing about the result, but it is the only way which is, in fact, normally in use in most countries of the modern world.

Thus—generally speaking—every change towards a new equilibrium price-level is initiated by a departure of profits from zero; and the significance of the above analysis lies in the demonstration that this condition of equilibrium comes to the same thing as (1) the equality of Savings and the value of Investment, and (2) the equality of the "market-rate" and the "natural-rate" of interest.

If, therefore, the banking system can regulate the amount which it lends in such a way that the market-rate of interest is equal to the natural-rate, then the value of investment will be equal to the volume of saving, total profits will be zero, the price of output, as a whole, will be at an equilibrium level, and there will be a motive moving productive resources between the production of consumption-goods and the production of capital-goods unless or until the purchasing power of money is also at an equilibrium level. The condition for the stability of purchasing power is, therefore, that the banking system should behave in this way and according to this criterion; though we may have to concede that this is not always practicable over short periods, since for short periods the natural-rate may sometimes fluctuate in an extreme degree.

(v.) THE BEHAVIOUR OF ENTREPRENEURS

We have spoken so far as if entrepreneurs were influenced in their prospective arrangements entirely by reference to whether they are making a profit or loss on their current output as they market it. In so far, however, as production takes time—and in Book VI. we shall be emphasising the fact that in many cases it does take an appreciable time—and in so far as entrepreneurs are able at the beginning of a production period to forecast the relationship between saving and investment in its effect on the demand for their product at the end of this production-period, it is obviously the anticipated profit or loss on new business, rather than the actual profit or loss on business just concluded, which influences them in deciding the scale on which to produce and the offers which it is worth while to make to the factors of production. Strictly, therefore, we should say that it is the *anticipated* profit or loss which is the mainspring of change, and that it is by causing anticipations of the appropriate kind that the banking system is able to influence the price-level. Indeed it is well known that one reason for the rapid efficacy of changes in bank-rate in modifying the actions of entrepreneurs is the anticipations to which they give rise. Thus entrepreneurs will sometimes begin to act before the price-changes which are the justification of their action have actually occurred. Since—to take an anticipated *fall* of price as our example—a reduction of costs or a reduction of output may, in the case of a single industry, actually prevent the incurring of losses or the feared fall of prices, each may hope by this means to avoid loss. Nevertheless—short of a complete cessation of output by the whole body of entrepreneurs

—avoidance of loss is impossible for entrepreneurs as a whole, however much they cut costs and reduce output, if the excess of saving over investment duly materialises.

Furthermore, widely held anticipations will tend for a short time to bring about their own verification, even if they have no basis outside themselves. For a reduced activity of entrepreneurs will diminish the volume of working capital required and so reduce investment; whilst an increased activity will have the opposite effect.

All the same, accurate forecasting in these matters is so difficult and requires so much more information than is usually available, that the average behaviour of entrepreneurs is in fact mainly governed by current experience supplemented by such broad generalisations as those relating to the probable consequences of changes in bank-rate, the supply of credit and the state of the foreign exchanges. Moreover, action based on inaccurate anticipations will not long survive experiences of a contrary character, so that the facts will soon override anticipations except where they agree.

Thus when I say that the disequilibrium between saving and investment is the mainspring of change, I do not mean to deny that the behaviour of entrepreneurs at any given moment is based on a mixture of experience and anticipation.

There is another matter which deserves a word in passing. When for any reason an entrepreneur feels discouraged about the prospects, one or both of two courses may be open to him — he can reduce his output or he can reduce his costs by lowering his offers to the factors of production. Neither course, if adopted by entrepreneurs as a whole, will relieve in the least their losses as a whole, except in so far as they have the indirect effect of reducing savings or of allowing (or causing) the banking system to relax the terms of credit and so increase investment (neither of which is what the entrepreneurs themselves have in mind); whilst, on the other hand, both courses are likely to aggravate their losses by reducing the cost of investment. Nevertheless these courses will in actual fact appeal to them, because, in so far as any class of entrepreneurs is able to adopt either of these courses in a degree greater than the average, they will be able to protect themselves. A discussion of the precise circumstances which determine the degree in which a class of entrepreneurs or an individual entrepreneur pursues the one course or the other over the short-period would, however, lead me too far into the intricate theory of the economics of the short-period. It must be enough here to repeat the indication already given on p. 125, that we do not require for the purposes of the present analysis to make any particular assumptions as to the time which has to elapse before losses (or profits), actual or anticipated, produce their full reaction on the behaviour of entrepreneurs. It is sufficient that the general tendency of a disequilibrium between saving and investment is in the sense described, and that, if the cause persists, the tendency must materialise sooner or later. Nor do any of the qualifications of this section affect in any way the rigour or the validity of our conclusions as to the quantitative effect of divergences between saving and investment on the price-levels ruling in the market.

(vi.) THE CONDITION OF EXTERNAL EQUILIBRIUM

We have stated the argument so far as though we were dealing with a *Closed System*, which was not susceptible of buying and selling and of borrowing and lending relations with an outside world. But it is typical of the world of to-day that the country whose currency system we are considering should not only buy goods from and sell goods to, but should have the same monetary standard as, and enter into borrowing and lending relations with, the outside world.

Nothing is required, however, in the extension of our argument to an International System which is not already adequately provided for in the terms of the Fundamental Equations. The main consequence is to introduce an additional condition of equilibrium.

For let L and B stand for the values of Foreign Lending and of the Foreign Balance respectively in accordance with the definitions given on pp. 131-2; G for the exports of gold; S_1 for the difference between S, the total volume of Saving, and L, so far as L is not financed by exports of gold—which we will call the volume of Home Saving; I_1 for the difference between I, the total value of Investment, and B— which we will call the value of Home Investment; and I_1' for $I_1 - Q_2$—which we call the "adjusted" cost of Home Investment; then we have:

$$L = B + G,$$
$$S_1 = S - L + G,$$
$$I_1 = I - B,$$

so that $\quad I - S = I_1 - S_1;$

and since $\quad I_1 - I_1' = Q_2 = I - I',$
$$I' - S = I_1' - S_1.$$

Thus we are entitled to substitute $I_1 - S_1$ for $I - S$ and $I_1' - S_1$ for $I' - S$ in our Fundamental Equations. Accordingly the equilibrium of the price-level of output as a whole requires that the volume of Home Saving should be equal to the value of Home Investment, and that of the Purchasing Power of Money requires that the volume of Home Saving should be equal to the *adjusted* cost of Home Investment, which is the same thing as its actual cost less the profit on the Foreign Balance, *i.e.* less the excess of value of B over its cost. In accordance with the definitions on p. 132, I includes an allowance for exports and imports of gold, but I_1 does not; that is, say, I is equal to the sum of the home investment, the foreign lending, and the imports of gold.

These are the conditions of internal equilibrium. But when we are no longer dealing with a Closed System, we require also a condition of external equilibrium. Clearly there can be no such equilibrium so long as there is a continual movement of gold into or out of the country. The condition of external equilibrium is, therefore, that $G = 0$, *i.e.* that $L = B$, so that the value of Foreign Investment (*i.e.* of the Foreign Balance) is equal to Foreign Lending.

Thus complete equilibrium requires *both* that $I_1 = S_1$ and $I_1 = I_1'$, and that $L = B$.

With the implications of this condition of external equilibrium we shall deal in Chapter 21 below. But there are one or two broad conclusions which may be mentioned here.

In the first place, the amount of the Foreign Balance in any given situation depends on the relative *price-levels* at home and abroad of the goods and services which enter into international trade. The amount of Foreign Lending, on the other hand, depends on relative *interest rates* (corrected, of course, for variations of risk, etc., so as to represent the net advantage of lending) at home and abroad. Now there is no direct or automatic connection between these two things; nor has a Central Bank any direct means of altering relative price-levels. The weapon of a Central Bank consists in the power to alter interest rates and the terms of lending generally. Thus when there is a change in the price-level abroad or in the demand-schedules of foreign borrowers (*i.e.* in their eagerness to borrow at given rates of interest) not reflected in corresponding changes at home, the only means open to the Central Bank for the preservation of external equilibrium is to change the terms of lending at home. But if $I_1 = S_1$ at the old terms of lending, they will be unequal at the new terms, so that the first effect of the effort to preserve external equilibrium will be to produce internal disequilibrium. We shall show in Chapter 13 that action by a Central Bank along these lines is capable at long last of producing a new situation in which internal and external equilibrium are both simultaneously restored. But this does not remove the fact of a tendency towards an initial disharmony between the two conditions of equilibrium.

In the second place, with an international currency system, such as gold, the primary duty of a Central Bank is to preserve *external* equilibrium. Internal equilibrium must take its chance, or, rather, the internal situation must be forced sooner or later into equilibrium with the external situation. For the duty of preserving the parity of the national currency with the international standard, which is laid on the Central Currency Authority by law, is incompatible with a long continuance of external disequilibrium; whereas no corresponding obligation of a binding character exists relating to internal equilibrium. The same thing applies, in greater or less degree, wherever the Central Currency Authority is required to preserve the parity of its money in terms of any objective standard other than the purchasing power of money itself.

The degree, however, to which an individual country can so dominate the international situation as to bend the position of external equilibrium to suit the conditions of its own internal equilibrium, and the period for which it can afford to disregard external disequilibrium in the interest of preserving its own internal equilibrium (allowing gold to flow freely in or out), are very different in different cases, depending on the various elements of its financial strength. Before the War Great Britain and since the War the

United States have had a considerable power of influencing the international situation to suit themselves. Since 1924 France and the United States are examples of countries which have been in a situation to ignore external disequilibrium for long periods at a time in the interests of their own internal equilibrium, whilst Great Britain is an example of a country which has been forced to disregard internal equilibrium in the effort to sustain a self-imposed external equilibrium which was not in harmony with the existing internal situation.

The acuteness of the possible disharmony between the conditions of internal and of external equilibrium depends on whether the volume of foreign lending is large relatively to total saving, whether it is susceptible to *small* changes in relative rates of interest at home and abroad, and whether the volume of the foreign balance is susceptible to *small* changes in relative prices; and the duration of such disharmony depends on the ease with which changes can be effected in the internal money-costs of production. If the volumes of foreign lending and of the foreign balance and the internal money-costs of production are all of them very susceptible to small changes in interest-rates, prices and the volume of employment respectively, then the simultaneous preservation both of external and of internal equilibrium will present no difficult problem. Much current theory assumes too lightly, I think, that the above conditions of susceptibility are in fact fulfilled in the present-day world. But this assumption is unsafe. In some countries (but not all) the volume of foreign lending is easily influenced, and in most countries the money-costs of production show but little resistance to an upward movement. But in many countries the volume of the foreign balance is sticky when it is a question of increasing it to meet a change in the external situation; and so are the money-costs of production when it is a question of a movement downwards.

In pre-war days no one troubled much about anything but the condition of external equilibrium. But since the War the progress of ideas about Monetary Management and the importance of stabilising the Purchasing Power of Money have led to a more general concern about the preservation of internal equilibrium, without its being clearly realised how far the one is compatible with the other. This, however, is a matter of which we must postpone the further discussion to the later chapters of this Treatise.

(vii.) Changes in Price-Levels due to "Spontaneous" Changes in Earnings

We have assumed in previous sections that rates of efficiency-earnings do not, as a rule, change " spontaneously " so to speak, but only as a result of a change in the offers made by entrepreneurs acting under the influence of profits or losses. But this is not the whole of the truth and we must now supplement it.

If money-rates of earnings were uniformly fixed in relation to output, being as it were piece-wages, so that they tended to increase or decrease automatically with every change in the coefficient of efficiency, then we should need to add nothing to what we have written above about the causation of price changes.

If, on the other hand, money-rates of earnings were uniformly fixed in relation to effort, being as it were time-wages, so that they tended to remain the same irrespective of changes in the coefficient of efficiency, then the price-level would change (assuming Investment and Saving to be in equilibrium) with every change in efficiency and in inverse proportion to such change. That is to say, there would be a spontaneous tendency for price-levels to change in the opposite direction to changes in efficiency, any further change due to a disparity between Investment and Saving being superimposed on this.

In actual fact, earnings are probably fixed on the whole somewhere between an effort-basis and an efficiency-basis. If, as before, W stands for effort-earnings and W_1 for efficiency-earnings, and if W_2 stands for actual earnings, then, if actual earnings are fixed in a proportion a on an effort-basis and in a proportion b on an efficiency-basis, then $W_2 = (a \cdot e + b)W_1$, where e is the coefficient of efficiency. In this case, there will be a tendency towards spontaneous changes in P (or Π) inversely proportional to such changes as occur in $(a \cdot e + b)$ for reasons other than a change in entrepreneurs' profits.

Let the reader observe that changes in the average rate of earnings have no direct tendency in themselves to bring about profits or losses, because—so long as the Currency Authority allows the change without attempting to counteract it—entrepreneurs will always be recouped for their changed outlay by the corresponding change in their receipts, which will result from the proportionate change in the price-level. But if such spontaneous changes in the rate of earnings as tend to occur require a supply of money which is incompatible with the ideas of the Currency Authority or with the limitations on its powers, then the latter will be compelled, in its endeavour to redress the situation, to bring influences to bear which will upset the equilibrium of Investment and Saving, and so induce the entrepreneurs to modify their offers to the factors of production in such a way as to counteract the spontaneous changes which have been occurring in the rates of earnings.

Thus we can conveniently distinguish what we have already called "spontaneous" changes in the rates of efficiency-earnings and in the price-levels due to the character of the Wages System (including in this, *e.g.*, the powers and activities of Trade Unions), from what we may call the " induced " changes arising from the existence of profits or losses due to the Currency Authority permitting or promoting a disparity between Investment and Saving. If the spontaneous changes which occur do not suit the Currency Authority, the only remedy of the latter lies in promoting induced changes in an equal and opposite degree.

Since this is a Treatise on Money, and not on the Wages System, we shall be more concerned in what follows with the close analysis of induced changes than with that of spontaneous changes. Moreover, whilst it is important to recognise spontaneous changes which are incompatible with the currency situation as one of the contingencies which will force the Currency Authority, from time to time, deliberately to upset the equilibrium between Investment and Saving, this case merges, analytically speaking, into the case— common enough for a country which belongs to an unmanaged international Currency System and one which we shall have to examine in considerable detail —where the monetary position forces the Currency Authority to upset the equilibrium between Investment and Saving, not because there has been a spontaneous *change* in the rates of efficiency-earnings, but because the *existing* level of the latter has ceased (perhaps because of changes abroad) to be compatible with the monetary situation. Also, induced changes are likely to be much more important than spontaneous changes over the short-period—which is another reason why in much of what follows we can confine our attention to the former.

In conclusion, it may be well to say a word at this point about the bearing of the above on the problem of price-stabilisation.

If we have complete control both of the Earnings (or Wages) System and of the Currency System, so that we can alter the rate of earnings by *fiat*, can accommodate the supply of money to the rate of earnings which we have decreed, and can control the rate of investment, then we can afford to follow our fancy as to what we stabilise—the purchasing power of money, its labour power, or anything else—without running the risk of setting up social and economic frictions or of causing waste.

If, on the other hand, we have control of the Earnings System but not of the Currency System, then it lies outside our power to determine what the equilibrium price-level shall be ; and the best we can do is to use our power so as to ensure that the equilibrium rate of earnings, which is dictated to us by outside forces, shall come about with the minimum of friction and waste. That is to say, we had better fix the rate of earnings at a level which will be compatible with the currency situation without any disturbance of the equality of I and S.

But if—which is the case usually assumed by Monetary Reformers—we have at least a partial control of the Currency System but not of the Earnings System, so that we have some power of deciding what the equilibrium price-level and rate of earnings is to be, but no power of bringing about this equilibrium except by setting into operation the mechanism of induced changes, then we may do well in choosing our standard to consider what will fit in best with whatever may be the natural tendencies of spontaneous change which characterise the Earnings System as it actually is.

If, for example, the Earnings System, left to itself, tends to approximate more nearly to steady efficiency-earnings than to steady effort-earnings, then we shall do well, perhaps, to stabilise the purchasing power of money ; but if the facts are the other way round, then to stabilise the labour power of money. Or, if money-rates of earnings have a rising tendency (from the power of Trade Unions or the mere human inclination to think in terms of money and to feel an increase of money-earnings as a betterment), then in a progressive Society where efficiency is increasing it may be better to stabilise purchasing power, but in a declining Society where efficiency is decreasing, to stabilise labour power.

At any rate, some account should be taken of these considerations, based on social expediency and the avoidance of waste and friction, along with considerations of social justice, in deciding what it is best to do.

For my own part I am somewhat inclined to think, without having reached a final conclusion, that it is more important to have a system which avoids, so far as possible, the necessity for induced changes, than it is to attempt to stabilise the price-level according to any precise principle, provided always that the rate of change in the price-level is kept within narrow limits. At least this is the first thing to do. For the worst of all conceivable systems (apart from the abuses of a *fiat* money which has lost all its anchors) is one in which the Banking System fails to correct periodic divergences, first in one direction and then in the other, between Investment and Saving, and where, besides, spontaneous changes in earnings tend upwards, but monetary changes, due to the relative shortage of gold, tend downwards, so that, even apart from fluctuations from the side of Investment and superimposed upon them, we have a chronic necessity for induced changes sufficient not only to counteract the spontaneous changes but to reverse them. Yet it is possible that this is the sort of system which we have to-day.

This line of thought anticipates much that is to come. If it is not fully clear, the reader will nevertheless pick up its drift easily enough if he returns to it on a second reading.

CHAPTER 12

A FURTHER ELUCIDATION OF THE DISTINCTION BETWEEN SAVINGS AND INVESTMENT [1]

(i.) SAVINGS AND INVESTMENT

In the previous chapters we have been dealing on the one hand with the earnings or money-income of the community and its division into two parts, one of which is spent by the recipient on current consumption and the other of which is " saved " ; whilst on the other we have dealt with the community's output of actual goods and services and its division into two parts, one of which is marketed and sold to con-

---

[1] The notion of the distinction which I have made between Savings and Investment has been gradually creeping into economic literature in quite recent years. The first author to introduce it was, according to the German authorities,* Ludwig Mises in his *Theorie des Geldes und der Umlaufsmittel* (1st edition, pp. 227 ff. and 411 ff.) published in 1912. Later on the idea was adopted in a more explicit form by Schumpeter, and " Forced Saving " † (*i.e.* the difference between Savings and Value of Investment as defined by me, though without there being attached to the idea—so far as I am aware —anything closely corresponding to the analysis of chapters 10 and 11 above) has become almost a familiar feature of the very newest German writings on Money. But so far as I am concerned—and I think the same is true of most other economists of the English-speaking world— my indebtedness for clues which have set my mind working in the right direction is to Mr. D. H. Robertson's *Banking Policy and the Price Level*

---

* See Hahn's article on " Kredit " in *Handwörterbuch der Staatswissenschaften* (4th edition) vol. v. p. 951, and Schumpeter, *Theorie der wirtschaftlichen Entwicklung* (2nd edition, 1926), p. 156. These references are given by Mises himself, *Geldwertstabilisierung und Konjunkturpolitik* (1928), p. 45.

† " Erzwungenes Sparen " or " gezwungenes Sparen ". I should prefer not to use the word " saving " in this connection. See further footnote, p. 172.

sumers and the other of which is "invested". Thus "saving" relates to units of money and is the sum of the differences between the money-incomes of individuals and their money-expenditure on current consumption; and "investment" relates to units of goods. The object of this chapter is to illustrate further the significance of the distinction between these two things.

Saving is the act of the individual consumer and consists in the negative act of refraining from spending the whole of his current income on consumption.

Investment, on the other hand, is the act of the entrepreneur whose function it is to make the decisions which determine the amount of the non-available output, and consists in the positive act of starting or maintaining some process of production or of withholding liquid goods. It is measured by the net addition to wealth whether in the form of fixed capital, working capital or liquid capital.

It might be supposed—and has frequently been supposed—that the amount of investment is necessarily equal to the amount of saving. But reflection will show that this is not the case, if we exclude from income and from saving—as we must for reasons already given—the windfall profits and losses of entrepreneurs.

---

published in 1926.‡ More recently Mr. Abbati's *The Final Buyer* (1928) has reached—independently I think—some substantially similar results. Mr. Abbati has probably failed to make his thought fully intelligible to those who have not already found the same clue themselves. But the essence of the distinction between saving and investment is to be found in his chapter v. Moreover, by the aggregate of "final buying", Mr. Abbati means expenditure on consumption *plus* investment, and he attributes depressions to a failure of this aggregate to reach the aggregate of money-incomes.

---

‡ I do not much like Mr. Robertson's term "automatic lacking". I should prefer "lacking" *simpliciter* for his "automatic lacking", "Saving" for his "spontaneous lacking" and no special term for his "induced lacking". And looked at from the other point of view, we might speak of "profiteering" as the equivalent for the entrepreneur of what "lacking" is to the recipient of income.

Let us, for the moment, ignore the possibility of variations in hoarded goods, which as we shall see later are in fact likely to be small compared with the variability of the other factors; which amounts to the same thing as to assume that available output is perishable. In this case the amount of consumption is exactly equal to the amount of the available output. But the proportion of the total output which shall be available has been determined unequivocally by the amount of investment which the entrepreneurs have decided to make. Thus when positive investment is taking place, consumption falls short of output quite irrespective of the volume of saving; and when investment is negative, consumption exceeds output also quite irrespective of the volume of saving. In short, the increase or decrease of capital depends on the amount of investment and not on the amount of saving.

That saving can occur without any corresponding investment is obvious, if we consider what happens when an individual refrains from spending his money-income on consumption. It does not matter what he does with the surplus—whether he deposits it at his bank, pays off a loan or buys a house or a security —provided it is not accompanied by an additional act of investment by an entrepreneur. There is now in the market one purchaser less for consumption-goods, with the result that their prices fall. This fall of prices increases the purchasing power of the money-incomes of the rest of the community and they are able, therefore, to increase their consumption by the amount which the saver has foregone, whilst spending the same amount of money as before. If, however, these others then proceed to reduce correspondingly their money-expenditure on consumption and, consequently, to increase their savings, this only has the effect of still further increasing the purchasing power of the balance of their income which they do spend.

Meanwhile the savers are individually richer by the amount of their savings, but the producers of consumption-goods, who have sold their current output at a lower price than they would have got if the savings had not taken place, are poorer by an equal amount. Thus in such circumstances the saving, instead of resulting in an increase of aggregate wealth, has merely involved a double transference—a transference of consumption *from* the savers to the general body of *consumers*, and a transference of wealth *to* the savers from the general body of *producers*, both total consumption and total wealth remaining unchanged. Thus, in Mr. Robertson's language, the saving has been "abortive". There is no increase of wealth in any shape or form corresponding to the increase of saving; — the saving has resulted in nothing whatever except a change and change-about between those who consume and between those who own titles to wealth. The saving has been balanced by the losses of the entrepreneurs who produce consumption-goods.

If, on the other hand, investment has taken place *pari passu* with saving, the equilibrium of consumers' expenditure and producers' available output will be maintained at the pre-existing price-level. For if the investment takes the form of an increase of fixed capital or of working capital unaccompanied by an increase of employment, balanced by an equal volume of saving, the producers' output of available goods will be reduced by the act of investment to the same extent as the consumer's expenditure on such goods is reduced by the act of saving ; and if the investment takes the form of an increase of working capital, accompanied by an increased volume of employment and an increased remuneration of the factors of production, balanced by an equal volume of saving, the reduction of consumers' expenditure by the savers will be exactly balanced by an equal increase of consumers' expenditure from the increased earnings of the factors of production.

Finally, if investment exceeds saving, then—as is easily seen in the light of the preceding argument—consumers' expenditure will be increased relatively to producers' output of available goods, with the result that the prices of consumption-goods will rise ; and the new investment in excess of the volume of saving will be made possible, not by voluntary abstention from consumption by refraining from spending money-income, but by involuntary abstention as the result of money-incomes being worth less (Mr. Robertson's " automatic lacking ").

Now if the decisions as to the proportions of the flow of future output to be in available and in non-available form respectively at a given date were to be made by the same people who decide how much is to be " saved " at that date, no trouble would arise. But if they are made—as in fact they are—by different people, then (except in so far as relief is obtainable from variations in the amount of hoarded goods) the net increment to the capital wealth of the community as a whole will differ to a certain extent (more or less) from the aggregate of the cash-savings of individuals, meaning by the latter the portions of their cash-incomes which they abstain from spending on consumption.

There need be no feeling of paradox about this when we remember that Income does not include Profits or Losses, and that it is these which represent the mysterious difference between savings and the value of investment. The vital point to appreciate is this. An act of saving by an individual may result either in increased investment or in increased consumption by the individuals who make up the rest of the community. The performance of the act of saving is in itself no guarantee that the stock of capital goods will be correspondingly increased.

(ii.) An Illustration

A parable or illustration may possibly make the conclusion clearer—or at least more vivid. Let us suppose a community owning banana plantations and labouring to cultivate and collect bananas and nothing else; and consuming bananas and nothing else. Let us suppose, further, that there has been an equilibrium between saving and investment in the sense that the money-income of the community, not spent on the consumption of bananas but saved, is equal to the cost of production of new investment in the further development of plantations; and that the selling price of bananas is equal to their cost of production (including in this the normal remuneration of entrepreneurs). Finally, let us suppose, what is plausible, that ripe bananas will not keep for more than a week or two.

Into this Eden there enters a Thrift Campaign, urging the members of the public to abate their improvident practices of devoting nearly all their current incomes to buying bananas for daily food. But at the same time there is no corresponding increase in the development of new plantations—for one or other of many reasons: it may be that counsels of prudence are influencing entrepreneurs as well as savers, fears of future over-production of bananas and a falling price-level deterring them from new development; or technical reasons may exist which prevent new development at more than a certain pace; or the labour required for such development may be highly specialised and not capable of being drawn from labour ordinarily occupied in harvesting bananas; or there may be a considerable time-lag between the initial preparations required for development and the date of the bulk of the expenditure eventually required by it. What, in such a case, will happen?

SAVINGS AND INVESTMENT

The same quantity of bananas as before will continue to be marketed, whilst the amount of current income devoted to their purchase will, by reason of the thrift campaign, be diminished. Since bananas will not keep, their price must fall; and it will fall proportionately to the amount by which saving exceeds investment.[1] Thus, as before, the public will consume the whole crop of bananas, but at a reduced price-level. This is splendid, or seems so. The Thrift Campaign will not only have increased saving; it will have reduced the cost of living. The public will have saved money, without denying themselves anything. They will be consuming just as much as before, and virtue will be sumptuously rewarded.

But the end is not yet reached. Since wages are still unchanged, only the selling-price of bananas will have fallen and not their cost of production; so that the entrepreneurs will suffer an abnormal loss. Thus the increased saving has not increased in the least the aggregate wealth of the community; it has simply caused a transfer of wealth from the pockets of the entrepreneurs into the pockets of the general public. The savings of the consumers will be required, either directly or through the intermediary of the banking system, to make good the losses of the entrepreneurs. The continuance of this will cause entrepreneurs to seek to protect themselves by throwing their employees out of work or reducing their wages. But even this will not improve their position, since the spending power of the public will be reduced by just as much as the aggregate costs of production. By however much entrepreneurs reduce wages and however many of their employees they throw out of work, they will continue to make losses so long as the community continues to save in excess of new investment. Thus

---

[1] The case where the bananas will keep will be considered in detail in Chapter 19. It will be found not to differ from the above as much as might have been expected.

there will be no position of equilibrium until either (*a*) all production ceases and the entire population starves to death ; or (*b*) the thrift campaign is called off or peters out as a result of the growing poverty ; or (*c*) investment is stimulated by some means or another so that its cost no longer lags behind the rate of saving.

(iii.) THEORIES OF OVER-SAVING

Economists are familiar with a class of theories which attribute the phenomena of the Credit Cycle to what is described as " Over-saving " or " Under-consumption ". At bottom these theories have, I think, some affinity to my own. But they are not so close as might be supposed at first sight. The theories of Bouniatian and the European writers influenced by him, of Mr. J. A. Hobson in England and of Messrs. Foster and Catchings in the United States, who are the best-known leaders of this school of thought, are not in fact over-saving or over-investment theories, if these terms be given the same sense that I have given to them. They have, that is to say, nothing to do with saving running ahead of investment or *vice versa*. They are concerned, not with the equilibrium of saving and investment, but with the equilibrium of the production of instrumental capital-goods and the demand for the use of such goods. They attribute the phenomena of the Credit Cycle to a periodic over-production of instrumental goods, with the result that these instrumental goods facilitate a greater production of consumption-goods than the purchasing power in the hands of the public is capable of absorbing at the existing price-level.

In so far as these theories are capable of any reconciliation with mine, it is at a later stage in the course of events ; for in certain cases a tendency for the rate of investment to lag behind the rate of savings might come about as the result of a reaction from over-investment in the above sense. In so far, however, as these theories maintain that the existing distribution of wealth tends to a large volume of saving, which leads in turn to over-investment, which leads to too large a production of consumption-goods, they are occupying an entirely different *terrain* from my theory: inasmuch as, on my theory, it is a large volume of saving which does *not* lead to a correspondingly large volume of investment (not one which *does*) which is the root of the trouble.

Mr. J. A. Hobson and others deserve recognition for trying to analyse the influence of saving and investment on the price-level and on the Credit Cycle, at a time when orthodox economists were content to neglect almost entirely this very real problem. But I do not think they have succeeded in linking up their conclusions with the theory of money or with the part played by the rate of interest.

(iv.) A Summary of the Argument

It may help the reader if I endeavour at this stage to give a broad summary (with some sacrifice of exact accuracy) of the argument of the preceding chapters.

The price-level of output as a whole during any period is made up of two components—the price-level of the goods coming forward for consumption and the price-level of the goods added to the stock of capital.

In conditions of equilibrium both these price-levels are determined by the money-cost of production, or, in other words, by the money-rate of efficiency-earnings of the factors of production.

The question whether the price-level of the goods which are consumed is in fact equal or unequal to their cost of production, depends on whether the proportion of the income of the community which is spent on consumption is or is not the same as the proportion of the output of the community which takes the form of the goods so consumed; in other words, on whether the division of income between savings and expenditure on consumption is or is not the same as the division of the cost of production of output between the cost of the goods which are added to capital and the cost of the goods which are consumed. If the former proportion is greater than the latter, then the producers of the goods which are consumed make a profit; and if the former proportion is less than the latter, then the producers of the goods which are consumed make a loss.

Thus the price-level of the goods which are consumed (*i.e.* the inverse of the Purchasing Power of Money) exceeds or falls short of their cost of production, according as the volume of savings falls short of or exceeds the cost of production of new investment (*i.e.* of the goods which are added to the stock of capital). Hence, if the volume of savings exceeds the cost of investment, the producers of the goods which are being consumed make a loss; and if the cost of investment exceeds the volume of savings, they make a profit.

What happens to the price-level of new investments, *i.e.* of the goods which are added to the stock of capital? For a detailed answer to this question I must ask the reader to be patient and to wait for what he will find in later chapters. It is important for him to understand that the account of this matter which I have given in Chapter 10 is not intended to be more than a preliminary treatment of this subject. Broadly speaking, it depends on the anticipated price-level of the utilities which these investments will yield up at some future date and on the rate of interest at which these future utilities are discounted for the purpose of fixing their present capital value. Thus, whether producers of investment-goods make a profit or loss depends on whether the expectations of the market about future prices and the prevailing rate of interest are changing favourably or adversely to such producers. It does *not* depend on whether the producers of consumable goods are making a profit or a loss.

Nevertheless, movements in our two types of price-level are connected at one remove and are, generally speaking, in the *same* direction. For if producers of investment-goods are making a profit, there will be a tendency for them to endeavour to increase their output, *i.e.* to increase investment, which will, therefore, tend—unless savings happen to be increasing in the same proportion—to raise the prices of consumable goods; and *vice versa*. If, on the other hand, producers of consumable goods are making a profit, but those of investment-goods are making a loss, then there will be a tendency for output to be changed over from the latter to the former, which will—unless savings happen to be decreasing in the same proportion—lower the price-level of consumable goods and obliterate the profits of the producers of such goods. Thus, whilst it is not impossible for the two types of price-level to be moving in opposite directions, it is more natural to expect them to move in the same direction.

Let us now move first of all forwards, and then backwards, in the causal sequence; and for simplicity of statement let us restrict ourselves to the case where the two price-levels are moving in the same direction.

If producers as a whole are making a profit, individual producers will seek to enlarge their output so as to make more profit. They can do this by employing more of the factors of production, either at the old rate of remuneration or at an enhanced rate. We shall find in Book VI. that either of these things means an increase in the total cost of investment, so that this effort of the producers to make more profit serves, at first at least, to aggravate the rising tendency of prices and profits. Thus we may conclude that, as a rule, the existence of profit will provoke a tendency towards a higher rate of employment and of remuneration for the factors of production ; and *vice versa*.

Next let us step backwards. In order that producers may be able, as well as willing, to produce at a higher cost of production and to increase their non-available output, they must be able to get command of an appropriate quantity of money and of capital resources ; and in order that they may be willing, as well as able, to do this, the rate of interest which command over such resources costs must not be so high as to deter them. How much bank-credit they have to borrow in order to obtain command over a sufficient quantity of money depends on what the public is doing with its savings—on the relative attractions of savings-deposits and of securities respectively. But whatever the public may be doing, and whatever may prove to be the strength or weakness of the motive of producers to increase that proportion of their output which is non-available, the banking system comes in as a balancing factor; and by controlling the price and quantity of bank-credit the banking system necessarily controls the aggregate expenditure on output.

Thus the first link in the causal sequence is the behaviour of the banking system, the second is the cost of investment (so far as the purchasing power of money is concerned) and the value of investment (so far as the price-level of the output as a whole is concerned), the third is the emergence of profit and loss, and the fourth is the rate of remuneration offered by the entrepreneurs to the factors of production. By varying the price and quantity of bank-credit the banking system governs the value of investment; upon the value of investment relatively to the volume of savings depend the profits or losses of the producers ; the rate of remuneration offered to the factors of production tends to rise or fall according as entrepreneurs are making a profit or a loss ; and the price-level of the community's output is the sum of the average rate of efficiency-earnings of the factors of production and the average rate of profit of the entrepreneurs. Thus, to bring first and last together, the price-level of output as a whole oscillates above or below the rate of efficiency-earnings, according as the banking system is causing the *value* of investment to exceed or fall short of the volume of savings ; and the purchasing power of money oscillates below or above the rate of efficiency-earnings according as the banking system is causing the *cost* of investment to exceed or fall short of the volume of savings.

This is not to assert that the banking system is the *only* factor in the situation ;—the *net* result depends on the policy of the banking system in conjunction with all kinds of other factors. But, in so far as the banking system is a free agent acting with design, it can, by coming in as a balancing factor, control the final outcome.

If the banking system controls the terms of credit in such a way that savings are equal to the value of new investment, then the average price-level of output as a whole is stable and corresponds to the average rate of remuneration of the factors of production. If the terms of credit are easier than this equilibrium level, prices will rise, profits will be made, wealth will increase faster than savings as the result of the incomes of the public being worth less—the difference being transferred into the pockets of entrepreneurs in the shape of the ownership of increased capital; entrepreneurs will bid against one another for the services of the factors of production, and the rate of remuneration of the latter will be increased—until something happens to bring the actual terms of credit and their equilibrium level nearer together. And if the terms of credit are stiffer than the equilibrium level, prices will fall, losses will be made, wealth will increase slower than savings by the extent of the losses, unemployment will ensue, and there will be a pressure towards a reduction of the rate of earnings of the factors of production—until something happens to bring the actual terms of credit and their equilibrium level nearer together.

Booms and slumps are simply the expression of the results of an oscillation of the terms of credit about their equilibrium position.

When the comparative simplicity of a closed system is replaced by the complexity of an international system, the effect is—as we shall see—that the necessity of preserving international equilibrium may force the domestic banking system to establish terms of credit which diverge from their domestic equilibrium level. Thus the conditions of international equilibrium may be incompatible for a time with the conditions of internal equilibrium; and it is necessary for the restoration or maintenance of complete equilibrium that *two* elements in the domestic situation should be mobile—not only the terms of credit, but also the money-rate of efficiency-earnings of the factors of production.

CHAPTER 13

THE " MODUS OPERANDI " OF BANK-RATE

(i) THE TRADITIONAL DOCTRINE

BANK-RATE does not appear explicitly as a factor in the Fundamental Equation of Price. It cannot, therefore, affect price-levels directly but only indirectly through its influence on one or more of the factors which do appear in the Fundamental Equation. We must not be satisfied, therefore, with any statement to the effect (*e.g.*) that an increase in bank-rate will cause price-levels to fall, unless it is explained to us at the same time by what intermediate action on the factors in the Fundamental Equation the fall is brought about.

In Chapter 11 I have anticipated very briefly the general character of the solution which I shall offer. Bank-rate operates primarily on the second term of the Fundamental Equation. It is the instrument by which a disturbance is set up or equilibrium restored between the rates of Saving and of Investment; for to raise it stimulates the one and retards the other, and conversely if it is reduced. This does not preclude it from affecting sooner or later the first term of the Fundamental Equation, or from having secondary effects on other elements in the Fundamental Equation, in particular on the quantity of bank-money, the velocities of circulation, and the proportion of savings-deposits.

Before, however, we embark on a detailed development of these ideas, it may be useful to outline the accepted doctrine as it has been developed historically and as it exists to-day. It is surprisingly difficult to do this. No systematic treatment of the subject exists in the English language, so far as I am aware. You will search in vain the works of Marshall, Pigou, Taussig or Irving Fisher. Even Professor Cassel's treatment, which is somewhat fuller, does not examine the train of causation in any detail.[1] Mr. Hawtrey has a little more to say; but he is somewhat unorthodox on this matter and cannot be quoted as an exponent of the accepted doctrine. There remains, however, one outstanding attempt at a systematic treatment, namely Knut Wicksell's *Geldzins und Güterpreise*, published in German in 1898, a book which deserves more fame and much more attention than it has received from English-speaking economists. In substance and intention Wicksell's theory is closely akin (much more closely than Cassel's version of Wicksell) to the theory of this Treatise, though he was not successful, in my opinion, in linking up his Theory of Bank-rate to the Quantity Equation.

"Bank-rate Policy", in the modern sense, was originated in the discussions which followed the monetary crisis of 1836-37 and preceded the Bank Act of 1844. Before 1837 such ideas did not exist—in the works of Ricardo, for example, nothing of the sort is to be found; and the explanation is not far to seek. For throughout the life of Ricardo, and up to the repeal of the Usury Laws in 1837, the rate of interest was subject to a legal maximum of 5 per cent.[2] For

---

[1] There are many incidental references to Bank-rate scattered through Prof. Cassel's post-war writings. But the most systematic treatment with which I am acquainted is to be found in his *Theory of Social Economy*, chap. xi.

[2] I believe that there is still a legal maximum (of 6 per cent) in force in the Isle of Man.

seventy-six years—from 1st May 1746 to 20th June 1822, the Bank-rate stood unchanged at 5 per cent. From 1822 to 1839 there were small fluctuations between 4 and 5 per cent. The rate of 5½ per cent established on 20th June 1839 (and raised six weeks later to 6 per cent) was the first occasion on which the official rate of the Bank of England had ever exceeded 5 per cent.[1]

The traditional doctrine, which has been developed in the ninety years which have since elapsed, has been woven of three distinct strands of thought, difficult to disentangle, to which different writers attach differing degrees of stress. All of them have been obscurely present from the beginnings of the discussion.

1. The first of these regards Bank-rate merely as a means of regulating the *quantity* of bank-money. This is the basis on which the practical method of Bank-rate as the characteristic instrument of the Bank of England was developed in the middle of the nineteenth century. Lord Overstone, for example [2]—who may be taken as typical of the reformers of this period —regarded Bank-rate as the correct and efficacious method for reducing the demand on the Bank for discounts, and so for contracting the volume of the circulation.

This notion, that an upward change in Bank-rate is associated with a diminished quantity of bank-money, either as cause or effect—or at least with a less quantity of money than if Bank-rate had not gone up—and conversely, so that the alleged association of high Bank-rate with falling prices follows directly from the usual Quantity Theory of Money, runs, indeed, through all the later nineteenth century literature of the subject. It was an important part of

[1] For elaborate statistics of Bank-rate during the nineteenth century and its relation to market-rate, see Gibson's *Bank Rate; the Banker's Vade Mecum.*

[2] "Thoughts on the Separation of the Departments of the Bank of England" (1844); *vide* his *Collected Tracts*, p. 264.

Marshall's thought in his *Evidence before the Gold and Silver Commission*,[1] none the less because he believed that it was through speculation or speculative investment that the new money found its way out into the world.[2] An account of the matter almost identical with Marshall's had been published a short time previously (1886) by Sir Robert Giffen.[3] Professor Pigou's theory of Bank-rate seems to descend almost exclusively from this strand of Marshall's thought. He conceives of Bank-rate as acting directly on the quantity of bank credit and so on prices in accordance with the Quantity Equation.[4] Mr. Hawtrey's scattered remarks in his *Currency and Credit* seem to be on the same lines.[5]

In the same way Professor Cassel explains that the price-level is regulated by the Bank-rate because the Bank-rate regulates the supply of the means of payment. I do not gather from his *Theory of Social Economy*, chap. xi. § 57, that he conceives of a fall of Bank-rate as operating to raise the price-level, except in so far as it causes, or is associated with, the supply of "newly created bank media of payment": "If the banks thus succeed in getting new bank media of payment into circulation, and if on that account the quantity of media of payment increases in a larger proportion than the production and exchange of commodities, the general level of prices is bound to rise."[6]

---

[1] *E.g., Official Papers*, p. 48: "I do not myself put the rate of discount into the first place; my own way of looking at it was rather to lay stress upon the actual amount of money in the market to be loaned".

[2] Cf. *Official Papers*, p. 52: "There is more capital in the hands of speculative investors, who come on the markets for goods as buyers, and so raise prices".

[3] *Essays in Finance*, second series, Essay II., *Gold Supply, the Rate of Discount and Prices.*

[4] *E.g., Industrial Fluctuations*, p. 241. At least so I understand him; for he has written no clear or systematic account of his views.

[5] *Currency and Credit*, chap. ix. pp. 132, 133 (3rd edition).

[6] *Op. cit.* (Eng. trans.) p. 478. Cf., also, *Fundamental Thoughts in Economics*, p. 128: "The supply of means of payment, and therefore also the purchasing power of the unit of money, is regulated essentially by the bank-rate".

To the question whether Prof. Cassel's theory contains or implies more than this, we shall return later.

Now the association of changes in Bank-rate with changes in the supply of bank-money is often or generally a factor in the situation. But the association is certainly not invariable; nor is the effect on prices proportionate to the change in the supply of money. Numerous qualifications and complications have to be introduced, and, by the time these are complete, the theory will really have become a different one. At any rate I shall argue that a discussion of Bank-rate on these lines alone is incomplete, and overlooks an essential element.

2. The second strand is that which is generally uppermost in discussions by practical bankers. They regard Bank-rate policy primarily, not as a means of regulating the price-level, but as a means of protecting a country's gold-reserves by regulating the rate of foreign lending. The point of raising Bank-rate, that is to say, is to make it higher relatively to the interest rates current in other international financial centres and so turn the balance of international indebtedness in our favour by influencing the international short-loan market.

The use of Bank-rate for this purpose was developed by the Bank of England as a practical expedient in the two decades following 1837. The first clear account of how it worked was given in Goschen's *Foreign Exchanges*,[1] first published in 1861. But Goschen regarded changes in Bank-rate as being in the main a reflection of market conditions rather than

[1] See particularly chap. vi., "Review of the so-called Correctives of the Foreign Exchanges". Prof. Clapham, however, has drawn my attention to a passage in Tooke's *History of Prices*, vol. ii. p. 296 (published in 1838), in which Tooke attributes to a rise of bank-rate the effect of "diminishing the facility, consequently the extent, of negotiations of foreign securities and of the financial arrangements of the banks of the United States. . . . But more especially would a moderate pressure on the money market . . . have restrained the extravagance of extent to which credits were granted in America upon this country."

as determining them. It was left to Bagehot (*Lombard Street*, chap. v.) to complete the story by emphasising the extent of the Bank of England's power, though "the Bank of England has no despotism in the matter", to determine what the market conditions should be.

It is obvious that this too is an important aspect of the question. But it is by no means obvious how it is connected with our first strand, and I know of no author who has attempted the synthesis. Moreover—superficially at least—it seems to pull in the opposite direction. For the object of raising Bank-rate is to attract gold or to prevent the loss of gold, so that its effect is to *increase* the basis of credit above what it would have been otherwise. It may be objected that the higher Bank-rate can only be made effective if the Central Bank reduces its other assets by more than it increases its stock of gold, so that the effect on balance is to decrease the aggregate of credit.[1] But it is questionable how exactly or invariably this corresponds to the observed facts.

3. The third strand of thought is the one which comes nearest to what seems to me to be the essence of the matter. It also winds through many previous discussions, but seldom or never in a clear or distinct fashion. This strand of thought conceives of Bankrate as influencing in some way the rate of investment, or at least the rate of some kinds of investment, and, perhaps in the case of Wicksell and Cassel, as influencing the rate of investment relatively to that of savings.

The simplest way of putting the point, as I conceive it, is to say that to raise the Bank-rate discourages investment relatively to saving, and therefore lowers

---

[1] This is probably the underlying assumption of the traditional doctrine, *i.e.* that high bank-rate simultaneously reduces the aggregate superstructure of credit whilst increasing that part of its basis which consists of gold. Cf. Withers, *Meaning of Money*, pp. 276, 277. But I do not remember to have seen the accuracy of this assumption tested by reference to statistics. According to my theory, it would not be true invariably but would require various special conditions for its fulfilment.

prices, which, by causing the receipts of entrepreneurs to fall below the normal, influences them to offer less employment all round; and this, sooner or later, brings down the rate of earnings in the same proportion as that in which prices have fallen; at which point a new position of equilibrium can be established. Now no writer, so far as I know, has clearly distinguished these two stages, *i.e.* the fall of prices and the fall of the costs of production, the initial fall of prices having been treated as if it were the end of the story. But how far previous writers have perceived that to discourage investment relatively to saving is *in itself* calculated to reduce prices is more difficult to say.

The published observations of Marshall, mainly in his evidence before the Gold and Silver Commission (1887) and the Indian Currency Committee (1898) leave me with no clear conviction as to what his position was. Marshall certainly conceived of an additional supply of money as reaching the price-level by means of a stimulation of investment (or speculation) through a lower Bank-rate. His position is most clearly stated in the three passages following:

> "If there is an extra supply of bullion, bankers and others are able to offer easy terms to people in business, including the bill brokers, and consequently people enter into the market as buyers of things, as starting new businesses, new factories, new railways, and so on." [1]

> "The supply of loans on the one hand and the desire of people to obtain loans on the other, having fixed the rates of discount at anything, 8, 6, 5, or 2 per cent., then the influx of a little extra gold, going as it does into the hands of those who deal in credit, causes the supply to rise relatively to the demand; the rate of discount falls below its equilibrium level, however low that was, and therefore stimulates speculation. . . . This new rate affects the equilibrium by causing capital to go into the hands of speculators who would not take capital at the old rate, but do take it at the new; and whatever form

[1] *Gold and Silver Commission*, No. 9677, *Official Papers*, p. 49.

192 A TREATISE ON MONEY BK. III

their speculation may take, it is almost sure, directly or indirectly, to raise prices. This is the main issue. It is this : when the gold comes to the country it is known, and people expect that prices will rise. Now if a person doubting whether to borrow for speculative purposes has a reason to believe that prices will rise, he is willing to take a loan at 3 per cent., which before he would not have taken at 2½ per cent., and consequently the influx of gold into the country by making people believe that prices will rise increases the demand for capital, and raises, therefore, in my opinion, the rate of discount." [1]

" Having this extra supply, lenders lower still more the rate which they charge for loans, and they keep on lowering it till a point is reached at which the demand will carry off the larger supply. When this has been done there is more capital in the hands of speculative investors, who come on the markets for goods as buyers, and so raise prices. . . . This then is my account of the way in which this extra supply of the precious metals would bring prices up. Having been raised they would be sustained because the methods of business remaining stationary, if a man with an income of £1000 keeps on the average £12 in his pocket, and if there is more currency in the country so that his share is increased from £12 to £14 ; then what was bought by £12 would in future be bought by £14. . . ." [2]

The emphasis here is on " speculation ", which lends a false colour ; though in the first quotation, investment seems to be suggested. On the whole I am inclined to think that uppermost in Marshall's mind was the idea that what raises prices is the creation of additional purchasing power, but that in

[1] *Gold and Silver Commission*, No. 9981, *Official Papers*, p. 130. There seems here to be some perplexity in Marshall's mind as to whether the new gold raises or lowers the rate of discount. Before the Indian Currency Committee he makes the chronological sequence clearer : " The new currency . . . increases the willingness of lenders to lend *in the first instance*, and lowers discount ; but *afterwards* raises prices and, therefore, tends to increase discount "—(*Official Papers*, p. 274 ; my italics). But here it is higher prices which increase discount, whereas in the passage quoted above it is the demand for *capital* due to the *expectation* of higher prices which does so.

[2] *Gold and Silver Commission*, No. 9686, *Official Papers*, p. 51.

"MODUS OPERANDI" OF BANK-RATE

the modern economic world the organisation of the credit system is such that the "speculators" are the people into whose hands new money is most likely to find its way in the first instance, Bank-rate playing an obvious part in this causal train. This seems to me to be the doctrine on which I was brought up, and which certainly did not bring home to my mind any clear idea of the relationship between the volume of earnings at any time, the volume of savings, and the volume of goods coming forward available for consumption, or of the connection of these things with the equilibrium between savings and investment.

When we come to the earlier writings of Mr. Hawtrey, we seem to get much nearer to the idea of Bank-rate as affecting the rate of investment; but the whole emphasis is placed on one particular kind of investment, namely, investment by dealers and middlemen in liquid goods—to which a degree of sensitiveness to changes in Bank-rate is attributed which certainly does not exist in fact. It will be necessary to quote a somewhat lengthy passage to make clear his line of thought:[1]

> "What precise effect will this rise in the rate of interest have on the borrowers? The two principal classes of borrowers are the producers and the dealers. The producers will, of course, find the cost of production of commodities slightly increased. . . . But, in general, changes in the rate of interest such as we are considering are too small to affect retail prices immediately. . . . But the dealers themselves will be influenced by the rate of interest. One of the special functions of a dealer is to keep a stock or 'working balance' of the goods in which he deals. This is necessary to enable him to meet the varied needs of his customers without delay. Now a dealer borrows money to buy goods, and repays the money as the goods are sold. Consequently when his stocks are large, his indebtedness to his banker will be correspondingly large. The extent of the stocks which he sees fit to

[1] *Good and Bad Trade* (pp. 61-63).

keep will be based on experience, but can, of course, be varied within fairly wide limits without much risk of inconvenience. When the rate of interest goes up he will be anxious to reduce his indebtedness, so far as he can, without incurring serious inconvenience. He can reduce his indebtedness if he can reduce his stocks of goods, and he can reduce his stocks of goods by merely delaying replenishment when they are sold. But the orders received by manufacturers come from the dealers who want to replenish their stocks. Consequently the manufacturers will at once find that they are receiving fewer and smaller orders. The money which the dealers would otherwise have been using to pay the manufacturer for goods, they are using to extinguish their indebtedness to their bankers. . . . That is to say, he (the manufacturer) experiences a slackening of demand, and in order to relieve the resulting restriction of output he lowers prices so far as the existing expenses of production will permit. This lowering of prices will enable the dealers to lower retail prices, a measure which would ordinarily stimulate demand. But in the meanwhile the reduction of stocks by the dealers and the restriction of output by the producers will have been accompanied by a diminution of indebtedness of both producers and dealers to the banks, and this diminution of the bankers' assets will have been accompanied by a diminution in their liabilities, *i.e.* in the supply of credit money. The balances of money in the hands of the public are therefore decreasing, and the superstructure of incomes erected thereon is simultaneously shrinking."

Now, I believe this to be a very incomplete account of the normal *modus operandi* of a higher bank-rate. It relies, let the reader observe, exclusively on the increased costs of business resulting from dearer money. Mr. Hawtrey admits that these additional costs will be too small materially to affect the manufacturer, but assumes without investigation that they do materially affect the trader. He does not base his argument on the arousing of an expectation of falling price-levels in the minds of the dealers, and he makes the diminution of the supply of credit money the *last* event in his causal train. Yet probably the question whether he is paying 5 per cent. or 6 per cent. for the accommodation he obtains from his banker influences the mind of the dealer very little more than it influences the mind of the manufacturer, as compared with the current and prospective rate of off-take for the goods he deals in and his expectations as to their prospective price-movements.

I have not quoted this passage, however, in order to criticise Mr. Hawtrey. I doubt if he would express himself to-day exactly in these words. I quote it because it gives in a form so clear that it can be confuted *one* of the elements which underlies some current opinion on this matter.

The classical refutation of Mr. Hawtrey's theory was given by Tooke[1] in his examination of an argument very similar to Mr. Hawtrey's, put forward nearly a hundred years ago by Joseph Hume. Before the crisis of 1836–37 the partisans of the " currency theory "— according to Tooke—considered that the influence of the Bank of England on the price-level only operated through the amount of its circulation ; but in 1839 the new-fangled notion was invented that Bank-rate also had an independent influence through its effect on " speculation ". Tooke was not concerned to deny the association of an excessive issue of paper with an injudicious cheapening of money or the effect of a declining rate of interest in stimulating investment of all kinds. But Hume had laid chief emphasis on the effect of cheap money in stimulating speculation in commodities, *e.g.* cotton and corn, to which Tooke retorts in a passage which deserves to be quoted :[2]

"There are, doubtless, persons who, upon imperfect information, and upon insufficient grounds, or with too sanguine a view of contingencies in their favour, speculate improvidently ; but their *motive* or *inducement* so to

[1] Tooke, *History of Prices*, 1838–39, pp. 120 *et seq*. Hume's theory was propounded in a famous speech on the Management of the Bank of England delivered in the House of Commons on July 8, 1839.
[2] *Op. cit.* pp. 153–54.

speculate is the opinion which, whether well or ill-founded, or whether upon their own view or upon the authority or example of other persons, they entertain of the probability of an advance of price. It is not the mere facility of borrowing, or the difference between being able to discount at 3 or at 6 per cent. that supplies the *motive* for purchasing, or even for selling. Few persons of the description here mentioned ever speculate but upon the confident expectation of an advance of price of at least 10 per cent. . . . But the utmost difference between the rate of discount of 3 per cent. and 6 per cent. for three months, would on a quarter of wheat amount only to $4\frac{1}{2}$d. per quarter, a difference which, I will venture to say, never induced or deterred a single speculative purchase. But, given the force of the motive, the extent to which it can be acted upon is doubtless affected as regards persons who can buy only on credit, or who must borrow in order to be able to buy, by the greater or less facility of borrowing."

Moreover—Tooke adds (as many others have since)—falling commodity prices are often associated in actual experience, not with a rising rate of interest, but with a falling rate.[1]

Whilst Marshall, unless I have misunderstood him, regarded the influence of Bank-rate on investment as the means by which an increase of purchasing power got out into the world, and Mr. Hawtrey has limited its influence to one particular kind of investment, namely investment by dealers in stocks of liquid goods, Wicksell—though here also there are obscurities to overcome—was closer to the fundamental conception of Bank-rate as affecting the relationship between investment and saving. I say that there are obscurities to overcome, because Wicksell's theory in the form in which it has been taken over from him by Professor Cassel seems to me to be reduced to practically the

[1] The explanation of this on my theory is, of course, that movements of bank-rate have so often represented a belated and inadequate effort to follow a movement of the natural-rate.

"MODUS OPERANDI" OF BANK-RATE

same thing as the first strand of thought mentioned above, namely that the level of Bank-rate determines the volume of bank-money and hence the price-level. But I think that there was more than this in Wicksell's own thought, though obscurely presented in his book.

Wicksell conceives of the existence of a "natural rate of interest", which he defines as being the rate which is " neutral " in its effect on the prices of goods, tending neither to raise nor to lower them, and adds that this must be the same rate as would obtain if in a non-monetary economy all lending was in the form of actual materials.[1] It follows that if the actual rate of interest is lower than this prices will have a rising tendency, and conversely if the actual rate is higher.[2] It follows, further, that so long as the money-rate of interest is kept below the natural-rate of interest, prices will continue to rise—and without limit.[3] It is not necessary for this result, namely the cumulative rise of prices, that the money-rate should fall short of the natural-rate by an ever-increasing difference; it is enough that it should be, and remain, below it.

Whilst Wicksell's expressions cannot be justified as they stand and must seem unconvincing (as they have to Professor Cassel) without further development, they can be interpreted in close accordance with the Fundamental Equation of this Treatise. For if we define Wicksell's natural-rate of interest as the rate at which Saving and the value of Investment are in equilibrium

---

[1] *Geldzins und Güterpreise*, p. 93.

[2] Wicksell also used the term " real " interest in the above sense. But the " natural " rate of interest as defined above is on no account to be confused with Irving Fisher's " real " rate of interest, namely the money-rate corrected by reference to any change in the value of money between the loan's being advanced and its being repaid. *Cf.* Hayek, *Geldtheorie und Konjunkturtheorie*, pp. 124-25.

[3] Though this will involve—which Wicksell does not bring out—a continual rise in the rate of money-earnings, but one which is never quite sufficient to wipe out profits; and this rise will require, in turn, to be fed by a continual increase in the quantity of money.

(measured in accordance with the definitions of Chapter 10 above), then it is true that, so long as the money-rate of interest is held at such a level that the value of Investment exceeds Saving, there will be a rise in the price-level of output as a whole above its cost of production, which in turn will stimulate entrepreneurs to bid up the rates of earnings above their previous level, and this upward tendency will continue indefinitely so long as the supply of money continues to be such as to enable the money-rate to be held below the natural-rate as thus defined. This means, in general, that the market-rate of interest cannot be continually held even a little below the natural-rate unless the volume of bank-money is being continually increased; but this does not affect the formal correctness of Wicksell's argument. Professor Cassel's belief, that Wicksell was making a very odd mistake in arguing in this way,[1] may be justified by the incompleteness of Wicksell's expression, but it probably indicates that, whilst Wicksell was thinking along the same lines as those followed in this Treatise, Cassel is not,—in spite of the fact that Cassel expresses himself elsewhere in practically the same terms as Wicksell, namely that the true rate of interest is that at which the value of money is unchanged.[2]

At any rate, whether or not I have exaggerated the depth to which Wicksell's thought penetrated,[3] he was the first writer to make it clear that the influence of the rate of interest on the price-level operates by its effect on the rate of Investment, and that *Investment* in this context means *Investment* and not speculation. On this point Wicksell was very explicit, pointing out that the rate of investment is capable of being

---

[1] *Vide* his *Theory of Social Economy* (Eng. trans.), p. 479.
[2] *E.g. op. cit.* p. 480; *Fundamental Thoughts on Economics*, p. 129.
[3] There are many small indications, not lending themselves to quotation, by which one writer can feel whether another writer has at the back of his head the same root-ideas or different ones. On this test I feel that what I am trying to say is the same at root as what Wicksell was trying to say.

affected by small changes in the rate of interest, *e.g.* ¼ per cent., which could not be supposed to affect the mind of the speculator; that this increased investment causes an increased demand for actual goods for use and not for " speculative " purposes, and that it is this increased actual demand which sends up prices.[1]

More recently a school of thought has been developing in Germany and Austria under the influence of these ideas, which one might call the neo-Wicksell school, whose theory of bank-rate in relation to the equilibrium of Savings and Investment, and the importance of the latter to the Credit Cycle, is fairly close to the theory of this Treatise. I would mention particularly Ludwig Mises's *Geldwertstabilisierung und Konjunkturpolitik* (1928), Hans Neisser, *Der Tauschwert des Geldes* (1928), and Friedrich Hayek, *Geldtheorie und Konjunkturtheorie* (1929).[2]

4. There is a fourth factor by reference to which some writers (*e.g.* Professor Pigou) reinforce such other explanation as they may offer of the influence of bank-rate on the price-level, namely its *psychological* effect. But the fact of the *expectation* of lower prices aroused by a rise in bank-rate scarcely constitutes an independent explanation of why a higher bank-rate should cause prices to fall. For such an expectation could not persist year after year, as a mere illusion, if it was, in fact, groundless. Business men would be quite capable of entertaining the opposite expectation,

---

[1] *Geldzins und Güterpreise*, pp. 82-84.

[2] I should have made more references to the work of these writers if their books, which have only come into my hands as these pages are being passed through the press, had appeared when my own thought was at an earlier stage of development, and if my knowledge of the German language was not so poor (in German I can only clearly understand what I know already !—so that *new* ideas are apt to be veiled from me by the difficulties of language). I find Dr. Neisser's general attitude to monetary problems particularly sympathetic, and am hopeful that he may feel the same about my work. There are also some other recent German writers covering the same line of country, whose work I have only glanced at.

namely that a higher bank-rate would *raise* prices, if only for the very plausible reason that it would raise costs of production; but such an expectation could not persist if in fact, apart from the expectation, higher bank-rate was *not* calculated to raise prices. And even if the expectation did persist, the realisation of it would not. At any rate, I do not imagine that those who advance this explanation mean that the effect of higher bank-rate is traceable to a psychological mistake on the part of the business world. They mean rather that, because higher bank-rate does, quite apart from any expectations, actually tend towards lower prices, the business world " discounts " this tendency, so that it realises itself in terms of the price-level sooner, and perhaps in a more extreme degree, than it would otherwise. Thus the fact that the result is correctly anticipated is not in itself the reason, and does not help us to discover the reason, *why* the result follows.

I hope the reader will not feel that I have spent too much time on matters which are mainly of historical interest. But Bank-rate being a question about which the truth has long been confusedly and incompletely known, a history of opinion is of more value as an introduction to a constructive theory than it would be if progress had been made by well-defined stages.

(ii.) *The General Theory of Bank-rate.*

It is convenient to mean by " Bank-rate " in this section of this chapter the *effective* rate for lending and borrowing which prevails in the market, *i.e.* not necessarily the official published rate of the Central Bank at which it will discount three months' bills of a specified type, but the complex of interest rates effective in the market at any time for the borrowing and lending of money for short periods. If a change in the official rate does not alter the rates effective in the market, we shall say that it is " ineffective ". It will also be convenient to use the term " Bond-rate " to designate the complex of interest rates effective in the market for the borrowing and lending of money for longer periods; and we shall use the term " market-rate of interest" for the complex of bank-rate and bond-rate. The relationship between the official bank-rate, the " effective " rate of discount, and the market-rate of interest will be discussed in Chapter 37. We shall here assume that changes in bank-rate affect the market-rate of interest in the same direction.

The General Theory of Bank-rate, apart from the complications and elaborations which will occupy many succeeding chapters, can be broadly enunciated as follows :

We have argued that a rise (*e.g.*) in the market-rate of interest upsets the balance between the value of investment and saving, unless a corresponding rise in the natural-rate occurs at the same time. It may do this either by stimulating saving or by retarding investment.

In the case of saving, the effect of a change in the rate of interest is direct and primary and needs no special explanation, though the amount of the effect may often be quantitatively small in practice, especially over the short period. Thus a rise will have a direct tendency to increase the rate of saving, unless it is needed to offset a decline in saving which would have occurred, for other reasons, in its absence.

But its effect in retarding investment needs a little more explanation. Investment-goods are not identical with capital-goods (*cf.* their definitions on p. 130 above), being somewhat more comprehensive. But a retardation of investment will result, sooner or later, from a a reduction in the output of capital-goods. Now, from the point of view of individual entrepreneurs, there will be no occasion for a reduction in the output of such goods, unless their price is falling relatively to their cost of production, or unless the demand for them is falling off at the existing price. In what way can a rise in bank-rate tend to bring this about?

Upon what does the demand-price of capital-goods depend? It depends on *two* things—on the estimated net prospective yield from fixed capital (estimated by the opinion of the market after such allowance as they choose to make for the uncertainty of anticipation, etc.), measured in money, and on the rate of interest at which this future yield is capitalised. It follows that the price of such goods can change for either of two reasons—because the prospective yield has changed or because the rate of interest has changed. And we can pursue the analysis a step further: since the prospective yield must be measured for the present purpose in terms of money, a change in it may be due either to a change in the real yield, its price remaining the same, or to a change in the prospective price (or money value) of the real yield.

Now a change in bank-rate is not calculated to have any effect (except, perhaps, remotely and of the second order of magnitude) on the prospective real yield of fixed capital. It may conceivably affect the prospective price of the real yield, but only, as a rule, on goods the future yield of which will be spread over a comparatively short period of time and if the change of bank-rate constitutes a new fact in itself—by throwing new light, for example, on the policy and intentions of the currency authority. This conceivable effect, however, is one which we will for the present neglect. The connection between bank-rate (and, more particularly, bond-rate as affected by bank-rate) and the third influence on the price of capital-goods, namely, the rate of interest at which the prospective money-yield of fixed capital is capitalised in order to arrive at its present money-value, is, on the other hand, immediate, direct, and obvious. The connection will not, indeed, be quantitatively important, except on goods of which the future yield will be spread over a very short period, unless the bond-rate is sensitive to changes in bank-rate. But this is, in fact, the case, and in a higher degree than might have been expected. If, for example, a rise of 1 per cent. in bank-rate has the effect of raising bond-rate from 5 per cent. to $5\frac{1}{8}$ per cent., this means an average decrease of $2\frac{1}{2}$ per cent. in the price of new fixed capital—the prices of some categories of such goods falling, of course, more than the average and those of others less, according to their length of life and other considerations. This must necessarily be deterrent to the production of such goods, until, as a result of it, the falling off in their prospective supply has raised the money-value of their prospective yield sufficiently to offset the effect of the higher rate of interest. At any rate, the initial consequence of a higher bank-rate will be a fall in the price of capital-goods, and therefore in P′, the price-level of new investment-goods. Moreover, the deterrent or attractive effect on the demand for new capital-goods is often greater than one might expect if one was to concentrate all one's attention on the mere change of (say) $2\frac{1}{2}$ to 5 per cent. in the value of such goods due to the change in the rate of interest. For investment is much more capable of postponement or anticipation without serious disadvantage (or is so, at least, in the minds of those who make the decisions) than is consumption. If, therefore, the change in bank-rate is considered by the market to be a departure from its normal value, which is likely to be of a temporary character, the effect is to cause borrowers for investment purposes to put off or to anticipate their investment plans, and thus to cause the immediate rate of investment to fluctuate much more than would be the case if borrowers believed that the change in the rate of interest had come to stay. The actual organisation of the market is also an influence in the same direction. For issue houses will be inclined to "protect" the price of their recently previous issues —which may not have been wholly digested by permanent investors at the date when the bank-rate is changed—by damping down the rate of new issues, both in their own interest and in that of their clientele. That is to say, it will be abnormally difficult (if bank-rate has recently risen) or abnormally easy (if it has recently fallen) for new borrowers to float their wares at a price approximating to the prices quoted in the market for existing loans; so that market quotations are not at all times an equally good index of the ease with which new borrowers for investment purposes can be accommodated. Thus changes in bank-rate are calculated in the actual conditions of the contemporary capital-market to have a decided effect on the rate at which producers of capital-goods will be able to find buyers for their products at a satisfactory price, even if the change in the rate is believed to be a short-period fluctuation; and all the more so, for other and more obvious reasons, if the change is expected to last.

At least this will be the case unless the rise in the market-rate of interest (*i.e.* bank-rate and bond-rate) is compensated by a simultaneous rise, for other reasons, in the estimated prospective yield of fixed capital. Only if the higher rate of interest merely offsets market optimism about the prospective yield of new fixed capital, will the change be without direct effect on the output of capital goods.

Thus, generally speaking (*i.e.* unless the change in bank-rate happens to be balanced by other contemporary changes), we may expect the direct and *primary* effects of a rise of bank-rate to be a fall in the price of fixed capital and, therefore, in P', the price-level of investment-goods, and an increase of saving—of which the former is more likely to be quantitatively important than the latter.

What are its *secondary* effects ? The fall in the attractiveness of fixed capital at the existing price will make it impossible for producers of capital-goods to market their output on terms as satisfactory as before in relation to their cost of production and will be followed, therefore, by a fall in the output of such goods. At the same time, any increase of saving must mean a diminution in the flow of income directed towards the purchase of liquid consumption-goods and will be followed, therefore, by a fall of P.

Only if the rise in the rate of interest coincides with a reduction in the rate of saving for other reasons will this not be the case ; *i.e.* if the change in the market-rate coincides with a change in the natural-rate. For the natural-rate is the rate which balances the resultant effect of a change in the prospective yield of capital-goods and a change in the rate of saving, in such a manner that the change in the price-level of investment-goods, due to the combined effect of changes in their prospective yield and in the rate of interest, is equal and opposite to the change in the price-level of liquid consumption-goods, due to the change in the volume of saving, each price-level being weighted in proportion to the output of the goods to which it relates ; so that the price-level of output as a whole remains unchanged.

Thus a change in the natural-rate of interest will be accompanied by a temporary upset both of P and of P', though in opposite directions ; but profits as a whole will remain at zero, the gains of one category of producers being balanced by the losses of the other. Thus there will be a direct and double stimulus to shift the character of output from the one category to the other, and, when this has been effected, both P and P' will return to their previous positions of equilibrium without there having been any occasion to disturb the average rate of earnings (though the process of transfer may have required a temporary upset of relative earnings in the two categories of production). The process will, indeed, have been essentially similar to what must needs occur every day when changes in relative conditions of demand and supply require some sort of shift and turnover in the character of production ;—nothing will have occurred calculated to disturb profits or earnings as a whole.

But if the change in the market-rate does *not* exactly correspond to a change in the natural-rate, what will be the *tertiary* effects of the rise of bank-rate which we have been considering ? The decline in the rate of investment will cause a fall in P additional to any fall caused by the increase of savings, since there will be a reduction in the incomes of the producers of investment-goods available for the purchase of liquid consumption-goods, as necessarily follows from the Fundamental Equation.

At this stage, therefore, we have a fall both in P and in P', consequent losses to *all* classes of entrepreneurs, and a resulting diminution in the volume of employment which they offer to the factors of production at the existing rates of earnings. Thus a state of unemployment may be expected to ensue, and to continue, until the rise in bank-rate is reversed or, by a chance, something happens to alter the natural-rate of interest so as to bring it back to equality with the new market-rate.

Moreover, the longer this state of affairs continues, the greater is the volume of unemployment likely to be. For, at first, entrepreneurs may continue to offer employment on the old terms, even though it involves them in losses, partly because they are tied up with long-period contracts with the factors of production which they cannot quickly get out of, and partly because it will be worth while, so long as they hope and believe that the period of loss will be fairly short, to avoid the expenses of closing down and starting up again. But as time goes on, these motives will gradually lose their effect and cease to operate.

There is also one more aggravation. So long as there is a prospect of losses, the natural-rate of interest will fall below its normal level, thus widening the gap between the natural-rate and the market-rate, and requiring a reduction of the latter perhaps beyond what is practicable.

Finally, under the pressure of growing unemployment, the rate of earnings—though, perhaps, only at long last—will fall. This is the consummation of the whole process of pressure, if we can assume—as ordinarily we can—that the change in bank-rate had been dictated in the first instance by monetary reasons, local or international. For by this time two things will have occurred—the one sooner but temporarily, the other later but more permanently—which will tend to relieve the monetary situation and so permit, at last, a reversal of the bank-rate policy; and a third factor may also be relevant.

In the first place the decline in output due to unemployment will reduce the requirements of the Industrial Circulation. Also the fall in prices will tend to improve the foreign balance of the country and so enable it to retain or increase its gold. These things will happen quickly, and are real alleviations of the purely monetary position, so long as they last. Their mere occurrence is, therefore, often greeted with satisfaction, as though it were a final solution of the problem. Yet it is evident that these occurrences are of illusory advantage if they are regarded as anything more than a stage in a transition. For they are unreliable aids. If prices are low because entrepreneurs are accepting losses and not because costs of production have been reduced, a continuance of them can only result in a progressive increase of unemployment; and if the pressure on the supply of money has only been relaxed by the expedient of reducing output and employment, then monetary equilibrium will continue to require the indefinite prolongation of chronic unemployment.

Thus it is only when what I have called the consummation of the process has been achieved, namely, the reduction of the rate of efficiency-earnings, that a true equilibrium will be re-established.

The third factor, referred to above, which is also capable of bringing immediate relief, operates when the increase in the rate of interest is an increase relatively to rates abroad. For in this event there will be a reduction in the rate of foreign lending which will strengthen our country's gold position. But this also is incapable, as we shall see in the next section of this chapter and in more detail in Chapter 21, of restoring a true equilibrium, unless it is ultimately accompanied by a change in the rate of earnings.

There has been no more harmful confusion within the field of monetary practice, than the belief that bank-rate has done its work when it has produced a fall in the price-level, irrespective of whether this is due to selling at a loss or to a decline in the costs of production, *i.e.* irrespective of whether the deflation which it has produced is a Profit Deflation or an Income Deflation.[1]

Perhaps this discussion has been unnecessarily detailed and meticulous. The long and short of it is as follows:

1. Such changes in bank-rate, as cause the market-rate of interest to diverge from the natural-rate, have a direct effect, which is likely to be significant, on the profits of the producers of capital-goods and on their rate of production, partly by changing the demand-price for such goods and partly by influencing intending purchasers of such goods to postpone or

[1] For a classical example of this confusion, see *Report of the Committee on the Currency and Bank of England Note Issues* (Cmd. 2393, 1925)—the report on the strength of which Great Britain committed herself to a return in that year to the pre-War parity of the gold standard.

anticipate their purchases; and also a direct effect, which is less likely to be significant, on the price-level of liquid consumption-goods in so far as the rate of savings is affected.

2. The change in P' thus brought about will upset the balance between investment and saving, which will, as a secondary effect, cause P to move in the same direction as P'—whether or not it has done so already as a consequence of a change in the rate of saving—with the result that the profits of entrepreneurs producing consumption-goods will move in the same direction as the profits of those producing capital-goods.

3. The change in the average rate of profits, whether it is due to P' or to P, will alter the volume of employment which entrepreneurs will be prepared to offer at the existing rate of earnings.

4. A tendency will, therefore, be set up to change the prevailing rate of earnings in the same direction as P and P' and in the opposite direction to bank-rate.

(iii.) *Some Special Aspects of Bank-rate*

There are certain special points arising out of the above, which must be noticed before we pass on:

1. A change in the other factors of the situation may sometimes involve an inevitable instability unless there is an *anticipatory* change in the bank-rate. For a fall in the bank-rate required to stimulate investment so as to balance increased saving must—whenever the increased investment takes the form of an increased output of fixed capital—*precede* the increase of saving by an interval dependent on the length of the productive process. Moreover, the anticipatory change in bank-rate must also be correctly understood by the business world; otherwise it may stimulate the producers of capital-goods without any corresponding readiness on the part of the producers of

consumption-goods to reduce in-put—the latter not foreseeing the falling-off in the demand for their goods when the increased rate of saving, which is being anticipated, duly matures. Thus some fluctuations may be—practically speaking—unavoidable.

2. When there is a need to change the rate of earnings because some change is occurring which affects the Standard of Value, there is no ready means of doing this except by a change of bank-rate which is deliberately designed to provoke a (temporary) disequilibrium between Saving and Investment, in order that in this way entrepreneurs may be induced by abnormal profits to raise the money-earnings of the factors of production or—if a fall in the price-level is the objective—by abnormal losses to reduce the money-earnings of the latter. When, that is to say, we want to effect a quasi-permanent change in the purchasing power of money—which is the same thing as to alter the money-rates of efficiency-earnings of the factors of production —we can, in the existing economic system, only do this by allotting to entrepreneurs abnormal profits which will stimulate them to bid against one another for the services of the factors of production and so raise the money-rate of efficiency-earnings, or abnormal losses which will depress them into withdrawing offers of employment and so, by the pressure of unemployment, into (ultimately) reducing efficiency-earnings in terms of money. And our means for effecting this temporary stimulus or depression is to rupture the equilibrium between Savings and Investment by establishing a bank-rate which purposely causes the market-rate of interest to differ from the natural-rate.

3. There is often a confusion as to the way in which easier terms of credit affect different classes of entrepreneurs. Since cheaper borrowing lowers the cost of production of all types of entrepreneurs, it is often supposed that it stimulates all alike to increase their out-

put. But with correct forecasting this should not be the case. For—other things being equal—an all-round reduction of the cost of production should not stimulate anyone to increase his output, inasmuch as the aggregate incomes of consumers, which are simply the aggregate costs of production under another name, available to purchase the output, are also being reduced to exactly the same extent. In this case interest is simply the money-rate of earnings of one of the factors of production; so that reducing it will not enable entrepreneurs as a body to market profitably any more goods than before. Since entrepreneurs are not always acquainted with such reasoning, easier credit is, it is true, liable to provoke mistaken forecasting. But, apart from this, the effect of easier credit on the costs of production should be, not to stimulate production all round, but to cause a change-over from certain forms of production to other forms; namely, from those for which interest is a relatively unimportant cost to those for which it is a relatively important cost,—which partly depends on the duration of the process of production and does not even wholly coincide with the distinction between consumption-goods and capital-goods. That is to say, the effect of easier credit on the costs of production is *not* calculated in a closed system to stimulate the aggregate of productivity of all kinds. A fall in the rate of interest stimulates the production of capital-goods not because it decreases their cost of production but because it increases their demand-price.

4. It is not unusual for the stimulus to new investment to come about through a lower bank-rate first of all affecting the financial, as distinguished from the industrial, situation and so sending up the price-level of *existing* investments (including the price-level of working-capital, *i.e.* the wholesale standard). In so far as these investments are capable of reproduction, the prices of *new* capital-goods (in particular) will then

rise in sympathy. This is a matter to which we shall return later on.

5. As we have hinted above, a change in bank-rate may itself alter the natural-rate of interest in the opposite direction to that in which bank-rate has been changed, by altering expectations as to the future course of prices. For example, if bank-rate *falls*, this tends to *raise* the natural-rate of interest, if it arouses expectations of a tendency towards rising prices, thus increasing the attractiveness of investment in terms of money. This is an extra reason, in the first instance, for expecting a fall of bank-rate to stimulate investment relatively to saving. But it is a reason which will probably produce a reaction a little later on after prices have risen, whereas this will not be so with a rise in the natural-rate of interest due to other causes than monetary expectations.

6. If we assume that the lending of money takes place according to the principles of a perfect market, it is evident that, given the demand-schedule of borrowers, the effective bank-rate and bond-rate must uniquely determine the production of capital-goods and hence, generally speaking, the volume of investment. So far, however, as bank loans are concerned, lending does *not*—in Great Britain at least—take place according to the principles of a perfect market. There is apt to be an unsatisfied fringe of borrowers, the size of which can be expanded or contracted, so that banks can influence the volume of investment by expanding or contracting the volume of their loans, without there being necessarily any change in the level of bank-rate, in the demand-schedule of borrowers, or in the volume of lending otherwise than through the banks. This phenomenon is capable, when it exists, of having great practical importance. We shall discuss the practical conditions which are likely to lead to its existence, its limitations and the use which can be made of it in Volume ii., Chapter 37. Meanwhile

we are assuming that the Banking System works wholly by modifying its terms of lending and not by varying its attitude towards individual borrowers or by any form of rationing loans. This is for the sake of simplicity; for it is not difficult to adapt the general argument to the case where the rate of investment is partly determined (usually to quite a secondary extent) by the rationing policy of the Banking System as well as by its terms of lending.

(iv.) *The Function of Bank-rate in relation to External Equilibrium*

There remains the function of Bank-rate as a means of preserving external equilibrium, even at the cost of upsetting internal equilibrium.

We have seen in Chapter 11 (v.) that to a Central Bank, which adheres to an international gold standard (or to any objective standard other than the purchasing power of money itself), the problem of currency management presents itself not as a problem of keeping $I = S$, but as a problem of keeping $B = L$, where B is the value of the Foreign Balance and L the value of Foreign Lending, as defined in Chapter 9 (iv.). It deems it its business to take steps to cause B to exceed L, to cause L to exceed B, or to keep them equal to one another, according as it wishes to increase its gold reserve, to diminish it, or to maintain it unchanged. But although the problem presents itself to the Central Bank as one of keeping $B = L$, its national economic system will not in fact be able to maintain its equilibrium unless at the same time $I = S$. Thus the conditions for equilibrium in an international system are that we should simultaneously have

$$I = S, \text{ and } B = L.$$

It happens, however, that the Bank's recognised instrument for achieving the desired relationship between B and L is the instrument of bank-rate—just as it would be if I = S was its sole objective. For the instrument of Bank-rate has been found by experience to influence the movement of gold into and out of a country's reserves, a rise of bank-rate increasing B – L and a fall diminishing it. Now changes of bank-rate which are aimed at preserving equilibrium between B and L may be expected to exercise a disturbing effect in the first instance on the equilibrium between I and S. But we shall see that—apart from the difficulties of the transition—there is always a level of bank-rate which is compatible in the long run both with the equilibrium of B and L and also with that of I and S. What is the complete theoretical explanation of the phenomenon? When we understand that, we shall have reached the kernel of the *modus operandi* of bank-rate as the instrument of control in the modern world of an international gold standard.

We shall see that the extraordinary efficacy of bank-rate for effecting the above is due to the fact that it produces two reactions, one of them on L and the other on B, both in the right direction— one of them quick in action but not so durable, the other slow in action but calculated to establish gradually a new long-period equilibrium. Thus Bank-rate is both an expedient and a solution. It supplies both the temporary pick-me-up and the permanent cure— provided we ignore the *malaise* which may intervene between the pick-me-up and the cure.

The detailed theory of this matter we will postpone to Chapter 21. But the essence of the matter can be set out briefly. Raising the bank-rate obviously has the effect of diminishing L, the net amount of lending to foreigners. But it has no direct influence in the direction of increasing B. On the other hand, just as the dearer money discourages foreign borrowers, so also it discourages borrowers for the purposes of home investment,—with the result that the higher bank-rate diminishes I_1, the volume of home investment. Consequently total investment falls below current savings (assuming that there was previously equilibrium), so that prices and profits, and ultimately earnings, fall, which has the effect of increasing B, because it reduces the costs of production in terms of money relatively to the corresponding costs abroad. On both accounts, therefore, B and L are brought nearer together, until in the new position of equilibrium they are again equal.

Thus, where the evil to be cured was an excess of L over B leading to an export of gold, the increase of bank-rate will have done its work when B and L, continually approaching one another, have regained equality. Or rather, in practice, the high bank-rate will quickly diminish L, even to the extent of bringing it below B; but, nevertheless, it will not be safe to relax it until it has had time to increase B, by when it will be practicable to keep B and L at an approximate equality without so high a bank-rate; and if the original reason for disequilibrium between B and L was a change in price-levels and not in interest-rates abroad, with a bank-rate no higher than that which existed before—at the beginning of our story— the bank-rate was raised.

At the new level of equilibrium we shall once again have $P = \dfrac{M_1 V_1}{O}$ and $I = S$. But we shall also have $B = L$. For since B moves in the opposite direction to P and P in the opposite direction to $L - B$, whilst L moves in the opposite direction to bank-rate, for every value of bank-rate there is a value of P at which $B = L$; and since S moves in the same direction as bank-rate and I moves in the opposite direction, there is always a value of bank-rate for which $I = S$. Consequently there is always a pair of values of bank-rate and of P at which both $I = S$ and $B = L$.

For example, let us imagine an automatic international gold system in which the quantity of money is solely determined by the amount of gold in the Central Bank, and Bank-rate is left to find its own level as a result of free competition between borrowers for the amount of bank-money available on the basis of the amount of gold in the Central Bank. It then follows from the above that in such conditions (assuming an absence of economic frictions and of time-lag, and in particular that the rates of money-earnings are free to move in response to the competition of entrepreneurs for the services of the factors of production) an amount of gold will flow in which is just sufficient to establish a price-level and a bank-rate at home which shall be such, relatively to price-levels and bank-rates abroad, as to keep both $S=I$ and $L=B$ at the same time.

(v.) *The Relation of Bank-rate to the Quantity of Money*

In a free loan-market (*i.e.* in the absence of the rationing of loans) a given level of bank-rate, taken in conjunction with all other relevant factors, must be uniquely correlated, if it is to be effective, with a given quantity of bank-money. That is to say, every effective alteration of bank-rate must be associated, except in so far as it is balanced by simultaneous alterations in other factors, by *some* alteration in the quantity of bank-money.

But there is no simple or invariable relation between the effect of an alteration of bank-rate on the price-level, whether of liquid consumption-goods or of output as a whole, and the associated alteration in the quantity of bank-money. The volume of bank-money must be in due relation to the volume of output, the rate of earnings, the rate of profit, the velocities of different classes of deposits, and the requirements of the financial circulation. A change in bank-rate will have an effect, initially or subsequently, on all of these, and through them on price-levels. But its effect on these different factors will neither be in the same proportion on all of them at a given moment, nor in the same proportion on any one of them at different stages of a transition; so that it is not useful to say that a change in bank-rate changes price-levels *because* it is associated with changes in the quantity of bank-money—especially if this statement carries any suggestion that the price-levels will change more or less in the same proportion as the change in the quantity of bank-money.

In particular, we may note the following points:
(*a*) We have already seen that a rise in prices, which is due to an increase in the rate of earnings, will require a larger quantity of bank-money to support it than an equal rise which is due to the emergence of profits. Thus, as increased profits are gradually transmuted into increased earnings (in the manner to be examined in great detail in Book IV.), a larger and larger quantity of money is required;—which is part of the explanation of the cyclical character of some types of monetary fluctuation, inasmuch as a quantity of money which is adequate to support a rise of prices due to the second term of the Fundamental Equation is inadequate to support an equal rise due to the first term, with the result that as the first term increases, a reaction in prices becomes inevitable through lack of enough money to "finance" them.

(*b*) If there is a change in the natural-rate of interest, the *same* bank-rate as before will require, if it is to be effective, to be associated with a *changed* quantity of money. Thus it is not, strictly speaking, a change in bank-rate as such which needs to be associated with a changed quantity of money, but a change in the market-rate of interest relatively to the natural-rate.

(c) If the change in the market-rate of interest relatively to the natural-rate is due to a change in the volume of savings, it need not be accompanied by any change in the volume or character of output, but merely by the existing character of output being continued after this has ceased to be suitable to the changed volume of savings. In this case the change in the quantity of money required is likely to be small. But if, as is more commonly the case, the departure of the market-rate from the natural-rate is associated with a change in the volume of output and employment, this will involve a much more substantial change in the quantity of money—which, broadly speaking, will have to be changed in proportion to the change in the aggregate costs of production.

(d) A change in bank-rate may in itself modify the velocities of circulation, by changing the amount of sacrifice involved in holding balances. To the extent that this is the case, a fall in bank-rate will decrease velocities. On the other hand, as we shall see in Volume ii., Chapter 26, an increased briskness of trade is likely to increase velocities. Thus a reduction of bank-rate which is associated with a stagnation of trade may decrease velocities, but one which is associated with brisk trade may serve to increase them on balance.

(e) The reactions of a change in bank-rate on the financial situation will affect the volume of the Financial Circulation, and may affect it either in the same direction or in the opposite direction to its effect on the volume of the Industrial Circulation.[1]

Bank-rate may affect the Financial Circulation in two ways. In the first place, when—as in Great Britain—the rate of interest allowed on savings-

[1] For the distinction between the Financial Circulation and the Industrial Circulation, see Chapter 15 below.

deposits is largely governed by bank-rate (being fixed in many cases in a definite relationship to bank-rate), the volume of the former may sometimes tend to rise and fall with the level of the latter. More important, however, is its effect on what in Chapter 15 we shall call the "bear" position. We shall see there that an investment boom is likely to be associated with reduced requirements for money in the Financial Circulation in its early stages, but with increased requirements in the later stages.

(*f*) If there is an investment boom at home, associated with a sharp rise in the natural-rate of interest, the market-rate may fall behind the natural-rate and yet at the same time rise absolutely. This absolute rise in the market-rate may, if it is a rise relatively to market-rates abroad, have in the first instance a more pronounced effect on L, the volume of foreign lending, than the investment boom is having on B, the amount of the foreign balance; with the result that gold may flow into the country and so provide fodder for the rise of price at home consequent on the market-rate of interest not keeping pace with the natural-rate.

It appears, therefore, that the demand for money under (*a*) will be at first small, and that the total demand for money under (*a*) and (*c*) can sometimes be met wholly or in part, especially at first, by changes in true velocities under (*d*), by diminished requirements in the financial circulation under (*e*), or by gold imports under (*f*).

Thus the total requirements of the monetary circulation are not associated in any stable or invariable manner either with the level of bank-rate and its influence on the rate of investment or with the level of prices; so that we shall be misled if we lay much stress on the changes in the total quantity of money when we are trying to trace the causation and the stages of a transition.

But the fundamental reason for laying the stress

on changes of bank-rate as affecting the level of the market-rate of interest relatively to the natural-rate, rather than on changes in the quantity of money, is this. Given associated changes in the total quantity of money and in the effective level of bank-rate respectively, it is *viâ* the latter that the ultimate modification in the purchasing power of money is generated, looking at the problem dynamically. The order of events is *not* that a change of bank-rate affects the price-level because, in order to make the new bank-rate effective, the quantity of money has to be altered. It is, rather, the other way round. A change in the quantity of money affects the price-level in the first instance, because, other things being equal, this means a bank-rate which will change the market-rate of interest relatively to the natural-rate; and it is only through the complex movements thus set up that a new equilibrium position is eventually reached, with a price-level corresponding to the new quantity of money.

If we start from a position of equilibrium, then—provided that efficiency-earnings are stable—the condition for the continued stability of price-levels is that the total volume of money should vary in such a way that the effect of the corresponding volume of bank lending on the market-rate of interest is to keep the value of new investment at an equality with current saving.

CHAPTER 14

ALTERNATIVE FORMS OF THE FUNDAMENTAL EQUATION

THE Fundamental Equations of Chapter 10 are in themselves no more than identities, and therefore not intrinsically superior to other identities which have been propounded, connecting monetary factors. Indeed they have a disadvantage in that their elements are not those which it is easiest to determine statistically in the present state of our knowledge. They have, however, two principal advantages.

The first advantage is that which we have already emphasised, namely, that they do lead up to what are generally our real *quaesita*, namely, the Purchasing Power of Money and the price-level of output as a whole, whereas the alternative methods lead up, as we shall see, to various hotch-potch price-levels which are of no great interest in themselves; and if we try to argue on from these price-levels to the Purchasing Power of Money, then we are faced with statistical difficulties at least as great as those which attend our own Equation. Thus when we approach the monetary problem quantitatively, the statistical difficulties which the Equations of Chapter 10 bring to the surface are really latent in any method which we can adopt. In fact the statistical advantages of the other methods only exist so long as we are content with a price-level which is by no means the price-level we want.

The main advantage, however, to be claimed for the new Fundamental Equations is for the purposes of qualitative investigation. For they are, I think, a much more powerful instrument of analysis than their predecessors, when we are considering what kind of monetary and business events will produce what kind of consequences. The reader will find, as we have already found in dealing with the *modus operandi* of bank-rate, that we are compelled in any case to discard the alternatives when we advance to the later stages of the argument and attempt to analyse the actual monetary problems of the day—the problem of the Credit Cycle, for example—because we discover that they are quite ineffective for handling the elements which most matter. I must, however, leave the reader to judge whether or not the new instrument cuts better than the old, when he has become accustomed to the use of it in the various chapters of this Treatise. Meanwhile it will be useful to outline the older methods in their relation to the new.

(i.) The "Real-Balances" Quantity Equation

The first of these is that which I used in my *Tract on Monetary Reform* and have since developed into a more accurate shape. This method sets out from the idea that what a holder of money requires is a quantity of Real-balances which bears the appropriate relationship to the quantity of real transactions upon which he employs his balances. Consequently, if this appropriate relationship remains unchanged, the quantity of Cash-balances which he needs will be equal to the quantity of Real-balances as determined by the above " appropriate relationship ", multiplied by the Price-level corresponding to the prices applicable to the various real transactions against which the Cash-balances are held.

In my *Tract on Monetary Reform* (Chapter III. § 1) I measured Real-balances by what I called " Consumption Units ", namely units " made up of a collection of specified quantities of their (the public's) standard articles of consumption or other objects of expenditure"; and I designated by k and k' respectively the number of consumption units which the public required in cash and in bank-deposits respectively. I pointed out that "the amount of k and k' depends partly on the wealth of the community, partly on its habits", and that "its habits are fixed by its estimation of the extra convenience of having more cash in hand as compared with the advantages to be got from spending the cash or investing it". And I ended up with the Fundamental Equation

$$n = p(k + rk'),$$

where n is the total quantity of cash, r the proportion of the banks' cash reserves to their deposits, and p the price of a consumption unit.

Now the great fault of this treatment lay in the suggestion that the units relevant to its arguments are, strictly speaking, *consumption* units, so that p, being the price of a consumption unit, represents our *quaesitum*, the purchasing power of money. But this implied that Cash-deposits are used for nothing except expenditure on current consumption, whereas in fact they are held, as we have seen above, for a vast multiplicity of business and personal purposes. Our units of Real-balances must, therefore, correspond to the multiplicity of purposes for which Cash-balances are used, and the price-level measured by p must be the price-level appropriate to this multiplicity of purposes. In short p measures, not the purchasing power of money, but the Cash-balances Standard as defined in Chapter 6 above.

Its second fault lay in the suggestion that the possible causes of a variation of k' were limited to those which can be properly described as a change of habit on the part of the public. This use of language was not formally incorrect; but it is misleading in so far as it is intended to include, for example, a change in the proportions of the total deposits represented by Savings-deposits, Business-deposits and Income-deposits respectively, due to a change in bank-rate or in the business situation as a whole. In short, I was applying to the Cash-deposits, as a whole, conceptions which were only appropriate to the Income-deposits.

The argument can, however, be re-stated in a form which is formally free from these objections. We can make it clear that the Price-level (P_1) to which it leads up weights the different objects of expenditure, not in accordance with their relative importance to consumers, but in proportion to the anticipatory holding of real balances of which they are the occasion. Stated in its simplest form our Fundamental Equation can then be expressed as follows:

If M = the total volume of Cash-balances, and
C = the corresponding volume of Real-balances,
then $P_1 = \dfrac{M}{C}$.

This equation has—obviously—very little utility for quantitative purposes. But qualitatively it does bring out sharply one important point—namely the parts played by the decisions of the bankers and of the depositors respectively in the determination of prices —which can be embodied in the following proposition:

The volume of cash-balances depends on the decisions of the bankers and is "created" by them. The volume of real-balances depends on the decisions of the depositors and is "created" by them. The price-level (P_1) is the resultant of the two sets of decisions and is measured by the ratio of the volume of the cash-balances created to that of the real-balances created.

No one directly "decides" what the price-level shall be; all the relevant decisions are directed to the determination of the volumes of cash-balances and of real-balances respectively, and price-levels are the resultant of these. Every decision by an individual as to whether *at the existing price-levels* he desires to buy, to sell or to do neither is, in effect, a decision as to whether he desires to decrease, increase or leave unchanged his real-balances.

Thus this method of approach furnishes us with a clue to the manner in which the causation of the price-making process is related to human decisions. The train of thought is worth following a little further. For it makes apparent in what way harmony is established between the separate sets of decisions made by the body of depositors on the one side and the body of bankers on the other.

The normal state of affairs is a perpetual flow of exchanges of purchasing power for goods and *vice versa*, which temporarily increase both the Cash-balances and the Real-balances of some parties and decrease those of others, whilst leaving the aggregate balances approximately unchanged. In a state of equilibrium between the amount of Real-balances required, the amount of Cash-balances outstanding and the Price-level, the normal flow of purchases and sales has no tendency either to alter the relative aggregate volumes of Cash-balances and Real-balances or to modify the Price-level. If, however, at any moment the pressure of the individuals who wish to diminish their Real-balances (*i.e.* who wish to diminish their Cash-balances at the existing price-level) exceeds that of those who wish to increase their Real-balances (*i.e.* who wish to increase their Cash-balances at the existing price-level), the greater eagerness of the buyers than of the sellers at the existing price-level creates a tendency for the price-level to rise. The price-level will rise until there is again an equilibrium between the eagernesses of the two parties. The causation of the price-change is in the form of an *increase of demand* at the existing price-level, and the articles to which the additional buying pressure has been directed rise in price.

This, however, is only the first step in the process by which a final equilibrium is restored between Cash-balances, Real-balances and Price-level. The rise of price on the part of the articles first affected will in itself, by raising the price-level as a whole, diminish to a certain extent the amount of the Real-balances which are equivalent to a given amount of Cash-balances; so that, whilst the Cash-balances held by the sellers of the goods just exchanged will have increased by the same amount as that by which the Cash-balances held by the buyers has diminished, yet the Real-balances now held by the depositors as a whole will be *less* than they were before. Nevertheless it is unlikely that the initial rise of price on the part of the articles first affected will be sufficient to prevent any increase at all in the Real-balances held by the remaining depositors (including those who have just sold goods for balances) other than those who have just cleared out their balances in exchange for goods. For if the depositor who decides to reduce his Real-balances spends an amount of cash equal to a proportion r of the total cash on purchasing an article, the weight of which is q in the Cash-balances Standard, and thereby raises its price in the proportion p, it is unlikely that pq will be so great as r.

Unless, therefore, something has happened to change their ideas as to how much real-balances they require, the recent sellers, finding themselves with an increment, not only of cash-balances, but also of real-balances, become, in their turn, additional purchasers. Thus an endless chain of additional purchasing at something above the old price-level for goods in general is set up, affecting commodity after commodity, until equilibrium is brought about by a new and higher price-level being established at which the aggregate holdings of real-balances are diminished by the exact amount by which the original set of depositors, who turned buyers of goods, had decided to diminish their real-balances. This must necessarily come about in due course unless one of the individuals, into whose hands comes additional purchasing power in the course of the process, decides that he will take this opportunity to increase the amount of purchasing power which it suits him to keep at the bank, in which case the circle is broken, there will be no tendency to maintain the price-level at any higher figure than before, and the upward fluttering of prices will have been no more than temporary.

We are left, therefore, with the following proposition :

Whenever an individual makes a decision which means a diminution in his stock of real-balances, this occasions a rise in the price-level, except in so far as it may be balanced by decisions in the opposite sense, at the existing price-level, on the part of other individuals or by decisions on the part of the bankers to diminish correspondingly the stock of cash. If, however, the decision of this individual does not affect the decisions of the other individuals or of the bankers, then the eventual proportionate rise in the price-level is exactly in the proportion which the diminution in his stock of real-balances bears to the remaining stock of real-balances.[1]

We may observe, in passing, that whenever some individuals take steps to diminish their real-balances, this action is necessarily to the detriment of the other

[1] The second part of this proposition follows thus : If r is the stock of real-balances, m the stock of cash-balances (assumed constant), and p the price-level, whilst dp is the rise in the price-level when the depositor diminishes his stock of real-balances by dr, then : $rp = m = (r - dr)(p + dp)$
so that $$\frac{dp}{p} = \frac{dr}{r - dr}.$$
Let me repeat that the price-level in this equation is the Cash-Balances Standard.

holders of real-balances, who find that *their* cash-balances have been depreciated in value by the action of those who have cleared out (unless the volume of cash is also diminished *pari passu*). Similarly, if real-balances are increased, then (unless the volume of cash is also increased *pari passu*) pre-existing depositors are enriched by the extent of the increase. Thus any change in the volume of real-balances which is not balanced by a corresponding change in the volume of cash involves a somewhat arbitrary redistribution of wealth. The gain or loss corresponding to the loss or gain of the depositors as a whole does not, of course, accrue to the depositors who by taking steps to diminish or to increase their real-balances have been the *cause* of the disturbance, but to quite another set of people, namely to those who have *borrowed* from the banks (or otherwise) in terms of money.

Whenever depositors as a whole take steps to diminish the amount of their real-balances, their behaviour can only take the form of *an increased demand on their part at the existing level of prices*, which must result in a tendency for the price-level to rise. Thus the price-level (meaning by this the Cash-balances Standard) is the balancing factor which brings into appropriate relation the volume of real-balances which results from the collective decisions of the depositors and the volume of money-balances which results from the collective decisions of the bankers. The Quantity Theory of Money has been too often enunciated in a one-sided way, so as to make it appear that the price-level depends solely on the volume of money-balances created by the bankers. But the price-level can be affected just as much by the decisions of the depositors to vary the amounts of real-balances which they (the depositors) keep, as by the decisions of the bankers to vary the amounts of money-balances which they (the bankers) create.

ALTERNATIVE QUANTITY EQUATIONS

Provided we remember that the price-level to which these propositions relate is not the same thing as the purchasing power of money, that there are all sorts of assumptions underlying the argument as to what is happening to output, etc., and that the real-balances in question are an amalgamation of balances held for different kinds of purposes, the above analysis may contribute to our understanding of the monetary system. For it exhibits the broad aspects of the price-making process—the see-saw tilted in one direction by the volume of cash supplied by the bankers and in the other by the volume of real-balances which the public are willing to maintain.

Formerly I was attracted by this line of approach. But it now seems to me that the merging together of all the different sorts of transactions—income, business and financial—which may be taking place only causes confusion, and that we cannot get any real insight into the price-making process without bringing in the rate of interest and the distinctions between incomes and profits and between savings and investment.

(ii.) THE "CAMBRIDGE" QUANTITY EQUATION

The "Real-balances" Equation discussed above is descended from a method of approach long familiar to those who have heard Professors Marshall and Pigou in the lecture-rooms of Cambridge. Since this method has not often been employed elsewhere in recent times I call it the "Cambridge" Quantity Equation; but it has (*vide* the footnote ([1]), p. 230) a much longer descent, being derived from Petty, Locke, Cantillon and Adam Smith. Its essence cannot be summed up better than in the words of Dr. Marshall:

> "In every state of society there is some fraction of their income which people find it worth while to keep in the form of currency; it may be a fifth, or a tenth, or a

twentieth. A large command of resources in the form of currency renders their business easy and smooth, and puts them at an advantage in bargaining; but on the other hand it locks up in a barren form resources that might yield an income of gratification if invested, say, in extra furniture; or a money income, if invested in extra machinery or cattle." A man fixes the appropriate fraction " after balancing one against another the advantages of a further ready command and the disadvantages of putting more of his resources into a form in which they yield him no direct income or other benefit ". " Let us suppose that the inhabitants of a country, taken one with another (and including therefore all varieties of character and of occupation), find it just worth their while to keep by them on the average ready purchasing power to the extent of a tenth part of their annual income, together with a fiftieth part of their property; then the aggregate value of the currency of the country will tend to be equal to the sum of these amounts." [1]

This theory has been put into the form of a Quantity Equation by Professor Pigou [2]:

In the ordinary course of life, people are continually needing to make payments in discharge of obligations

[1] *Money, Credit and Commerce*, I. iv. 3. Dr. Marshall shows in a footnote as follows that the above is in fact a development of the traditional way of considering the matter : " Petty thought that the money ' sufficient for ' the nation is ' so much as will pay half a year's rent for all the lands of England and a quarter's rent of the Houseing, for a week's expense of all the people, and about a quarter of the value of all the exported commodities '. Locke estimated that ' one-fiftieth of wages and one-fourth of the landowner's income and one-twentieth part of the broker's yearly returns in ready money will be enough to drive the trade of any country '. Cantillon (A.D. 1755), after a long and subtle study, concludes that the value needed is a ninth of the total produce of the country; or, what he takes to be the same thing, a third of the rent of the land. Adam Smith has more of the scepticism of the modern age and says : ' it is impossible to determine the proportion,' though ' it has been computed by different authors at a fifth, at a tenth, at a twentieth, and at a thirtieth part of the whole value of the annual produce '." In modern conditions the normal proportion of the income-deposits to the national income seems to be somewhere between a tenth and a fifteenth, and the proportion of the total deposits round about a half.

[2] *Quarterly Journal of Economics*, vol. xxxii., November 1917. I have abbreviated the quotation which follows without indicating where sentences have been omitted.

contracted in terms of legal-tender money. Most people have also a flow of claims that are similarly maturing in their favour. But the obligations and the claims that become due at any moment seldom exactly cancel one another, and the difference has to be met by the transfer of *titles to legal tender*. Hence everybody is anxious to hold enough of his resources in the form of titles to legal tender both to enable him to effect the ordinary transactions of life without trouble and to secure him against unexpected demands. For these two objects people in general elect to hold in the form of titles to legal tender the aggregate value of a given quantity of wheat.[1] There is thus constituted at any given moment a definite demand schedule for titles to legal-tender money. Let R be the total resources,[2] expressed in terms of wheat, that are enjoyed by the community; k the proportion of these resources that it chooses to keep in the form of titles to legal tender; M the number of units of legal tender, and P the value, or price, per unit of these titles in terms of wheat. Then the demand schedule just described is represented by the equation $P = \frac{kR}{M}$.

Professor Pigou then enlarges this equation to cover the case where cash is held partly in legal tender and partly in bank deposits, namely:

$$P = \frac{kR}{M}\{c + h(1-c)\}$$

where c is the proportion of their cash which the public keep in legal tender and h is the proportion of legal tender to deposits held by bankers.

Now it is evident that this equation is formally correct. The question is whether it brings out clearly the important variables. It seems to me to be open to the following criticisms, some of which are equally applicable to the form of the Quantity Equation which I propounded in my *Tract on Monetary Reform*:
 (i.) The introduction of the factor R, the current

---

[1] Prof. Pigou explains that there is no special significance in wheat being chosen in this connection rather than any other commodity.
[2] The context implies that "resources" means income over a period of time.

income of the community, suggests that variation in this is one of the two or three most important direct influences on the demand for cash resources. In the case of the income-deposits this seems to me to be true. But the significance of R is much diminished when we are dealing, not with the income-deposits in isolation, but with the total deposits. Indeed the chief inconvenience of the "Cambridge" Quantity Equation really lies in its applying to the total deposits considerations which are primarily relevant only to the income-deposits, and in its tackling the problem as though the same sort of considerations which govern the income-deposits also govern the total deposits. I have aimed in the formulae given at the end of Chapter 10 at keeping the essential advantages of the "Cambridge" method by segregating the income-deposits and applying it to them alone.

(ii.) The prominence given to k, namely the proportion of the bank-deposits to the community's *income*, is misleading when it is extended beyond the income-deposits. The emphasis which this method lays on the point that the amount of real balances held is determined by the comparative advantages of holding resources in cash and in alternative forms, so that a change in k will be attributable to a change in these comparative advantages, is useful and instructive. But "resources" in this connection ought not to be interpreted, as it is interpreted by Prof. Pigou, as being identical with current *income*.

(iii.) By measuring the quantity of Real Balances in terms of wheat, Professor Pigou is shirking, rather than solving, the question of the type of price-level to which our fundamental equation is intended to lead up. The object of any quantity equation is to discover, not the price of wheat, but, in some sense or other, the purchasing power of money. But his equation either makes no contribution to this or does so by implying that relative prices are unchangeable, all individual prices and therefore all price-levels being fixed in terms of wheat—which is remote from the facts.

(iv.) The equation entirely obscures disturbances—which in practice are one of the most important types of disturbances—arising out of a change in the proportions in which deposits are held for the different purposes distinguished above as Savings, Business and Income. Moreover it is intractable for the task of analysing disturbances to the price-level due to disparities between the rates of saving and of investment.

(iii.) The " Fisher " Quantity Equation

Since the publication of Professor Irving Fisher's *The Purchasing Power of Money* in 1911, the famous formula PT = MV therein propounded has held the field in the world at large as against any other variety. This formula has played a very great part in promoting the progress of monetary theory, and those of us who have been brought up on it must not be deemed ungrateful to the genius of Professor Fisher if we find that the requirements of our analysis are outgrowing it.[1]

This formula sets out neither from the flow of

[1] Professor Fisher's *The Purchasing Power of Money* is dedicated to Simon Newcomb, from whom *viâ* Professor Kemmerer the PT=MV formula ultimately derives. Newcomb was not a professional economist but a mathematician (Professor of Mathematics in the U.S. Navy and at Johns Hopkins). His *Principles of Political Economy*, published in 1886, is one of those original works which a fresh scientific mind, not perverted by having read too much of the orthodox stuff, is able to produce from time to time in a half-formed subject like Economics ; and it still to-day deserves perusal. His Fundamental Equation, which he calls the " equation of societary circulation " (*op. cit.* p. 328), is V.R=K.P, where V is the volume of currency, R the rapidity of circulation (for the whole volume of currency, including both cash and bank-money, for which he allows distinct rapidities R′ and R″, corresponding to Fisher's V and V′), P the price-level, and K " the industrial circulation on the scale of prices which we take as unity ". By the " industrial circulation " Newcomb means the volume of goods and services changing hands for money. He excludes from the " industrial

income against consumption goods, nor from Real Balances, nor from the proportion of resources held in cash, but from the total volume of cash-transactions, or of "expenditure" as Professor Fisher calls it. If B is the total volume of cash-transactions in a given period, M the volume of cash outstanding, and V the average number of times that a unit of cash is used in transactions during that period, *i.e.* the velocity of circulation, then by definition $B = M \cdot V$.

But we can also analyse B in a different way. Each transaction consists of a quantity of goods or services or securities traded, multiplied by the price of the article. That is to say $B = \Sigma p_r \cdot q_r$ where q is the quantity of anything traded and p the price at which it is traded. Let us take as our units of quantity the amount which has a unit value in the base year. We then have

$$B = \Sigma p_r q_r = P_2 \cdot T$$

where $P_2 = \Sigma \left(p_r \cdot \dfrac{p_r q_r}{\Sigma p_r q_r} \right)$ and $T = \Sigma \left(q_r \cdot \dfrac{p_r}{P_2} \right)$.

Otherwise interpreted P_2 is the price-level of the articles traded, the price of each individual article being weighted in proportion to the money-volume of the transactions in that article; that is to say, P_2 measures the Cash-transactions Standard as defined in Chapter 6. And T is the sum of the number of units traded (a unit of anything being the quantity worth a unit of money in the base year), weighted in proportion to their relative prices, *i.e.* to their prices in terms of P_2 in the year in question; that is to say T measures what Professor Fisher calls the Volume of

---

circulation" and, presumably, from the "rapidity of circulation", "all such transfers as loaning money, or depositing it in a bank, because these are not balanced by reverse transfers of wealth or services". The whole thing is worked out with much subtlety—more subtlety, perhaps, than is shown by Fisher.

ALTERNATIVE QUANTITY EQUATIONS

Trade. Hence the standard version of the formula
$$P_2 \cdot T = M \cdot V.[1]$$
The great advantage of this formula is the fact that one side of it, namely $M \cdot V$, fits in better than most with the actually available banking statistics. For quantitative inquiries it is possible, therefore, to make more progress with this formula than with any other. $M \cdot V$ corresponds, more or less, to the volume of Bank Clearings [2] and M to the volume of Deposits; for both of which figures are available, so that the value of V can be deduced.

Its weakness, on the other hand, is to be found in the other side of it, namely $P_2 \cdot T$. For neither P_2 nor T corresponds to the quantities in which we are likely to be interested for their own sakes. P_2 is not the Purchasing Power of Money and T is not the Volume of Output. Professor Fisher has not, indeed, been oblivious to these defects, but he has not, I think, rated them as high as he should. Nor do the approximations which he has employed for their evaluation command confidence. For example he tried to arrive at P_2 by combining the Wholesale Standard, the Wages Standard, and an index of forty stocks, giving a weight of 30 to the first, of 1 to the second and of 3 to the third. This, of course,

[1] If we choose to distinguish between M the volume of cash in circulation and M' the volume of bank-deposits, V and V' being their respective velocities of circulation, we reach the formula
$$P_2 \cdot T = M \cdot V + M' \cdot V'.$$
[2] There is a slight ambiguity about the meaning of the expression *Bank Clearings* according to whether it includes internal clearings within a bank or only clearings, which pass through the clearing house, between different banks. For the purposes of this argument it is necessary that *Bank Clearings* should be interpreted in the wider sense. But in Great Britain our statistics have related hitherto only to the narrower sense, though the English Clearing Banks have now agreed to publish the aggregate of their debits as well as of their clearings, beginning with January 1930. In the United States, where statistics have been available (in recent years) for the volume of clearings in both senses, a separate terminology has been adopted, the expression *Bank Clearings* being used for the narrower sense only and the expression *Bank Debits* for the wider sense.

represented pioneer work. We could calculate a more accurate P_2 now; which Mr. Snyder has endeavoured to do. But the more accurately we calculate P_2, the clearer does it become what a hotchpotch standard the Cash-transactions Standard is and how unreliable as a guide to the Purchasing Power of Money.

A further objection to the Fisher Equation, particularly in its application to British banking statistics, is to be found in its neglecting to take explicit account of the distinction between Cash-deposits and Savings-deposits and of the use of overdraft facilities. Implicitly fluctuations in these factors can be allowed for by variations in the velocity of circulation. But, from the standpoint of qualitative analysis, this fails to put us on the right track for discovering what sort of circumstances will change the velocity of circulation. I should add, however, that this objection may be less applicable to American banking statistics. For American statistics distinguish between Time-deposits and Demand-deposits (and it is the latter only which Professor Fisher includes in his M), which corresponds roughly to the distinction between Savings-deposits and Cash-deposits; whilst overdraft facilities may play a lesser part in America in economising the holding of cash.

In any case it is not difficult to remedy this defect; and it may be worth while to do so, as follows:

(1) Let w = the proportion of Cash-deposits to Total deposits,

so that Mw = the volume of Cash-deposits
and $M(1-w)$ = the volume of Savings-deposits.

(2) Let w' = the proportion of unused overdraft facilities to the Cash-deposits,

so that Mww' = the unused overdraft facilities,
and $Mw(1+w')$ = the total volume of cash facilities.

(3) Let V = the velocity of circulation of the Cash-deposits, *i.e.* the ratio of the total volume of money payments to the total volume of Cash-deposits, and V' = the velocity of circulation of cash-facilities,

so that $B = MVw = MV'w(1 + w')$, where B is the total turnover of cash transactions.

Then we have
$$P_2 T = B = MVw = MV'w(1 + w')$$
or
$$P_2 = \frac{MV}{T} w = \frac{MV'}{T} w(1 + w').$$

This equation, like the Fisher Equation, is merely an amplification of the statement that the total cash facilities multiplied by their velocity of circulation equal the bank clearings.

Where there are no overdraft facilities and no savings-deposits, *i.e.* where $w = 1$ and $w' = 0$, equation (ii.) reduces to the form $P_2 = \frac{MV}{T}$, which is identical with the Fisher equation.

Where there are no deposits and nothing but overdrafts, *i.e.* where $M = 0$, it reduces to the form $P_2 = \frac{M'V'}{T}$, where M' is the volume of unused overdraft facilities.

(iv.) THE RELATIONSHIP BETWEEN THE "CAMBRIDGE" AND THE "FISHER" EQUATIONS

We have seen in Chapter 6 (pp. 76-78) that the relative importance of different articles of exchange is not necessarily the same in respect of the volume of cheque transactions to which they give rise as in respect of the balances which they cause to be held.

That is to say, the Cash-balances Price-level, which we have designated P_1, is not identical with the Cash-transactions Price-level, which we have designated P_2. This is evident when we remember that the date and the amount of some types of cheque transactions can be foreseen or can be provided against more accurately than others, so that of two cheque transactions of equal amount one may have led to a greater amount (in time multiplied by quantity) of anticipatory holding of cash-balances than the other. Furthermore the price quotations appropriate to the former index are not the same as those appropriate to the latter, inasmuch as the price-quotations which affect the face-value of the cheques being cleared at any time relate on the average to an earlier date than the price-quotations which affect the amount of cash-balances required to be held. This point is particularly important when prices are changing. Thus when prices are falling, the proportion P_1 to P_2 will be lowered. Under stable conditions, however, the proportion will be a more or less constant one.

Now Quantity Equations of the "Cambridge" type lead up, as we have seen, to the Cash-balances Price-level, whilst Equations of the "Fisher" type lead up to the Cash-transactions Price-level. Thus the relationship between the two types of Equation is the same as between the two Price-levels.

Let us write $P_1 = P_2 . f$; so that we have

$$P_1 = \frac{M}{C} = P_2 . f = \frac{MV}{T} . w . f.$$

Thus if we define the Price-level by reference to the quantity of money in demand, rather than by reference to the quantity of money turnover or cash-transactions (as Professor Irving Fisher has done), we have to introduce this additional element f, representing the proportion of P_1 to P_2, into the final result of the "Fisher" Equation. It is particularly important not to overlook this element, since otherwise we may fail to allow for the fact that P_2 does not relate to the set of prices prevailing at the moment, but to the set prevailing at some previous date when the transactions, which are being completed to-day, were being initiated. Thus, in so far as the volume of balances held looks further ahead than to-day's cheque transactions, the velocity of circulation will, when prices are rising, *i.e.* when f is greater than its normal value, be somewhat less than its normal value.

Nevertheless, P_1 itself, *i.e.* the Price-level which determines the amount of the demand for Cash-Balances, will also relate to dates earlier on the average than to-day; for it will be more influenced by the volume of cash transactions at the moment and in near prospect than by the volume at the more remote date when to-day's price quotations for new transactions will be materialising in cash payments. For this reason a given quantity of money will, during a period of rapidly rising prices, support a higher price-level than will be possible when P_1 and P_2 have fully overcome the time-lag (greater in the case of P_2 than of P_1) and are restored to their normal relationship to current prices.

(v.) THE RELATIONSHIP BETWEEN THE "FISHER" EQUATION AND THE FUNDAMENTAL EQUATIONS OF CHAPTER 10

Since (in the notation of Chapter 10)
$$P = \frac{M}{O} \cdot \frac{wV_1(V_2 - V)}{V_2 - V_1} + \frac{I' - S}{R}$$
and since
$$P_2 T = MVw,$$
it follows that
$$P = P_2 \cdot \frac{T}{O} \cdot \frac{V_1(V_2 - V)}{V(V_2 - V_1)} + \frac{I' - S}{R}.$$

I do not know that this equation is worth much. But it is interesting as showing what variables have to be introduced in order to bring P and P_2 into a definite relationship with one another.

BOOK IV

THE DYNAMICS OF THE PRICE-LEVEL

CHAPTER 15

THE INDUSTRIAL CIRCULATION AND THE FINANCIAL CIRCULATION

(i.) INDUSTRY AND FINANCE DISTINGUISHED AND DEFINED

WE must now devote ourselves to the analysis of the factors which tend to bring about changes in the value of money and to their mode of operation.

For this purpose it is necessary to make yet a further classification cutting, to a certain extent, across our division of the total quantity of money (in Chapter 3) into the Income-deposits, the Business-deposits and the Savings-deposits,—namely a division between the deposits used for the purposes of Industry, which we shall call the *Industrial Circulation*, and those used for the purposes of Finance, which we shall call the *Financial Circulation*.

By *Industry* we mean the business of maintaining the normal process of current output, distribution and exchange and paying the factors of production their incomes for the various duties which they perform from the first beginning of production to the final satisfaction of the consumer. By *Finance*, on the other hand, we mean the business of holding and exchanging existing titles to wealth (other than exchanges resulting from the specialisation of industry), including Stock Exchange and Money Market transactions, speculation and the process of conveying current savings and profits into the hands of entrepreneurs.

Each of these two branches of Business utilises a certain part of the total stock of money. Broadly speaking, Industry requires the use of the Income-deposits and of a part of the Business-deposits, which we will call Business-deposits A ; whilst Finance requires the use of the Savings-deposits and of the remainder of the Business-deposits, which we will call Business-deposits B. Thus the sum of the two former is the Industrial Circulation and the sum of the two latter the Financial Circulation. Since we shall argue that the *absolute* variability of the Business-deposits B is, as a rule, only a small proportion of the total quantity of money, this being a consequence of their very high velocity, changes in the Cash-deposits (*i.e.* Income-deposits *plus* Business-deposits) are generally a good index of changes in the Industrial Circulation; and, similarly, changes in the Savings-deposits of changes in the Financial Circulation—which fortunately brings us back to classes of deposits of the magnitude of which we have in practice moderately good statistical indications.

(ii.) FACTORS DETERMINING THE VOLUME OF THE INDUSTRIAL CIRCULATION

Since $M_1V_1 = E$, the amount of money M_1 required for the Income-deposits depends partly on E, the volume of income, and partly on V_1, the velocity of the Income-deposits; and since $E = W_1O$, E depends on W_1, the money-rate of efficiency-earnings, and O, the volume of output. The causes which determine the variability of V_1 we shall consider in detail in Vol. ii. Chapter 24.

As regards the Business-deposits A, it is evident in the first place that the volume of a part of them tends to move much in the same way as that of the Income-deposits. For the Income-deposits are constantly flowing into the Business-deposits through purchases of goods and out again through payment of wages. Those parts of the Business-deposits which represent the proceeds of sales to consumers and the remuneration of the factors of production must, therefore, bear the same proportion to the Income-deposits as the velocity of the latter (V_1) bears to that of the former (V_2), so that the two fluctuate together so long as the ratio of their velocities is unchanged.

In the second place, the prices of unfinished goods (*i.e.* of working capital) will in conditions of equilibrium reflect the prices of finished goods. Further, the costs of production, and therefore the prices, of fixed capital goods will, in equilibrium, also move with the money-rate of efficiency-earnings in the same way as the prices of other goods. Moreover, the relation between the volume of these transactions and the volume of output will be much the same as in the case of the Income-deposits. Thus the quantity of that part of the Business-deposits which is required for the exchange of unfinished goods and of newly finished fixed capital-goods between entrepreneurs will also tend in these conditions to vary in the same proportion as do the Income-deposits.

But there remain certain reasons why the amount of the Business-deposits A can vary differently from that of the Income-deposits, namely :

(*a*) The comparative importance of different articles for the Income-deposits and the Business-deposits respectively varies considerably—*i.e.* they are differently " weighted " ; so that changes in *relative* prices are liable to upset the ratio between the two classes of deposits. For the same reason the ratio may be upset by a change in the *character* of production.

(*b*) An assumption of stability in the ratio between the velocities of the Income-deposits and of the Business-deposits A respectively is not reliable. The latter is not tied down to a measure of stability, as the former is, by the regularity in the dates of payment which generally characterises the disbursement of wages and salaries.

The evidence, which we shall consider in Chapter 24, indicates that V_2, the velocity of the Business-deposits as a whole, is highly variable. Although this variability may often be due, in major part, not to changes in the velocities of Business-deposits A and of Business-deposits B, but to changes in the proportionate distribution of the total Business-deposits between A and B, nevertheless there can be no doubt that there are also short-period fluctuations of some magnitude in the velocity of the Business-deposits due to variations in the amount of sacrifice involved in holding balances, as well as to other causes. For when business is active and the cost of borrowing high, firms will tend to economise in the amount of Business-deposits A which they keep. Moreover, when real-incomes are falling through a decline in employment, the public may endeavour for a time to maintain their standard of life by reducing their Income-deposits, thus increasing the velocity V_1 at a time when V_2 is likely to be decreasing; though apart from changes due to a distrust of the currency, which can, as we know, be catastrophic, I incline to the opinion that the short-period fluctuations of V_1 are inconsiderable.[1] In any case, V_1 and V_2 may show different trends over long periods, due to progressive changes in business habits or in the character of production.

(c) Thirdly, the Business-deposits A and the Price-level appropriate to them may be influenced by the emergence of Profit or Loss, which, in some circumstances, can affect price-levels and the requirements of the monetary circulation out of proportion to the change, if any, in the volume of the Income-deposits.

Nevertheless, the requirements of the monetary circulation will be much less affected by a given change

---

[1] The variability of the velocities of circulation is a matter to which we shall return in detail in Chapter 24.

of price arising in this way than by an equal change due to a rise in the rate of efficiency-earnings. This is particularly the case where the profits are emerging in respect of a rise in the price of working capital which has not yet communicated itself to finished consumption-goods. We can conveniently call this state of affairs *Commodity Speculation*, meaning by this movements in the prices of goods in process of production which are not yet reflected in the purchasing power of money. For fluctuations in the price of Working Capital, of which the index-number of raw materials at wholesale may be taken as fairly representative, may be supported by expectations as to the prices which will be obtained on the re-sale of the goods at a subsequent date either in the same or in a more finished form. Thus for a time, the length of which will be determined by the duration of productive processes and the cost of carrying stocks, the rise in the wholesale standard can be sustained without a corresponding rise in the consumption standard.

It follows that a speculative rise in the wholesale standard, unaccompanied by a rise in the consumption standard, is particularly unlikely to be held back by a shortage in the quantity of money. Moreover, there is a further time-lag between the price-rise and the demand for money, in that the current price-quotations reflect the prices at which contracts for future completion are now being entered into; so that it is not until the date of completion that the higher prices will call for increased Business-deposits. If, indeed, the speculative movement is not supported in due course by a rise in the consumption standard, it is not likely to survive for long. For in this case the expectations on which it was based will have been disappointed. Nevertheless the time which elapses before the reaction may be quite substantial; and during this interval the movements of the wholesale standard and of that part of the Business-deposits which relate to transactions in working capital will be more or less divorced not only from those of the Income-deposits but also from those of the consumption standard.

For these various reasons the changes in the volume of the Industrial Circulation as a whole will not correspond accurately to changes in the volume of the Income-deposits. Nevertheless, in the main the volume of the Industrial Circulation—though it is also influenced to a certain extent by changes in the character of production, in the habits of the public and of the business world, and in the sacrifice involved in keeping resources in the form of money—will vary with E, the aggregate of money incomes, *i.e.* with the volume and cost of production of current output.

(iii.) Factors determining the Volume of the Financial Circulation

The amount of money required for the purposes of Finance, which we call the *Financial Circulation*, is, however, determined by quite a different set of considerations. In this case, also, the amount of Business-deposits B required to look after financial business depends—apart from possible variations in the velocity of these deposits—on the volume of trading × the average value of the instruments traded. But the volume of trading in financial instruments, *i.e.* the *activity* of financial business, is not only highly variable but has no close connection with the volume of output whether of capital-goods or of consumption-goods; for the current output of fixed capital is small compared with the existing stock of wealth, which in the present context we will call the volume of *securities* (excluding from this liquid claims on cash); and the activity with which these securities are being passed round from hand to hand does not depend on the rate at which they are being added to. Thus in a modern Stock-Exchange-equipped community the turnover of currently produced fixed capital is quite a small proportion of the total turnover of securities.

Nor does the price of existing securities depend at all closely over short periods either on the cost of production or on the price of new fixed capital. For existing securities largely consist of properties which cannot be quickly reproduced, of natural resources which cannot be reproduced at all, and of the capitalised value of future income anticipated from the possession of quasi-monopolies or peculiar advantages of one kind or another. The investment boom in the United States in 1929 was a good example of an enormous rise in the price of securities as a whole which was not accompanied by any rise at all in the price of the current output of new fixed capital. Furthermore, the values of the two categories of wealth traded, namely Loan Capital (*e.g.* bonds) and Real Capital (*e.g.* shares), will not infrequently move in *opposite* directions, thus partially compensating one another.

The fact of the financial turnover varying independently from the industrial turnover is not, however, of so much practical importance as might have been expected. For the velocity of the Business-deposits B is so very high—as a result of the great development of devices for economising the use of cash by Stock Exchange clearings and the like—that the *absolute* amount of the variations in the volume of money so employed cannot ordinarily be very great.

The main variation in the total demand for money for financial purposes arises, therefore, in quite a different way, namely in the volume of the Savings-deposits.

The existence of Savings-deposits is an indication that there are persons who prefer to keep their resources in the form of claims on money of a liquid character realisable at short notice. On the other hand, there is another class of persons who borrow from the banks in order to finance a larger holding of securities than they can carry with their own resources.

These Savings-deposits fall into two categories. They include, as a rule, a substantial stable substratum of Savings-deposits which are not held because the holder of them takes a view adverse to the prospects of the money-value of securities, but for one or other of the personal reasons enumerated in Chapter 3;—there are owners of wealth, that is to say, who permanently prefer to hold Savings-deposits in preference to securities. Since, however, the amount of this kind of Savings-deposits is likely to change slowly, any rapid change in the total of the Savings-deposits is apt to indicate that there is a change in the second category.

Let us call the two categories of Savings-deposits A and B respectively.

The second category of Savings-deposits comprise what, in language borrowed from the Stock Exchange, we will call the "bear" position,—including, however, as bears not only those who have sold securities "short", *i.e.* have sold securities which they do not own, but also those who would normally be holders of securities but prefer for the time being to hold liquid claims on cash in the form of Savings-deposits. A "bear", that is to say, is one who prefers at the moment to avoid securities and lend cash, and correspondingly a "bull" is one who prefers to hold securities and borrow cash—the former anticipating that securities will fall in cash-value and the latter that they will rise.

Now when bullish sentiment is on the increase, there will be a tendency for the savings-deposits to fall. The amount of this fall will depend upon how completely the rise in security-prices relatively to the short-term rates of interest offsets the bullishness of sentiment. There will be a level of security-prices which on the average of opinion just balances the bullishness, so that the volume of savings-deposits is unchanged. And if security-prices go still higher than this, then the volume of savings-deposits will be actually increased. But (apart from compensating variations in the requirements of the Industrial Circulation) the volume of savings-deposits can only be maintained or increased in face of an increase of bullish sentiment, if the banking system directly brings about the rise in security-prices by itself buying securities or if it takes advantage of the fact that *differences* of opinion exist between different sections of the public so that, if one section is tempted by easy credit to borrow for the purpose of buying securities speculatively, security-prices can be raised to a level at which another section of the public will prefer savings-deposits. Thus the actual level of security-prices is, as we have seen in Chapter 10, the resultant of the degree of bullishness of opinion and of the behaviour of the banking system.

It follows that any abnormal fall in the Savings-deposits, accompanied by a rise of security-prices, will probably indicate a *consensus* of opinion in favour of securities as against cash due to a bullishness of sentiment which is insufficiently offset by the rise in security-prices ; whilst an abnormal rise in the same circumstances may indicate a *diffe.ence* of opinion as to the prospects of securities, the party on the " bull " tack in effect buying securities and borrowing money *viâ* the banking system from the party on the " bear " tack ; such as appeared to exist on a large scale—to give an example—in the United States in 1928 and 1929. Thus during the Wall Street boom of 1929 attention was rightly paid to increases and decreases in the volume of "brokers' loans " ; for an increase meant that the rise of security-prices had gone still further beyond the point at which it would be just enough to offset the bullishness of average sentiment, in the sense that it had led to an increase in the " bear " position.

In modern conditions, both in Great Britain and in the United States, the total "bear" position can, of course, much exceed the amount of Savings-deposits B, since professional investors have other, and generally more profitable, means of lending "bear" funds against liquid claims on cash than through the Banking System, *e.g.* by buying Treasury Bills and by direct loans to the Money Market and the Stock Exchange; and in addition there are those transactions of bears who have sold what they do not own, which are directly offset against the transactions of bulls who "carry-over" what they have bought. Nevertheless the fluctuations in the amount of Savings-deposits B—including in this fluctuations in the deposits of industrial firms which are carrying less or more working capital than usual on account of a distrust of or confidence in the prospects, and also of the deposits of institutions which have thought it wise to take advantage of "bull" activity to raise funds by the sale of securities, new or old, in advance of their actual needs—are capable of being important. Thus the fluctuations in Savings-deposits B are probably the most important element of variability in the demand for money due to Finance.

The total amount of the Financial Circulation depends, therefore, partly on the *activity* of transactions but mainly on the magnitude of the "bear" position—both of these things being likely to be phenomena of rapidly *changing* prices rather than of an absolutely high or low level.

Now, whilst a tendency of the Savings-deposits (M_3) to increase or decrease is an indication of an increase or decrease of the "bear" position, there are altogether four possible types of speculative markets:

(i.) A "bull" market with a consensus of opinion, *i.e.* security-prices rising but insufficiently so that

M_3 is falling, and " bears " are closing their positions on a rising market.

(ii.) A " bull " market with a division of opinion, *i.e.* security-prices rising more than sufficiently so that M_3 is rising, and " bears " are increasing their positions on a rising market.

(iii.) A " bear " market with a division of opinion, *i.e.* security-prices falling more than sufficiently so that M_3 is falling, and " bears " are closing their positions on a falling market.

(iv.) A " bear " market with a consensus of opinion, *i.e.* security-prices falling insufficiently so that M_3 is rising, and " bears " are increasing their positions on a falling market.

Since an increase in the Savings-deposits, not balanced by an increase in the total assets of the Banks of an amount equal to this increase, will diminish the amount of money available for the Industrial Circulation, it follows that, failing compensatory action by the Banking System, speculations of type (i.) and type (iii.) both have the same effect on Industry as an increase in the supply of money, whilst those of type (ii.) and type (iv.) both have the same effect as a decrease in the supply of money.

On the other hand, when security-prices are rising, this is likely—in general but not necessarily—to stimulate a rise in P′, the price-level of *new* investment, and when security-prices are falling, the opposite is likely to be the case. Accordingly speculations of type (i.) tend to reduce the purchasing power of money on both headings, since by increasing the supply of money for the Industrial Circulation they allow increased investment, and by raising P′ they increase the attractiveness of investment. Similarly, those of type (iv.) tend to raise the purchasing power of money on both headings. But those of types (ii.) and (iii.) pull in opposite directions ; type (ii.), for instance, increases the attractiveness of new investment, but at the same time diminishes, other things being equal, the supply of money for the Industrial Circulation.

We conclude, therefore, that changes in the financial situation are capable of causing changes in the value of money in two ways. They have the effect of altering the quantity of money available for the Industrial Circulation; and they may have the effect of altering the attractiveness of Investment. Thus, unless the first effect is balanced by a change in the total quantity of money and the latter by a change in the terms of lending, an instability in the price-level of current output will result.

The awkwardness is that the two possible effects of a given change in the financial situation do not necessarily pull in the same direction. Perhaps, therefore, we may be permitted at this point (in anticipation of topics which belong more properly to Vol. ii.) an *obiter dictum* on the duty of a Central Bank which is endeavouring so to manage the monetary situation as to preserve a stable price-level of current output.

The dilemma before it—to take type (ii.) as our illustration—is as follows. If the Bank increases the volume of Bank-money so as to avoid any risk of the Financial Circulation stealing resources from the Industrial Circulation, it will encourage the " bull " market to continue, with every probability of a rising value of P' which will lead to over-investment later on; whereas if it refuses to increase the volume of Bank-money, it may so diminish the amount of money available for Industry, or so enhance the rate of interest at which it is available, as to have an immediately deflationary tendency.

The solution lies—so far as the stability of purchasing power is concerned—in letting both Finance and Industry have all the money they want, but at a rate of interest which in its effect on the rate of *new* investment (relatively to saving) exactly balances the effect of bullish sentiment. To diagnose the position precisely at every stage and to achieve this exact balance may sometimes be, however, beyond the wits of man. Moreover it may happen in practice that a rate of interest high enough to avoid future over-investment has the result of reducing present output below the optimum;—though I think this can only occur through inaccurate forecasting, or from the difficulties of changing over from one type of output to another. In this event some disturbance to stability may be inevitable. For there is then no way out except what has sometimes been attempted both in Great Britain and in the United States, though with dubious success, namely to discriminate in the terms of lending (either in the rate charged or by rationing the amount lent) between financial and industrial borrowers. If the terms of lending to both categories of borrowers have to be nearly identical, then, given inaccurate forecasting by certain purchasers of securities, it may be that a rate of interest high enough to avoid prospective over-investment is calculated to produce present unemployment.

We are left, therefore, with the broad conclusion that the stability of purchasing power and of output requires that the total deposits should be allowed to rise and fall *pari passu* with any changes in the volume of the Savings-deposits; but that the terms of lending should be adjusted—to the extent that this is practically possible—so as to balance the effect of bullish or bearish sentiment in the financial markets on the rate of new investment.

In the long run the value of securities is entirely derivative from the value of consumption-goods. It depends on the expectation as to the value of the amount of liquid consumption-goods which the securities will, directly or indirectly, yield, modified by reference to the risk and uncertainty of this expectation, and multiplied by the number of years' purchase corresponding to the current rate of interest for capital of the duration in question; and where the goods represented by the securities are capable of being reproduced, the anticipated value of the consumption-goods yielded by the capital-goods will be influenced by the cost of production of the capital-goods in question, since this affects the prospective supply of such goods.

But in the very short run, it depends on opinion largely uncontrolled by any present monetary factors. A higher value for securities is not immediately checked by monetary factors in the way that a similar enhancement of the prices of currently consumed goods would be checked by lack of sufficient income to purchase them. For we have seen that the amount of Business-deposits B required to transact financial business depends at least as much on the activity of markets as on the average value of the instruments traded, and also that on account of their very high velocity of circulation any necessary increase in them is easily supplied without much effect on the supply of money for other purposes; with the result that we cannot rely on this for a check.

Accordingly *opinion* has a dominating influence on the position to a degree which does not apply in the case of the quantity of money required to look after a given wages-bill. If everyone agrees that securities are worth more, and if everyone is a "bull" in the sense of preferring securities at a rising price to increasing their Savings-deposits, there is no limit to the rise in price of securities and no effective check arises from a shortage of money.

Nevertheless, as soon as the price of securities has risen high enough, relatively to the short-term rate of interest, to occasion a difference of opinion as to the prospects, a "bear" position will develop, and some people will begin to increase their Savings-deposits either out of their current savings or out of their current profits or by selling securities previously held. Thus in proportion as the prevailing opinion comes to seem unreasonable to more cautious people, the " other view " will tend to develop, with the result of an increase in the " bear " position—which does bring into existence a monetary factor, though one which is *corrective* only in a " bull " market— as described above.

Finally, if the value of existing securities of a kind which are capable of being reproduced comes to differ from the current cost of production, this will, by stimulating or retarding new investment, bring into operation certain other monetary factors in a manner to be elaborated in subsequent chapters.

I should say, therefore, that a Currency Authority has no *direct* concern with the level of value of existing securities, as determined by opinion, but that it has an important indirect concern if the level of value of existing securities is calculated to stimulate new investment to outrun saving, or contrariwise. For example, a boom in land values or a revaluation of the equities of monopolies, entirely dissociated from any excessive stimulus to new investment, should not divert a Currency Authority from keeping the terms of lending and the total supply of money at such a level as to leave over, after satisfying the Financial Circulation, the optimum amount for the Industrial Circulation (so far as this is compatible with the preservation of external equilibrium where our system is not a closed one). The main criterion for interference with a " bull " or a " bear " financial market should be, that is to say, the probable reactions of this financial situation on the prospective equilibrium between savings and *new* investment.

CHAPTER 16

A CLASSIFICATION OF THE CAUSES OF A DISEQUILIBRIUM OF PURCHASING POWER

ASSUME a state of equilibrium in which the price-level corresponds to the cost of production, profits are zero, the cost of investment is equal to that of saving, and (if we are dealing with a member of an international system) the rate of foreign lending is equal to the foreign balance. Assume also—if our community is a progressive one—that the supply of money is being increased at the same steady rate as that of general output, *e.g.* (say) 3 per cent per annum. In what way can this state of equilibrium be upset?

It follows from the Fundamental Equation of Chapter 10,

$$\Pi = \frac{E}{O} + \frac{I-S}{O},$$

that the Price-level of Output is wholly governed by the three factors: (i.) E, the volume of money-earnings of the factors of production, (ii.) O, the volume of current output, and (iii.) I − S, the relation between the volume of saving and the value of investment. Changes can only be effected, therefore, through one or other or all of these fundamental factors.

Bearing this in mind, we can best classify the possible initiating causes of disturbance under three heads, which we may call respectively changes due to Monetary Factors influencing the effective supply of money for income purposes, changes due to Investment Factors, and changes due to Industrial Factors influencing the volume of output and the demand for money for income purposes.

I. *Changes due to Monetary Factors*

A state of disequilibrium may be said to have been initiated by monetary factors, if we have :

(i.) A change in the total quantity of money which does not correspond to the secular trend in general economic activity ; or

(ii.) A change in the proportion of the total quantity of money needed to satisfy the requirements of Finance (*i.e.* the Financial Circulation), due to a change of financial sentiment or activity or of financial values relatively to the price-level of output ; or

(iii.) A change in the requirements of the Industrial Circulation, owing to a change in the velocity of the Income-deposits or of the Business-deposits A or in the turnover of the Industrial Circulation corresponding to a given volume of Earnings, due to a change in the habits and methods of the public or of the business world or to a change in the character (as distinct from the volume) of output.

Changes of any of these types mean that the supply of money available to entrepreneurs is no longer in equilibrium with the amount required by them to maintain the current income and output of the Factors of Production at their existing level. There will, therefore, be a tendency for a series of changes and adjustments to take place, of which a disturbance of the rate of investment is likely, as we shall see, to be the first stage.

II. Changes due to Investment Factors

The market-rate of interest may come to diverge from the natural-rate on account of :

A. A change in the market-rate, resulting from altered conditions in the loan market due to a change in Monetary Factors, uncompensated by a change in the natural-rate.

B. A change in the natural-rate, occasioned by a change in the attractiveness of Investment or in that of Saving, uncompensated by a change in the market-rate ;

C. A change in the market-rate, occasioned by the necessity of maintaining equilibrium between the rate of Foreign Lending and the Foreign Balance, uncompensated by a change in the natural-rate.

III. Changes due to Industrial Factors

There may be a change in the quantity of money demanded by entrepreneurs for the Industrial Circulation due to a change—away from the secular trend which we have already allowed for in our hypothetical conditions of equilibrium—in the volume of Current Output or to a change in its Cost of Production, due either to an "induced" or to a "spontaneous" change (see p. 166 above) in the rate of earnings.

These different types of disturbance can exist simultaneously with one another and they can tend to produce one another; but they are independent in the sense that their effects are superposable, the effect of one aggravating or counterbalancing the effect of another.

Now it is the argument of this Treatise that disturbances to the pre-existing position of equilibrium due to changes of Type I. normally work themselves out *viâ* changes of Type II. ; that disturbances due to changes of Type II., whether of category *A*, *B*, or *C*, tend to work themselves out *viâ* changes of Type III.,—though changes of Type II. *B* may also set up changes of Type I.; and that changes of Type III. finally establish a new position of equilibrium after a series of oscillations caused by their reacting on and interacting with a further series of changes of Type II.

We will deal in some detail with these various types of disturbance in the following chapters. Changes of Type II. *B*, and changes of Type II. *C* where the external disequilibrium is due to changes either at home or abroad of Type II. *B*, and not of Type II. *A*, correspond, I think, to what is usually discussed under the designation of the *Credit Cycle*. We shall see that there is a certain appropriateness in this description, because in this case we have an oscillation about an unchanged position of equilibrium and not a transition from one position of equilibrium to another. On the other hand, the oscillation is not necessarily of a strictly cyclical type, and its characteristics shade off into the not very dissimilar characteristics of the oscillations which attend *any* monetary change, including a transition from one position of equilibrium to another.

Spontaneous changes of Type III. need not be separately discussed, because when they occur their subsequent history will be the same as that of similar changes caused by prior changes of one of the other types.

Nor do we need to introduce *Changes due to Financial Factors* as a separate type, since these, as we have seen in the previous chapter, operate either *viâ* Type I. above by modifying the supply of money available for the Industrial Circulation, or *viâ* Type II. by modifying the attractiveness of new Investment or of Saving.

CHAPTER 17

CHANGES DUE TO MONETARY FACTORS

It does not make much difference to the subsequent course of the argument whether the balance between the demand and supply of money for the Industrial Circulation is changed as a result of a change in the total supply of money or of a change in the requirements of the Financial Circulation, or of a change in the requirements of the Industrial Circulation relatively to the value of output, or of a change in the volume of Incomes. For example, if the requirements of the Industrial Circulation are falling relatively to the value of output, this means that entrepreneurs are getting back against current sales more money than they require to maintain output at the existing bill of costs, so that the Banking System finds itself with redundant lending power at the old equilibrium, just as it would if the total supply of money had been augmented. It will be sufficient, therefore, to consider the case of a change in the total supply of money.

(i.) THE INDUSTRIAL CONSEQUENCES OF A CHANGED SUPPLY OF MONEY

By what route will the injection of an increased quantity of money into the monetary system, or a withdrawal of money from it, bring about a new equilibrium at a changed price-level ?

Since the injection of an increased quantity of cash (using this word to include Central Bank reserves) into the monetary system will increase the reserve-resources of the member banks, it will, for reasons already explained, render the latter more willing lenders on easier terms ; that is to say, the new money stimulates the banks to put resources at the disposal of those borrowers who are ready to employ them, if they are offered on satisfactory terms. Conversely, a withdrawal of cash from the monetary system, by reducing the reserve-resources of the member banks, influences the latter to withdraw resources from borrowers.

Now it may be that part of the proceeds of the new loans will find their way indirectly to the Savings-deposits or to the Business-deposits B, thus augmenting the Financial Circulation. But the rest must, directly or eventually, find its way into the hands of the entrepreneurs. This being so, it is, in general, probable that the greater ease of borrowing will—whatever other effects it may also have—influence entrepreneurs in one or other of three ways :

(i.) The lower rate of interest will stimulate the production of capital-goods by raising their prices. Moreover this tendency may be further encouraged if at the same time the effect of ampler and cheaper money for the Financial Circulation is having the effect of raising security-prices.

(ii.) In so far as there was previously an unsatisfied fringe of would-be entrepreneur borrowers (which, as we shall see subsequently, is sometimes the case) who were ready to borrow, if they had been able, even at the old terms, and also, on the other hand, an unemployed fringe of the factors of production, certain entrepreneurs will now be enabled to offer employment to an additional quantity of the factors of production at the existing rates of remuneration.[1]

---

[1] Since the rate of remuneration to the factor Capital is less than before, owing to the fall in the rate of interest, the above is compatible with an *increase* (but probably only a small one) to the other factors of production.

(iii.) Certain entrepreneurs may now be willing to increase their output even if this means making higher offers than before to the factors of production because (as the ultimate result of the influx of new money) they foresee profits.

Thus in all three cases there will be, sooner or later, an increase in the value of new investment, whether in the form of fixed capital or of working capital; and, probably, an increase in output as well. Yet there is no reason to suppose that the effect of a change in the quantity of money on the rate of saving will be such as to compensate the change in the rate of investment. There is, indeed, a general presumption that the effect on saving, if any, will be opposite in direction to the effect on investment, the easier terms to borrowers meaning less satisfactory terms to lenders, so that what stimulates the one retards the other. Therefore, whatever rise of prices takes place as a result of a rise, if any, in the rate of earnings, a further rise, superimposed on this, must occur as the result of an increase of investment relatively to saving. In other words, whether or not the aggregate of O is increased, the part of O which consists in the output of available income will not be increased as much as the part of $M_1 V_1$ which is spent on the purchase of available income, so that P will rise in excess of $\frac{M_1 V_1}{O}$ by an amount which, as we have seen, is measured by $\frac{I' - S}{O}$; whilst Π will rise by an amount which is measured by $\frac{I - S}{O}$.[1]

In the most straightforward case where there is in

---

[1] In this and the succeeding chapters I shall sometimes ignore the distinction between the purchasing power of money and the price-level of output as a whole, and the extra complication due to the fact that I and I' are not necessarily equal. But where the essence of the argument is affected, I shall, of course, draw attention to this.

the first instance no change in the rates of efficiency earnings, *i.e.* where entrepreneurs do not improve their offers to the factors of production, the whole of the *initial* rise in prices is due to the second term, *i.e.* to the stimulus to investment caused by the easier conditions of borrowing. It may even be that in the first instance there will be no change either in the rates of efficiency-earnings or in the volume of employment, so that M_1V_1 is unaltered, the initial effect of the new money on prices operating wholly through the stimulus to investment. In this case it is probable that comparatively little new money will be needed to augment the Industrial Circulation, and any surplus beyond this will have to be temporarily absorbed by a decrease of Velocities or an increase in the Financial Circulation.

But the consequence of a change in prices due to the inequality of I and S is, as we have seen in Chapter 11, to give a windfall profit to entrepreneurs. Under the stimulus of this profit the secondary phase of the transition is introduced. For the stimulus of profit influences entrepreneurs to bid more eagerly for the services of the factors of production, and so causes the rate of efficiency-earnings $\frac{M_1V_1}{O}$ to increase, whether or not this has already occurred to a certain extent in the primary phase.

So far we have assumed that the supply of money has been increased and that the terms of lending are easier. But the same argument applies *mutatis mutandis* where it is a case of a diminished supply of money and stiffer terms for lending.

(ii.) THE DIFFUSION OF A CHANGE IN THE TOTAL DEPOSITS BETWEEN THE DIFFERENT KINDS OF DEPOSITS

We may now—at the expense of some recapitulation—consider in more detail by what routes an increase in the total deposits distributes itself between the Savings-deposits, the Business-deposits and the Income-deposits.

Obviously, the first effect of a new loan by a bank is to increase the deposits of the borrower by the amount of the loan. Now it is uncommon for a borrower to borrow, not for any business or investment purpose, but to meet his personal expenditure on consumption;—at any rate, bank loans of this kind are so small a proportion of the whole that we can in general neglect them. Further, it would be unusual to borrow merely in order to add the money to the Savings-deposits, since the interest payable by borrowers always exceeds the interest allowed to depositors; so that this contingency also we can neglect. Generally speaking, therefore, the proceeds of a new loan are added in the first instance to the Business-deposits.

Some part of this addition to the Business-deposits will probably find its way, more or less directly, into the hands of entrepreneurs, who are encouraged by the easier terms of borrowing, to be used by them to meet an increased earnings-bill M_1V_1. This increased earnings-bill—as we have seen above—may or may not be associated with an increase in $\frac{M_1V_1}{O}$, the rate of efficiency-earnings. Thus a part of the new money will quickly find its way from M_2 into M_1, the Income-deposits, and a corresponding part will remain in the Business-deposits A to look after the increased turnover of the entrepreneurs corresponding to their increased earnings-bill. Some small increase in Business-deposits A may also be required as a result of the emergence of profits.

The rest of the addition to the Business-deposits—which may conceivably amount in the first instance to the whole of the additional money—will fall into the hands of speculators and financiers, *i.e.* of persons who wish to buy commodities or securities with borrowed money. This will raise the price of securities, and the boom in securities thus brought about will probably increase the Stock Exchange turnover. Thus a part, but usually a very small part, of the new money will have to be retained in the Business-deposits B to look after the increased money-turnover of securities. Now for every buyer of a security (or commodity) there must be a seller. The seller may use the proceeds to buy some other security, in which case the rise in price of securities will spread from one category to another. But as the price of securities continues to rise, one or other of two things must, sooner or later, happen. It may be that this price-rise will furnish windfall profits to the producers of *new* investments, with the result that, viâ the new issue market or otherwise, increased funds will reach the hands of entrepreneurs for the purpose of increasing, or endeavouring to increase, the output of investments. The further course of events will then be the same as in the case already considered.

The other alternative is that the rising prices of securities will cause a difference of opinion to develop between two sections of the financial community,—one section (the " bulls ") believing in the continuance of the price-rise and willing to buy with borrowed money, the other section (the " bears ") doubting the continuance and preferring to sell securities for cash or bills or other liquid assets. Or, in so far as the banks are themselves buying securities, it will be sufficient if a "bear" position develops. Now in so far as the bears' funds are lent to the bulls otherwise than through the Banking System, the Stock Exchange boom can continue with the aid not only of the new money but also of the proceeds of the bears' sales. But in so far as the bears add the proceeds of their sales (or of their refraining from buying securities with their current savings) to the Savings-deposits, this uses up part of the new money in appropriately increasing M_3.

Thus all the new money will eventually find its way either to M_1, corresponding to (1) the increased earnings-bill M_1V_1, or to M_2 to look after either (2) the increased entrepreneurs' turnover or (3) the increased Stock Exchange turnover, or to M_3 to provide for (4) the enlargement of the " bear " position.

Now so long as the new money is absorbed by (3) and (4), without, however, stimulating the output of new investment, there will be no effect on the purchasing power of money, since, although I (the value of the output of new investment) will have increased, I' (the cost of this output) will not have increased. But in so far as the earnings-bill M_1V_1 is increased, and also in so far as entrepreneurs change over from the production of consumption-goods to that of capital-goods under the influence of the profits obtainable from the production of the latter on account of their rise in price, not only will P increase (*i.e.* the purchasing power of money decline) but I' - S will increase, with the result that P will increase (temporarily) by more than $\frac{M_1V_1}{O}$ has increased.

Thus the effect of the new money in the first instance is—unless it is needed to balance changes in V_1 or V_2:

(i.) To increase M_3, M_2 and P' (the price-level of new investment-goods), whilst leaving I' - S, M_1V_1 and P unchanged; or

(ii.) To increase I' - S and P, whilst leaving M_1V_1 unchanged; or

(iii.) To increase I' - S, M_1V_1 and P, whilst leaving $\frac{M_1V_1}{O}$ unchanged; or

(iv.) To increase I' - S, M_1V_1, $\frac{M_1V_1}{O}$ and P.

Changes in M_3, M_2 and P' can, of course, also occur in cases (ii.), (iii.) and (iv.).

In the last three cases P rises and to a greater extent, in the first instance, than can be accounted for by any increase in $\frac{M_1V_1}{O}$. Nevertheless, so long as $P' > P$ or $P > \frac{M_1V_1}{O}$, there can be no position of equilibrium. For the increase of P' relatively to P and the increase of P, in so far as it is due to an increase in $I' - S$, cause profits, and thereby stimulate entrepreneurs to improve their bids for the services of the factors of production. This must continue until $\frac{M_1V_1}{O}$ has settled down at a higher figure, which is in equilibrium with the new total quantity of money and also with values of P and P' which are enhanced relatively to their old values in a degree corresponding to the amount by which $\frac{M_1V_1}{O}$ has been increased.

(iii.) THE PROBLEMS OF THE TRANSITION

We have seen that the price-level will have responded to the increased (or decreased) quantity of money as soon as the second term of the Fundamental Equation is affected. Thus the effect of the new money on prices will be rapid. But, as we have also seen, we must not, therefore, assume that a new equilibrium has been established at this stage. So long as entrepreneurs are enjoying windfall profits (or losses), the position is unstable. If it is a case of profits, they bid against one another for the services of the factors of production, until the latter have risen to a level at which costs of production and sale proceeds are again equal. If it is a case of losses, they throw factors of production out of employment until the latter agree to accept a rate of remuneration at which the costs of production no longer exceed the sale proceeds. Only when the stimulation (or retardation) of investment has worked itself out in an increase (or decrease) of M_1V_1 will the lending capacity of the banks be again restored to equilibrium with saving (for the excess loans will be balanced by the accrual of profits at the end of each production period and will, therefore, be again available, directly or indirectly, for the next production period) and with the task of furnishing an Industrial Circulation appropriate to the now increased (or decreased) earnings-bill. But, finally, the second term $\frac{I' - S}{O}$ will have to fall back again to zero; the banks no longer commanding a surplus lending power wherewith to stimulate investment to outstrip savings (or *vice versa*). A new equilibrium will have been established with both P and $\frac{M_1V_1}{O}$ at a higher (or lower) level corresponding to the increased (or decreased) volume of money.

It must not be supposed, however, that this transition from an enhancement of prices as a result of an increase in the second term of the Fundamental Equation to their enhancement as a result of an increase in the first term will necessarily take place smoothly. If it is a case of reducing the rate of earnings, the factors of production may resist the fall, with the result that their period of unemployment may be prolonged. Moreover investment may continue to exceed (or fall short of) saving *after* what should be a sufficient alteration of M_1V_1 has taken place, with the result of driving prices to a higher (or lower) value than can be permanently sustained. Thus a series of minor oscillations backwards and forwards will be set up before the final position has been reached.

Furthermore, if we are not dealing with a closed system, part of the initial increase (or decrease) in the supply of money relatively to the demand at the old equilibrium will probably be obliterated by an export or import of gold. For—to take the case of an increased supply—the easier terms for lending will tend to increase Foreign Lending, whilst the Foreign Balance, so far from increasing so as to balance this, will tend to diminish under the influence of the rising domestic price-level.

Since the movement of gold will tend to reproduce abroad (though presumably on a relatively smaller scale) the same situation as at home, the effect of the above will be to diffuse the effects of the change of the supply of money over a wide area and so diminish their degree.

If, however, the increased supply of money is in fact due to an import of gold, resulting from a previous excess of the Foreign Balance over Foreign Lending, then the changes at home, which this import of gold sets in train, will all be in the direction of restoring, instead of disturbing, our country's external equilibrium.

We may remark that there is an element of disequilibrium which may continue even when *average* efficiency-earnings have been reduced to a level which is in equilibrium with the reduced volume of money. If the money-rates of remuneration of the *different* factors of production could be reduced simultaneously and in an equal proportion, no one need suffer, when once this point has been reached. But there is generally no means of securing this. The effect of contraction is not to secure an equal reduction all round, but to concentrate the reduction on those particular factors which are in the weakest bargaining position or have the shortest contracts governing their rate of money-earnings. It may be a very long time before *relative* rates of efficiency-earnings are restored to their former proportions. Nor is this an evil peculiar to deflation; there is an analogous mal-distribution of earnings which is equally characteristic of an inflation.

The essential awkwardness lies in the fact that a change in the total quantity of bank-money is algebraically consistent for a time with more than one set of consequences. A change in the quantity of money will change the rate of investment; the change in the rate of investment will bring with it profit or loss; and the stimulus of profit or loss, if carried far enough and continued long enough, will change sooner or later the average rate of earnings; and at long last the change in individual rates of earnings will again conform appropriately to the change in the average rate of earnings, instead of being dispersed inequitably about the average as they will be at first and perhaps for a period of years. But there is no necessity for these adjustments to come about at once.

Since neither economists nor bankers have been quite clear in their minds as to the character of the causal process through which a reduction in the quantity of money leads eventually to a new equilibrium at a lower level of money-earnings and of prices, they have been apt to contemplate a deflation too light-heartedly. Bankers are over-encouraged by the comparative ease with which they bring prices down, and think that the job is already done when only the first and easiest step has been accomplished; and they are then taken by surprise at the protracted period of unemployment and business losses which ensues before the money-earnings per unit of output are adjusted to the new equilibrium. For economists have tended to overlook both the *possibility* of a short-period divergence between prices and efficiency-wages and the *impossibility* of a long-period divergence between them. We are often told (*e.g.*) that a rise of bank-rate causes *prices* to fall, which "makes a country a good one to buy in and a bad one to sell in", etc., etc. We are not told that a rise of bank-rate causes *wages* to fall. But if not, what is to happen to entrepreneurs and to employment? And if so, what is the nature of the transition from high bank-rate to low prices and from low prices to low wages?

It may be considered a defect that the Central Banking Authority has in most modern economic systems no means of acting directly on the first term of the Fundamental Equation—that it cannot directly influence the level of efficiency-earnings. In Bolshevist Russia or in Fascist Italy it may be possible *by decree* to change the money-rate of efficiency-earnings overnight. But no such method is available in the systems of Capitalistic Individualism which prevail in most of the rest of the world. It was not open to the British Treasury when at the time of the return to the Gold Standard the Standard of Value was by its decree raised 10 per cent to decree at the same time that efficiency-earnings should be reduced all round by 10 per cent. On the contrary, the first term of the equation can only be influenced indirectly—raised by stimulating entrepreneurs with abundant credit and abnormal profits, lowered by depressing them with restricted credit and abnormal losses. When bank-rate is raised, not in the interests of equilibrium to keep the second term from rising, but in order to bring the first term down, this means that the *object* of the higher bank-rate is to involve entrepreneurs in losses and the factors of production in unemployment, for only in this way can the money-rates of efficiency-earnings be reduced. It is not reasonable, therefore, to complain when these results ensue.

Thus there is a vital difference between a change in bank-rate which is intended to prevent a Profit Inflation (or Deflation) and one which is intended to cause an Income Deflation (or Inflation); for the former operates to preserve equilibrium by adjusting the market-rate of interest to the natural-rate, whereas the latter operates *viâ* disequilibrium by forcibly divorcing the market-rate from the natural-rate.

For these reasons our existing monetary mechanism, whilst capable of being used efficiently—as we shall see —for the avoidance or mitigation of credit fluctuations, is singularly ill-adapted for achieving an Income Deflation. I am doubtful, therefore, whether those are right who believe that a period of deflation generally does less harm than a period of inflation. It is, of course, true that real wages are apt to be higher (for those who are still employed) during the deflationary phase than during the inflationary phase ; for during the former phase entrepreneurs are paying the factors of production more, and during the latter phase less, than the equivalent of what they produce. From the standpoint of distributive justice it may be preferable to rob the entrepreneur for the benefit of the consumer than to rob the consumer for the benefit of the entrepreneur. But we must not overlook the fact that the former is associated with under-employment and with savings running to waste, whilst the latter means full employment, perhaps over-employment, and a large addition to capital wealth. The warmest advocates of the value of leisure would scarcely prefer the leisure of severe unemployment to the over-stimulated activity of a boom, and enthusiasm about a high level of real-wages may be cooled by a realisation that the increment of real-wages is being paid at the expense of the accumulation of wealth by the community.

At any rate, it is certain that the opinion, which I have sometimes heard expressed, that the real wealth of the community increases faster, in spite of appearances to the contrary, during a depression than during a boom, must be erroneous. For it is a high rate of investment which must necessarily by definition be associated with a high rate of increment of accumulated wealth. Thus I am more disposed to sympathise with Mr. D. H. Robertson, who thinks that much of the material progress of the nineteenth century might have been impossible without the artificial stimulus to capital accumulation afforded by the successive periods of boom, than with the puritans of finance—sometimes extreme individualists, who are able, perhaps, to placate in this way their suppressed reactions against the distastefulness of Capitalism—who draw a gloomy satisfaction from the speculative and business losses, the low prices, and the high real-wages, accompanied, however, by unemployment, which characterise the typical depression.[1] Nor is it a sufficient justification of the latter state of affairs, that, necessity being the mother of invention, there are certain economies and technical improvements which the business world will only make under the stimulus of distress; for there are other improvements which will only mature in an atmosphere of optimism and abundance.

Finally, where our Central Bank is a member of an international monetary system, bank-rate policy will sometimes have to be brought into action, neither to prevent credit fluctuations nor to establish a new equilibrium level of prices, but deliberately to provoke a profit inflation or deflation in order to keep step with a similar disturbance occurring in the outside world.

[1] See, however, Chapter 19 § (i.) below.

CHAPTER 18

CHANGES DUE TO INVESTMENT FACTORS

THE causes of disequilibrium to be discussed in this chapter are not always separated by a sharp line from those discussed in the preceding chapter, and, after the initial stage has been passed, they shade off into one another.[1] For a disturbance initially due to monetary factors will soon set up some disturbance on the investment side, and similarly a disturbance due to investment factors is likely, as we shall see, to cause some modification to monetary factors. But there is, nevertheless, the broad distinction that the former are due to changes on the supply side and the latter, generally speaking, to changes on the demand side.

Moreover there is a further characteristic of great importance which differentiates monetary disturbances (whenever, that is to say, the monetary change is of a quasi-permanent nature) from investment disturbances; namely that the former represents a passage from one equilibrium price-level to another, whereas the latter (even when the investment change is of a quasi-permanent nature) is an oscillation about an approximately unchanged price-level. Thus the former ends up in a new price structure; whereas the latter is calculated to generate an equal and opposite reaction later on. It is this characteristic which

[1] This is particularly the case where the change in the supply of money for the Industrial Circulation is due to a change in the requirements of the Financial Circulation; which latter should perhaps have been classified as a change due to Investment Factors.

CH. 18 CHANGES DUE TO INVESTMENT FACTORS

makes it appropriate to designate investment disturbances as *Credit Cycles*.

(i.) THE DEFINITION OF THE CREDIT CYCLE

Our Fundamental Equation has demonstrated that, if Costs of Production remain constant, the Purchasing Power of Money suffers a see-saw movement up and down according as the volume of savings exceeds the cost of investment or the cost of investment exceeds the volume of savings. On the other hand, if the volume of savings is equal to the cost of investment, then the Purchasing Power of Money fluctuates inversely with the Costs of Production. Moreover, the effect on the Purchasing Power of Money of a change in the Costs of Production and the effect on it of a disequilibrium between the volume of saving and the cost of investment are additive and superposable.

We have called increases and decreases in the Costs of Production *Income Inflation* and *Deflation* respectively, and excesses and defects in the cost of investment over the volume of saving *Commodity Inflation* and *Deflation* respectively. We now define the *Credit Cycle* to mean the alternations of excess and defect in the cost of investment over the volume of saving and the accompanying see-saw in the Purchasing Power of Money due to these alternations. In any given circumstances, however, Costs of Production are unlikely to remain stable throughout the course of a Credit Cycle. Indeed, as we shall see subsequently, Commodity Inflation and Deflation are likely in themselves to set up influences tending towards Income Inflation and Deflation. Moreover where the initial stimulus to change comes from monetary changes, we have already seen that these in their turn must set up credit disequilibria. Thus the actual course of events observable at any time will be a complex phenomenon resulting from the combined effects of changes in the

Costs of Production and of the phases of the Credit Cycle proper. In common usage the term *Credit Cycle* has been applied to this complex phenomenon; and it will often be convenient to follow this looser usage—provided that the initial impulse comes from investment disequilibria and the changes in the Costs of Production are a reaction to these disequilibria and not to some independent or lasting change in the monetary situation.

We shall see that there is an appropriateness in using the term *Cycle* in this connection, because an excess movement in one direction tends to bring into operation not only its own remedy but a stimulus to an excess movement in the other direction, so that the swing of the pendulum is positively to be expected unless something occurs to interrupt it. Moreover the time-interval between the beginning of an upward swing on one side of the equilibrium position and the beginning of the reaction will sometimes depend on physical facts connected with the average duration of productive processes, whilst the interval between the beginning of a downward swing on the other side of the equilibrium position and the beginning of the reaction may be connected with the length of life of important capital-goods and, more generally, with the duration of the existing contracts between entrepreneurs and the factors of production; so that a certain measure of average regularity in the time-phases of the so-called cycle is not inconsistent with what we might expect on *à priori* grounds.

Nevertheless, we should not overstate the truly cyclical character of these phenomena. Credit Cycles can be of many distinct types and many disturbances can arise to interrupt their course. Above all, the behaviour of the banking system can always intervene to mitigate or aggravate their severity.

(ii.) The Genesis and Life-history of a Credit Cycle

It is not surprising that Saving and Investment should often fail to keep step. In the first place—as we have mentioned already—the decisions which determine Saving and Investment respectively are taken by two different sets of people influenced by different sets of motives, each not paying very much attention to the other. Especially is this the case over short periods. There are many reasons, as we shall see in Vol. ii., why the volume of investment should suffer fairly wide fluctuations. The development of an investment boom certainly does not mean that the entrepreneurs who initiate it have deliberately decided that the public are going to save out of their incomes on a larger scale than before. Nor is an investment slump to be explained by entrepreneurs having decided beforehand that the public's savings are going to fall off. There is, indeed, no possibility of intelligent foresight designed to equate savings and investment unless it is exercised by the banking system; for it is the facilities allowed by the banks which are the marginal factor determining the precise degree to which entrepreneurs will be in a position to carry out their enterprises. Yet hitherto the banking system has been mainly preoccupied with a different objective.

Not only are the decisions made by different sets of persons; they must also in many cases be made at different times. When the increased investment represents an increase of working capital, the act of saving is required, it is true, immediately. But when there is a change-over in the character of production which will lead later on to an increased output of fixed capital, the additional saving is only needed when the process of production is finished. This results from the duration of the process of production, whether of capital-goods or of consumption-goods. The time occupied in building a house may be no longer than the time occupied between ploughing the wheat-fields and eating a loaf of bread raised therefrom. That is to say, the two processes employ the same amount of working capital, and it is only when they emerge from the process of production in a finished form that the first adds to the volume of net investment and therefore needs an act of saving to balance it. Thus when the collective decisions of the entrepreneurs are of such a character that they will result in investment running ahead of saving at some later date, the results will not be apparent until this later date is actually reached, when there will have been time for many reactions to have been set up which cannot be immediately reversed.

The business of saving is essentially a steady process. If there are disturbances in the economic world, these by affecting prosperity may react on the rate of saving. But a disturbance will seldom or never be initiated by a sudden change in the proportion of current income which is being saved. Investment in fixed capital, on the other hand, has been accustomed to proceed irregularly and by fits and starts. We shall examine in Book VI. the nature and extent of fluctuations of investment. It is sufficient for our immediate argument to claim the support of common knowledge and experience for the conclusion that the development of disequilibria between the rates of saving and of investment under the existing economic system is nothing to wonder at.

Many writers on the Credit Cycle have emphasised the irregularity of the rate of investment in fixed capital as being the major cause of disturbance.[1] If we have in mind *initiating* causes this is probably true. But the most characteristic *secondary* phase of a Credit Cycle is due to the growth of investment in

[1] See Vol. ii., Chap. 27.

CH. 18 CHANGES DUE TO INVESTMENT FACTORS 281

working capital. Moreover, whenever we have to deal with a boom or a slump in the total volume of employment and current output, it is a question of a change in the rate of investment in working capital rather than in fixed capital; so that it is by increased investment in working capital that every case of recovery from a previous slump is characterised.

Credit Cycles can be analysed into three types,— though those which actually occur are generally complex in type and partake of the character of all three. Let us take the case where investment is increasing relatively to saving:

(i.) The increased investment may take place, without any change in the total volume of output, by the substitution of the production of capital-goods in place of consumption-goods; in this case the increase of investment will not materialise until after the elapse of a production period.

(ii.) The increased investment may take the form of an increase of working capital corresponding to an increased total output due to an additional production of capital-goods being superimposed on the existing output; in this case the increase of investment will begin from the outset, being first of all in the shape of working capital and, after the elapse of a production period, in the shape of fixed capital.

(iii.) The increased investment may take the form of an increase of working capital corresponding to an increased total output due to an additional production of consumption-goods being superimposed on the existing output; in this case the increase of investment will only continue for the duration of a production period.

A phenomenon partaking of the characters of (i.), (ii.) and (iii.), in varying degrees may also be complicated by the presence of some measure both of Income Inflation (*i.e.* of rising costs of production) and of Capital Inflation (*i.e.* a rise of the price-level of new investment-goods relatively to their cost of production).

The occurrence either of 'a Commodity Inflation or of a Capital Inflation will tend to cause a Profit Inflation; and a Profit Inflation will bring about an Income Inflation through the eagerness of entrepreneurs to secure the services of the factors of production. But—theoretically at least—it is possible to disentangle from these complications the element of Commodity Inflation which constitutes a Credit Cycle. Moreover, a Commodity Inflation of Type (iii.) above may be considered as the most characteristic of a Credit Cycle, because—as we shall see—all Credit Cycles tend to end up, however they may begin, with an admixture of this type.

The possible varieties of the paths which a Credit Cycle can follow and its possible complications are so numerous that it is impracticable to outline all of them. One can describe the rules of chess and the nature of the game, work out the leading openings and play through a few characteristic end-games; but one cannot possibly catalogue all the games which can be played. So it is with the Credit Cycle. We will begin, therefore, by examining the three openings and then proceed to an analysis of the characteristic secondary phase.

A. *The Primary Phase*

(i.) Let us suppose that circumstances have come about which lead entrepreneurs to believe that certain new investments will be profitable; for example, a new technical discovery, such as steam or electricity or the

CH. 18 CHANGES DUE TO INVESTMENT FACTORS 283

internal-combustion engine, or a shortage of houses due to a growth of population, or more settled conditions in a country where previously the risks of normal development had been excessive, or a Capital Inflation due to psychological causes, or a reaction stimulated by cheap money from a previous period of under-investment, *i.e.* a previous slump.[1] If they are to put their projects into operation, they must either attract factors of production from other employments or employ factors previously unemployed.

Let us begin with type (i.) above where factors previously producing consumption-goods are now turned on to producing capital-goods. In this case no effect will be produced on prices until after an interval of time equal in length to the process of production of the consumption-goods which were previously, but are no longer, being made. For during this interval earnings are as before and the output of available goods is also as before. But after the expiry of the appropriate interval, whilst earnings will be unchanged, the amount of available output will fall off to an extent corresponding to the amount of consumption-goods previously, but no longer, made—with the result that the Consumption Price-level will rise, unless there is a corresponding increase in the proportion of earnings saved. The upward-price phase of the Credit Cycle will have made its appearance.

It is to be observed that prices will necessarily have risen *more* than in proportion to a rise, if any, in the costs of production. It is not necessary to assume that the change-over from one kind of production to another is achieved without an increase in the cost of production (*i.e.* in earnings)—that is to say, without any Income Inflation. Indeed the change-over will often, perhaps usually in the contemporary world, come

---

[1] War-expenditure, not covered by taxation, is most conveniently regarded for the purposes of the present argument as a sudden increase of investment; cf. Vol. ii., Chapter 30.

about by the new entrepreneurs attracting factors of production to themselves by bidding up the rate of earnings. In this case earnings being increased from the very start out of proportion to output, the Consumption Price-level will rise proportionately to the amount of Income Inflation. But however large or small the amount of the Income Inflation, the effects of the Commodity Inflation will be superimposed on it and will essentially consist in a rise of prices *relatively* to costs and earnings. After the necessary interval of time has elapsed, the available output coming on to the market will be diminished and real earnings must fall, *i.e.* the Consumption Price-level must rise *more* than earnings. Income Inflation, however great, leaves the equilibrium of earnings, costs and prices just where it was; it is only Commodity Inflation which can disturb this equilibrium. The commonest form of Type (i.) in practice is an Income Inflation, possibly slight in degree, brought about by the insistence of new producers, followed by a Commodity Inflation after an appropriate interval. In any case the characteristic conclusion of the Primary Phase of a Credit Cycle consists in a rise of the Consumption Price-level out of proportion to costs.

(ii.) Type (ii.), however, is the more usual, namely, that in which the increased investment is accompanied by an increase in the total volume of production ; *i.e.* where there is from the outset a growth of working capital not balanced by additional saving. For the increased production of capital-goods is more likely to be additional to, than in substitution for, the previous production of consumption-goods ; if only because the factors of production engaged on the latter are not easily turned over to the former at short notice. This assumes, of course, that the factors of production are not fully employed at the moment when the Cycle begins its upward course ; but then that generally is the case, whether as the result of the slump which had ensued on the previous Cycle or for some other cause. In this case the earnings of the factors of production increase from the outset, without there being any increase in available output. Prices rise, therefore, at once relatively to earnings and costs; the difference between this case and case (i.) being that the upward-price phase of the Credit Cycle begins immediately.

(iii.) Let us next take type (iii.) where factors of production previously unemployed are put to work on producing, not fixed-capital goods as in type (ii.), but particular categories of consumption-goods. The course of events is exactly as in type (ii.) for a period of time equal to the duration of the process of production, after which the available output coming on to the market is increased by the same amount—assuming that the rate of efficiency-wages is unchanged—as total earnings had been increased at the earlier date, so that prices fall back again to their previous level.

It is to be noticed that expansions of types (ii.) and (iii.) cannot come about without a substantial change in the monetary situation, since they involve an increase in aggregate earnings as well as in profits. Thus it requires the acquiescence of the banking authorities; though if the banks have got into the habit of concentrating their attention on the volume of the total deposits to the exclusion of other factors, the monetary adjustment may come about without arousing their notice. For an increased volume of money may be furnished for the Industrial Circulation as the result of a decrease of the Financial Circulation, *i.e.* of the savings-deposits, since it is particularly likely that in the earliest phases of a boom there will be a unanimity of bull sentiment leading to a decrease of the "bear" position. Failing this, a slight rise in bank-rate, which is insufficient to counteract the tendency towards Commodity Inflation, may serve to increase monetary facilities sufficiently to look after the increased earnings; either by increasing the velocities of circulation as a result of the enhanced cost of maintaining balances (and a very slight change of velocities will usually be enough), or—if we are concerned with a country which belongs to an international system—by attracting gold from abroad.[1] An expansion, however, of type (i.)—where the volume of liquid goods coming on to the market is diminished because more productive effort has been concentrated on capital-goods—can come about with only a slight alteration in monetary factors, and therefore requires more positive action on the part of the banks if it is to be avoided.

We may note in passing that where the price of consumption-goods is raised, not by a falling off in their supply, but by an increase in the volume of employment not (immediately) compensated by an increase of their supply, the volume of employment will, as a rule, increase gradually, and entrepreneurs, entering into plans for increased production, will be inclined to place their orders ahead for some part of the half-finished goods which they are going to require. Thus the price of working capital, *i.e.* the wholesale standard, will tend to increase sooner and faster than the consumption standard. Such anticipatory price-movements, however, are still part of the Primary Phase.

We have taken as our standard case an increase of investment uncompensated by increased savings. But the same arguments apply, *mutatis mutandis*, when a Credit Cycle has been initiated by a drop in saving uncompensated by decreased investment. This is not very likely to occur in practice on an important scale, because the influences which determine the volume of saving are of such a kind that they are not so likely to

[1] In countries (such as most of those on the continent of Europe), where the volume of money partly depends on the volume of suitable bills available to be discounted at the Central Bank, an increase in the volume of output has a direct tendency to produce some corresponding increase in the volume of circulating money.

change suddenly as are those which determine the volume of investment. If, however, saving does fall off for any reason, this will mean a larger expenditure on the same available consumption-goods as before, so that, as in the other cases, prices move upward. Nor is there any theoretical reason why a Credit Cycle should not start with a downward phase, due to Investment falling off whilst Saving keeps up. This might result from some blow to the confidence of entrepreneurs in particular types of enterprise, or by a Capital Deflation which left unaffected the readiness of the public to save. Most often of all, perhaps, an upward phase is brought about as a reaction from a previous downward phase and a downward phase as a reaction from a previous upward phase, boom succeeding slump and slump succeeding boom; though the precise date at which the reaction commences will be usually determined by some independent change in the environment due to non-monetary factors.

B. *The Secondary Phase*

The price-movements so far considered belong to the Primary Phase of the Credit Cycle. They are brought about, not as the result of attempts to take advantage of the occurrence of profits, but because entrepreneurs see advantageous opportunities for increased activity in particular directions. The Secondary Phase, however, is of a different character. We have emphasised the point that it is of the essence of a Commodity Inflation that prices rise out of proportion to the increase, if any, in the costs of production. Consequently those entrepreneurs who have liquid consumption-goods emerging from the process of production are able to sell them for more than they have cost, or are costing, to produce, and so to reap a windfall profit. The high prices also act as an inducement to retailers and wholesalers to reduce their stocks—which they can now realise at an unusually satisfactory price—below their normal level. To the extent that this occurs it operates, indeed, by reducing investment in one particular kind of working capital, as a partial offset to the excessive investment in other directions. But the almost inevitable result of profits on current output and the visible depletion of stocks is to encourage manufacturers of consumption-goods to strain their efforts to increase their output. We thus have, under the influence of the windfall profits accruing from the price-rise consequent on the Primary Phase of the Credit Cycle, a secondary stimulus to an increased volume of production—which, this time, is of an all-round character and affects *all* types of goods which are the object of general consumption.

This secondary phase is even more likely than the primary phase to involve some measure of Income Inflation as well as of Commodity Inflation. For the attempt to increase still further the volume of employment will probably have the effect of stiffening the attitude of the factors of production and enabling them to obtain a higher rate of remuneration per unit of output. Moreover, in certain cases specialised factors of production will be fully employed, with the result that the emergence of profit will cause entrepreneurs to bid against one another for such supply of these factors as is available, thus raising the rate of remuneration in these particular cases. With the progress of Income Inflation the surplus bank-resources which gave the stimulus to entrepreneurs to extend their activities fade away (because of the increasing demands of the Industrial Circulation), but so long as any element of Commodity Inflation is still present the stimulus continues. Furthermore, in so far as a further rise of prices is expected, there may set in a tendency to hoard liquid goods, which aggravates the excess of investment over saving, and so precipitates the very rise in question.

C. *The Collapse*

Now whether or not the primary phase contains within it the seeds of a reaction, the secondary phase necessarily does. If the primary phase is caused by an increased production of capital-goods, the higher price level will continue so long as this capital output continues—which, in appropriate conditions, might be a long time, though the incentive to an increased output of capital-goods should diminish, just as the incentive to the production of consumption-goods increases. But if it is caused by an increased production of consumption-goods, then, after an interval governed by the length of the process of production, the supply of such goods coming on to the market will be increased fully in proportion to earnings. Thus there will no longer be any occasion for the higher price-level, and prices will drop back to their former figures. Only in so far as Income Inflation has occurred can a higher level be maintained. Now, since the secondary phase necessarily stimulates the production of consumption-goods, it follows that even where the primary phase is caused by an increased production of capital-goods, the secondary phase brings with it the seeds of a reaction, which will germinate as soon as the increased supply of consumption-goods is ready for the market. Thus, sooner or later, consumption-goods will be coming on to the market which can no longer be sold at the previously ruling price; so that the downward price phase of the Cycle now commences.

This downward price-movement, whilst obliterating in whole or in part the windfall profits which had been ruling previously, should not, taken by itself, involve entrepreneurs in an actual loss; and, indeed, so long as any element of over-investment continues, some degree of profit will still remain. For, provided saving does not exceed investment, entrepreneurs can always sell consumption-goods for an aggregate sum which is at least equal to their cost of production. Thus there is no theoretical necessity for a reaction leading to windfall losses; when the over-investment comes to an end, the boom may just cease. We shall examine a particular case of this in detail in Chapter 20.

Nevertheless, there are many reasons why in actual fact the downward price phase is likely to usher in, not merely the end of windfall profits, but the beginning of windfall losses.

First of all, on the investment side new influences will be coming into operation. Some entrepreneurs will, as a result of inaccurate forecasting, have been led into producing in conditions of sub-normal efficiency in which they cannot cover their costs of production unless prices are such that entrepreneurs as a whole are making a windfall profit. The fall of prices will, therefore, cause these entrepreneurs to cease such production—which will, by reducing investment in working capital, reduce the total rate of investment. The sight of falling prices, and perhaps of a declining volume of output also, may change financial sentiment in two ways,—" bear " views may develop, with the result of augmenting the demand for money in the Financial Circulation and so reducing the supply of money for the Industrial Circulation, thus causing the banks to force a reduction of investment, and the Capital Inflation (which, as we have seen, is influenced more by *opinion* than by the volume of money) may disappear, perhaps giving place to a Capital Deflation (*i.e.* a fall of P'), thus removing one of the stimuli to over-investment.

Meanwhile, on the monetary side also the position will be changing. Apart from the cessation of the bullish unanimity which had temporarily augmented the Industrial Circulation at the expense of the Financial Circulation, the other short-period factors, which had permitted a certain augmentation of the earnings-bill, will have come to the end of their tether. It may be that their tendency will be actually reversed, —for example, velocities of circulation may tend back to normal; and, if the Commodity Inflation has spread to other countries, or for other reasons, the existing level of bank-rate may cease to draw gold or may even cease to retain the existing stock. More probably, however, the potentialities of the factors of expansion will become exhausted rather than—in the first instance at least—reversed. For, as the Credit Cycle proceeds, the windfall profits of entrepreneurs will be continuously stimulating them to bid against one another for the services of the factors of production, so that the Profit Inflation will gradually pass over into an Income Inflation and, in proportion as it does so, more and more money will be required for the support of the Industrial Circulation.

A point will come, therefore, when the effort to expand or to maintain the volume of the Industrial Circulation will drive the effective bank-rate to a level which is, in all the circumstances, deterrent to new investment relatively to saving. At this point the slump sets in. The reaction from the boom will not merely have brought back prices and profits to the normal, but an era of business losses and sub-normal prices will have commenced.

All this presumes of course that the Banking System has been behaving according to the principles which have in fact governed it hitherto, and that it lies either outside its purpose or outside its power so to fix and maintain the effective bank-rate as to keep Saving and Investment at an approximate equality throughout. For if it were to manage the Currency successfully according to the latter criterion, the Credit Cycle would not occur at all.

I have in this Chapter described the genesis and life-history of the Credit Cycle in the most general possible terms. It is obvious that the actual course of events can follow innumerable courses differing from one another in detail. But a great many different cases can, I think, be fitted into the above generalised framework.

CHAPTER 19

SOME SPECIAL ASPECTS OF THE CREDIT CYCLE

(i.) THE "JUSTIFICATION" OF COMMODITY INFLATION

THE experiences of the post-war period led many of us to advocate stability of the price-level as the best possible objective of practical policy. Amongst other things, this would mean an attempt on the part of the banking authorities to eliminate the Credit Cycle at all costs. This advocacy has led to criticism, of which Mr. D. H. Robertson (in his *Banking Policy and the Price Level*) is the main author, to the effect that the Credit Cycle, though guilty of disastrous excesses and grave crimes, has a part to play in a progressive society, and that an attempt to check it altogether might produce stagnation as well as stability. It may be convenient, therefore, to examine at this point how much force there is in Mr. Robertson's contentions.

The main basis of Mr. Robertson's argument is that the Commodity Inflation phase of a Credit Cycle, so long as it lasts, causes the wealth of the community to increase faster than would otherwise be the case. This is undoubtedly true. The result of Commodity Inflation is to cause the current output of the community to exceed its current consumption to a greater extent than would be the case otherwise ; whilst, on the other hand, the higher real wages which are enjoyed during a slump are at the expense of normal capital accumulation. The amount of the excess due to a Commodity

Inflation over the increment of accumulated wealth represented by voluntary savings, Mr. Robertson calls " imposed lacking ", and he contends that there are occasions when it is desirable that the rate of increment of accumulated wealth should be greater than could be the case under a régime of voluntary saving unsupplemented by " imposed lacking ".

It should be noticed that the Commodity Inflation phase of a Credit Cycle cannot be of use for continuously raising the rate of wealth-accumulation. It is only useful for the purpose of producing a short, sudden spurt. Now it is quite conceivable that occasions may arise when a spurt of this character may be acutely needed. Commodity Inflation may be the most effective means of rapid transition in any case in which we have good reasons to be in a hurry. But I find it difficult to think of good examples,— except, of course, War, when the financial purist may find himself overwhelmed before his own more slow-moving devices have had time to produce their effect.

We must, therefore, set on the other side the losses to wealth-accumulation due to the Deflation phase of the Credit Cycle. And is it certain, when this has been done, on which side the balance lies ? It may very likely be the case that during the nineteenth century the greatly increased wealth of the world was predominantly accumulated by Commodity Inflation ; but this may have been due to the increasing abundance of money and at the same time the increasing efficiency of the factors of production which allowed a prolonged moderate excess of prices over efficiency-earnings, so that profits emerged and wealth was built up, rather than to the sharp oscillations of the Credit Cycle which were superimposed on this general trend. For there are enormous losses to be put on the other side ascribable to the cyclical Deflations. The loss during the latter arises not only out of consumption at the expense of savings but also out of the loss of output due to involuntary unemployment (which is a greater evil than the overtime of the booms is a benefit). Not nearly enough weight is generally given to this great loss of wealth during a Deflation ascribable partly to the loss of savings and partly to the involuntary idleness of the factors of production. A policy of monetary management which engineered a Commodity Inflation from time to time when it seemed that voluntary savings were insufficient, without ever allowing the reaction of a Deflation to follow, might indeed do good. But this would not be a Cyclical Inflation. If we are to have general rules relating to Credit Cycles, it seems unlikely that a general rule in their favour would be advantageous on balance.

Secondly, some weight must be given to considerations of social justice. In a Commodity Inflation the earnings of the factors of production are worth less than what they are producing, and the difference is arbitrarily distributed amongst the members of the entrepreneur class as a permanent addition to the latter's wealth; for they can usually secure more of the gains of the Inflation than they suffer of the losses of the Deflation. This forced and arbitrary transference of the ownership of the results of effort is in itself a considerable evil.

There are, however, certain secondary arguments which can be used to support Mr. Robertson's general position as follows:

(i.) In a progressive society, and indeed in a society which is subject to change of any kind, the instrument of temporary inflation may sometimes be a necessary one to secure the change-over from one type of production to another with the desirable degree of rapidity. In a Socialist system which was directed with perfect knowledge and wisdom, the diversion of productive resources could be effected by *fiat*. But in an individualist system this is not possible. Resources will tend to remain where they are. It will require not merely the expectation of higher profits elsewhere to move them, but the pinch of lower profits and even the threat of bankruptcy unless they move. It follows that the new men will not easily get hold of the resources, necessary to enable them to put their ideas into practice as soon as they should in the social interest, if they have to wait until the established entrepreneurs now controlling them voluntarily relinquish them in their favour. It is better therefore—so the argument runs—that the new borrowers should at times be given an opportunity of resources by an act of Commodity Inflation, or enabled to bid against the established firms by an act of Income Inflation, if progress is to proceed at its proper pace. We must concede real force to this. It is a by-product of strenuous times, and indeed of misfortunes generally, that the new men and methods rise more rapidly to the top than in eras of placid prosperity. But, obviously, it is a question of balancing advantages and of the price to be paid. Moreover, the usual ups and downs of individual industries will often provide quite an adequate stimulus without its being necessary to engineer the *general* disturbances which we are now discussing. Currency stability does not mean universal quiescence and a prevailing atmosphere of no change. The *average* stability at which it aims is one in which the losses of entrepreneurs in one direction are approximately balanced by the gains of this class in another direction, so that there is no general tendency to boom or slump super-imposed on the progress or on the decline of particular industries and particular entrepreneurs. It is not one in which the Survival of the Fittest by the operation of profit and loss has been suspended.

(ii.) Mr. Robertson contends that in certain circumstances changes in the general price-level, as distinct from particular price-changes, will enable the factors of production to adjust the degree of their effort to the degree of its reward with a closer approximation to maximum advantage than under a régime of stability. But even if this could be established in special cases—and many conditions have to be fulfilled for this—there remains the question of what *general rule* is best.

I conclude, therefore, that Mr. Robertson's contentions, though they deserve serious attention, are not sufficient to dispose of the *prima facie* presumption in favour of aiming at the stability of purchasing power as a general rule, in preference to the oscillations of the Credit Cycle. But the reader must please note emphatically that throughout this chapter I am dealing solely with a Commodity Inflation *which is part of a Credit Cycle*, *i.e.* an Inflation which is due to Investment Factors, unaccompanied by any lasting change in Monetary Factors. A prolonged Commodity Inflation due to progressive increases in the supply of money, as contrasted with a prolonged Commodity Deflation, is quite another thing—as we shall see in Vol. ii. Chap. 30—and may be a most potent instrument for the increase of accumulated wealth.

In any case the conclusion holds good that an expansion of the volume of investment, resulting in rising prices, may be extremely advisable as a general rule, when it is a corrective to a pre-existing Commodity Deflation. In this case the rising prices are tending to bring the price-level back again to equilibrium with the existing level of incomes. When, for example, a condition of widespread unemployment exists as the result of the downward phase of a Credit Cycle, but without the Commodity Deflation having passed over into an Income Deflation, it will be impracticable to bring about a recovery to a normal level of production and employment without allowing some measure of expansion and of rising prices as a corrective to the existing Deflation. This is not true of an Income Deflation, provided its incidence has been fairly equal on all the factors of production. But it is true of a Commodity Deflation. In short, to stabilise prices at the bottom of a Commodity Deflation would be a stupid thing to do. But with this all "stabilisers" would agree.

There is one other general conclusion which legitimately emerges from this discussion, namely that the principal evils of a Credit Cycle are due to its Deflation phase and not to its Inflation phase. Thus real advantages may ensue if, when a Commodity Inflation has passed over into an Income Inflation, no attempt is made to go back to the old state of affairs but stability is preserved at the new level of incomes. The state of affairs in which the supply of money allows the equilibrium price-level to rise over the long period a little faster than efficiency-earnings, so that there is a progressive moderate bias in favour of Commodity Inflation, is, therefore, vastly preferable to one in which the price-level is slowly falling relatively to earnings. The advantages to economic progress and the accumulation of wealth will outweigh the element of social injustice, especially if the latter can be taken into account, and partially remedied, by the general system of taxation ;—and even without this remedy, if the community starts from a low level of wealth and is greatly in need of a rapid accumulation of capital.

(ii.) The Incidence of Commodity Inflation

A Commodity Inflation really does increase the resources available for new investment and serves to augment Society's stock of wealth. This respect, in which it totally differs from an Income Inflation and from a Capital Inflation which do no such thing, has been commonly overlooked by those who do not distinguish different kinds of Inflation from one another.

But it also—and in this respect it resembles Income Inflation—causes a redistribution of existing wealth by transferring wealth from owners of money and debts to those who have borrowed and have liabilities expressed in terms of money. For not only do those in the possession of money-incomes find that their real incomes are diminished; those who are in possession of a stock of money also discover that this stock has less than its previous real value. Mr. Robertson has argued from this that the latter class may, therefore, be induced to save on a greater scale than they would otherwise, in order to make good the loss which they have involuntarily suffered in the value of their stock of money. In addition those in receipt of increased incomes, whether as a result of increased employment or of higher money-rate of efficiency earnings, may be expected to save part of their incomes to build up their income-deposits.

To savings arising in the former way, *i.e.* to replenish income-deposits, Mr. Robertson has given the name of " induced lacking ", as distinct from the " imposed lacking " (as he calls it) resulting from the reduction in the purchasing power of current money incomes which is caused by Commodity Inflation.

But there is something further to be said about the distinction between these two things. Mr. Robertson's "imposed lacking" is solely a characteristic of Commodity Inflation and is not present in the case of an Income Inflation; whereas his "induced lacking" is primarily a characteristic of an Income Inflation, and is only present in the case of Commodity Inflation when the latter is accompanied by an increase of output. For there is no reason to expect any increase in the Income Deposits except in proportion to the increase of money-earnings. Furthermore, whilst "imposed lacking" *necessarily* represents an augmentation of the resources available for new investment, this is only true of "induced lacking" when this results from genuine savings. Yet there are other ways of augmenting the Income Deposits,—for example, by a transfer from the Savings Deposits or by refraining from the purchase of securities with normal current savings; or the velocity of the Income Deposits, instead of their amount, may be increased. Thus "induced lacking" seems to me to be too precarious a source of additional savings to deserve separate notice.

The confusion between the loss in the value of current income and the loss in the value of existing stocks of money and money claims sometimes leads to a corresponding confusion as to the *incidence* of Commodity Inflation. When a bank increases the volume of credit to the accompaniment of a rise of prices, it is evident that the borrower, in whose favour the additional money-credit has been created, has at his command an increased purchasing power with which he can augment his fund of working capital; and this remains true even if prices rise, and however much they rise. At whose expense has this augmentation taken place? Or, in other words, whose real income has been diminished in order to supply the increased real income in the hands of the borrower? The obvious answer—but the wrong one—is to say that the transference has taken place at the expense of the depositor. It is true that the borrower, coming on to the market as an additional buyer without any diminution in the purchasing power of the existing buyers at the existing price-level, raises prices. It is also true that the increase of prices diminishes the value of the depositor's deposits, *i.e.* of his *command* of purchasing power. But unless we assume that the depositors as a body were about to diminish their real-balances, the increase in the price-level, although it diminishes the value of the money-deposits, does not for that reason necessarily diminish the consumption of the depositors. So long as depositors as a body are not drawing on their previous deposits for purposes of consumption, it is not with their existing deposits that they are paying for their consumption, but with their *current income*. This leads us to the correct answer. What the rise of prices diminishes is the value of all current incomes payable in cash. That is to say, the *flow* of purchasing power in the hands of the rest of the community is diminished by an amount equal to the fresh purchasing power obtained by the aforesaid borrower. Furthermore, as we have seen, a benefit exactly equal to this loss in the value of current income accrues in the shape of profits to the entrepreneurs who are able to sell their current output at the enhanced price. Thus the increment of capital acquired by the new borrowers by means of the loans accorded to them is at the expense of recipients of current income; but this increment of wealth, or rather the loan which it secures, belongs not to those at whose expense it has been built up but, directly or indirectly, to the entrepreneurs who have made windfall profits by being able to dispose of their output at an enhanced price.

To whom, on the other hand, has there accrued an increment of wealth corresponding to the loss of wealth of the depositors ? Obviously to the *old* borrowers—*i.e.* to the borrowers who have borrowed at the previous lower price-level but will be able to repay at the new higher price-level. But this transference, whilst it is a transference of wealth—not only between bank-depositors and bank-borrowers but between all classes of lenders and borrowers in terms of money—is not a transference which serves in any way to augment the stock of capital. For whilst the borrowers can repay when the due date of their loan arrives by parting with less purchasing power than what they had expected to part with, and therefore retain additional purchasing power which they may or may not employ to replenish working capital, the amount of credit available in the hands of the banks, as a result of these repayments of old loans, wherewith to make new loans to business, is worth correspondingly less.

(iii.) THE NORMAL COURSE OF A CREDIT CYCLE

Having emphasised sufficiently the endless variety of the paths which a Credit Cycle can follow, we may allow ourselves, by way of simplification, to pick out one path in particular which seems to us to be sufficiently frequented to deserve, perhaps, to be called the usual or normal course.

Something happens—of a non-monetary character—to increase the attractions of investment. It may be a new invention, or the development of a new country, or a war, or a return of "business confidence" as the result of many small influences tending the same way. Or the thing may start—which is more likely if it is a monetary cause which is playing the chief part—with a Stock Exchange boom, beginning with speculation in natural resources or *de facto* monopolies, but eventually affecting by sympathy the price of new capital-goods.

The rise in the natural-rate of interest, corresponding to the increased attractions of investment, is not held back by increased saving; and the expanding volume of investment is not restrained by an adequate rise in the market-rate of interest.

This acquiescence of the Banking System in the increased volume of investment may involve it in allowing some increase in the total quantity of money; but at first the necessary increase is not likely to be great and may be taken up, almost unnoticed, out of the general slack of the system, or may be supplied by a falling off in the requirements of the Financial Circulation without any change in the total volume of money.

At this stage the output and price of capital-goods begin to rise. Employment improves and the wholesale index rises. The increased expenditure of the newly employed then raises the price of consumption-goods and allows the producers of such goods to reap a windfall profit. By this time practically all categories of goods will have risen in price and all classes of entrepreneurs will be enjoying a profit.

At first the volume of employment of the factors of production will increase without much change in their rate of remuneration. But after a large proportion of the unemployed factors have been absorbed into employment, the entrepreneurs bidding against one another under the stimulus of high profits will begin to offer higher rates of remuneration.

All the while, therefore, the requirements of the industrial circulation will be increasing—first of all to look after the increased volume of employment and subsequently to look after, in addition, the increased rates of remuneration. A point will come, therefore, when the Banking System is no longer able to supply the necessary volume of money consistently with its principles and traditions.

It is astonishing, however,—what with changes in the Financial Circulation, in the Velocities of Circulation, and in the reserve proportions of the Central Bank—how large a change in the Earnings Bill can be looked after by the Banking System without an apparent breach in its principles and traditions.

It may be, therefore, that the turning-point will come, not from the reluctance or the inability of the Banking System to finance the increased Earnings Bill, but from one or more of three other causes. The turn may come from a faltering of financial sentiment, due to some financiers, from prescience or from their experience of previous crises, seeing a little further ahead than the business world or the banking world. If so, the growth of " bear " sentiment will, as we have seen, increase the requirements of the Financial Circulation. It may be, therefore, the tendency of the Financial Circulation to increase, on the top of the increase in the Industrial Circulation, which will break the back of the Banking System and cause it at long last to impose a rate of interest, which is not only fully equal to the market-rate but, very likely in the changed circumstances, well above it.

Or it may be that the attractions of new investment will wear themselves out with time or with the increased supply of certain kinds of capital-goods.

Or, finally,—failing a turn-about from any of the above causes—there is likely to be a sympathetic reaction, not much more than one production period after the secondary phase of the boom (the increased activity in the production of consumption-goods) has properly set in, owing to the inevitable collapse in the prices of consumption-goods below their higher level.

Thus the collapse will come in the end as the result of the piling up of several weighty causes—the evaporation of the attractions of new investment, the faltering of financial sentiment, the reaction in the price level of consumption-goods, and the growing inability of the Banking System to keep pace with the increasing requirements, first of the Industrial Circulation and later of the Financial Circulation also.

The order of events is, therefore, as follows. First, a Capital Inflation leading to an increase of Investment, leading to Commodity Inflation; second, still more Capital Inflation and Commodity Inflation for approximately one production period of consumption-goods; third, a reaction in the degree of the Commodity and Capital Inflations at the end of this period; fourth, a collapse of the Capital Inflation; and finally, a decrease of Investment below normal, leading to a Commodity Deflation.

CHAPTER 20

AN EXERCISE IN THE PURE THEORY OF THE CREDIT CYCLE

I PROPOSE in this chapter to take a particular type of Credit Cycle and to work it out in full detail. Owing to the simplifying assumptions which have to be introduced in order to rule out the various complexities which are usually present in actual life, the example taken is somewhat artificial. Since, moreover, it does not add to the previous argument but only illustrates it, some readers may prefer to leave this chapter out. The method and the ideas of the preceding chapters will, however, be better illustrated in this way than if I were to cover more ground less intensively.

The type taken is one at the inception of which some of the factors of production are unemployed. It is then assumed that the banks adopt a lending policy which allows the production of consumption-goods to increase, accompanied by a building up of an additional stock of working capital inadequately compensated by additional saving, sufficient to permit all the unemployed factors of production to return gradually to work. The chapter is, therefore, an essay in the internal mechanics of the price-wage-employment structure during the course of a Cycle which represents a recovery in the volume of employment from a preceding slump which has reached an equilibrium between prices and costs of production, but is still characterised by unemployment.

(i.) THE STANDARD CASE

Let us begin by simplifying the problem so as to set out the essential mechanism (which, as we shall find, is substantially similar in the more generalised cases) in a manner which is free from non-essential complications. Our initial assumptions, which will be removed later on, are as follows:

Assumption Alpha. It is assumed that current savings, exclusive of additions to the Income Deposits, are equal to the amount of net new investment other than the addition to working capital required to provide for the additional volume of employment; so that the additional working capital corresponds exactly to the amount of entrepreneurs' profits *plus* any additions to Income Deposits.[1]

Assumption Beta. It is assumed that the banks create just enough additional money for the Industrial Circulation, after allowing for any fluctuations in the amount of the Financial Circulation, to allow the absorption of the unemployed factors of production into employment at a steady rate, so that the last unemployed factors will just have been brought into employment when one production-period has passed by. This amounts to the bank's supplying the entrepreneurs with whatever they require, over and above their profits, to pay wages on the gradually increasing scale which is assumed and to increase their Business-deposits A.

Assumption Gamma. It is assumed that the whole of the increased employment is directed to the production of consumption-goods, and that the stocks, if any, of liquid capital are constant.

---

[1] This implicitly assumes that entrepreneurs are, at the commencement of the period, making neither profits nor losses, but this assumption is not essential, and it is easy to adjust the argument to its absence.

Assumption Delta. It is assumed that there is no Income Inflation, so that the rates of efficiency-wages of the factors of production are unchanged throughout : *i.e.* that the money-costs of production are constant.

Assumption Epsilon. It is assumed that the duration of the productive process is the same for all commodities, and that the process is a steady process.

Assumption Zeta. It is assumed that wages are paid at the end of regular intervals, which we will call " weeks ", in respect of work done during each week; that the wages thus paid are only available for expenditure by the recipients in the following week; and that expenditure during any week is at a steady rate ; that is to say, the expenditure in any week is governed by the income of the previous week, the income earned in respect of work done during the current week not being received in time to affect expenditure during that week. It is assumed further that consumers carry forward in their income-deposits over the week-end an amount equal to their incomes just received in respect of the current week *plus* a constant proportion of their incomes in the previous week.

When money-incomes are unchanged or are changing at a constant rate, the above means that the income-deposits carried forward at the end of each week are a constant proportion of the week's income and that the velocity of circulation of the income deposits is constant. But when money-incomes are changing, the position is not so simple. For if k_1 stands, as before, for the inverse of the velocity of circulation of the income-deposits, w_1 and w_2 for the income of two successive weeks, and $m \cdot w_1 + w_2$ for the carry-forward at the end of the second week (in accordance with the above assumption), then the expenditure in the third week is $w_2 + m(w_1 - w_2)$ and the average level of income-deposits is $m \cdot w_1 + w_2 - \tfrac{1}{2}\{w_2 + m(w_1 - w_2)\}$, which is the balance at the middle of the week, i.e. $\tfrac{1}{2}\{w_2 + m(w_1 + w_2)\}$, so that $k_1 = \tfrac{1}{2}\dfrac{w_2 + m(w_1 + w_2)}{w_2 + m(w_1 - w_2)}$, which is only constant if wages are stable or are increasing at a steady (geometrical) rate.

Assumption Eta. It is assumed that, whatever mistakes may have been made in the past, all those concerned accurately forecast the subsequent course of the Credit Cycle.

Let the length of the production period (assumed uniform in length and steady in intensity in accordance with assumption Epsilon) be equal to $2r - 1$ of these units of time or " weeks ".

Then if a = the flow of earnings in terms of money per unit of time, and

t = the proportion of earnings spent on consumption, and also—in virtue of Assumption Alpha—the proportion of output emerging in a form available for consumption,

we have initially,

$a \cdot r$ = cost of production of working capital;[1] and

$t \cdot a$ = the flow of consumption.

Let p be the price-level of goods available for consumption.

Now let us suppose that the proportion of the factors of production out of work to those in work is x, and that a movement starts to increase employment up to capacity and therefore working capital in the proportion x. We will assume, in accordance with

[1] For $\dfrac{a}{2r-1} + \dfrac{2a}{2r-1} + \dfrac{3a}{2r-1} + \ldots + \dfrac{(2r-1)a}{2r-1} = a \cdot r$.

CH. 20 PURE THEORY OF THE CREDIT CYCLE

assumption Beta, that this is done not in one jump but by steady equal increments, so that the rate of in-put $\frac{a}{2r-1}$ into the machine of process per week is increased in the proportion x and is then maintained at the level $\frac{a}{2r-1}(1+x)$. Thus after $2r-1$ weeks the earnings will be increased to $a(1+x)$ and will be maintained thereafter at this steady level.

This means that in the first week earnings will be increased to $a\left(1+\frac{x}{2r-1}\right)$, in the second to $a\left(1+\frac{2x}{2r-1}\right)$, in the third to $a\left(1+\frac{3x}{2r-1}\right)$; until in the $2r-1$th week they have reached $a(1+x)$ and employment is at full capacity.

The increased earnings will not affect the price-level in the first time-interval, because we have assumed wages to be paid at the end of the week, so that the additional earnings do not come on to the market as buying power until the second week. During the second week, however, the buying power, which will come on to the market against the same amount of available real output as before, will be increased to $a\left(t+\frac{x(1-m)}{2r-1}\right)$, since $\frac{ax}{2r-1}$ is the increase of income and $\frac{axm}{2r-1}$ is the proportion of this added to the carry-forward and not spent, so as to satisfy Assumption Zeta.[1] The result is that the price-level will rise to $p\left(1+\frac{x(1-m)}{t(2r-1)}\right)$.

---

[1] If m is greater than one, *i.e.* if the carry-forward is more than a week's income, this assumption is not likely to be fulfilled except after a time-lag; for, in this case, when incomes are increasing, it is probable that the carry-forward will be raised in the same proportion only gradually, so that the velocity of circulation of the income-deposits will temporarily fall below its normal value.

Thus the consumers lose a proportion $\frac{x(1-m)}{t(2r-1)}$ of the purchasing power of their money incomes, and those entrepreneurs whose goods have emerged in available form during the time-interval in question, and so fetch price $p\left(1+\frac{x(1-m)}{t(2r-1)}\right)$ instead of p, have gained a profit of the same amount.

The volume of earnings in the second week is $a\left(1+\frac{2x}{(2r-1)}\right)$, and the new price-level in the third week will be, by the same reasoning as before, $p\left(1+\frac{x(2-m)}{t(2r-1)}\right)$. This process then continues until $2r-1$ weeks have passed, at the end of which time the volume of earnings will be $a(1+x)$, and the price-level during the $(2r-1)$th interval will be $p\left(1+\frac{x(2r-2-m)}{t(2r-1)}\right)$, which—if $2r-1$ represents a substantial number of weeks—is practically equal to $p\left(1+\frac{x}{t}\right)$. That is to say, if r is large,[1] both absolutely and relatively to m, the rise of prices is retarded very little by the consumers maintaining the ratio of their income-deposits to their money incomes. Such retardation of the rise of prices as occurs is due partly to the earners being paid one week late, and partly to their increasing the unspent income carried forward from one week to another so as to keep their income-deposits in the appropriate relation to their money-incomes.

The increase in the volume of income-deposits will have amounted by this time (*i.e.* carried over at the end of the $(2r-1)$th week) to $a \cdot x \left(1+\frac{2r-2}{2r-1} \cdot m\right)$. Meanwhile the whole body of consumers, including

[1] As to the probable magnitude of r, see Vol. ii., Chap. 28.

CH. 20 PURE THEORY OF THE CREDIT CYCLE 311

those responsible for the new volume of production, will have consumed exactly the same amount as before, namely, at the rate of $a \cdot t$ per week. For although rates of real wages will have been falling steadily throughout, so that the old producers, excluding those responsible for the new volume of production, will have had their consumption curtailed, the new producers will have increased their consumption by the same amount.[1] Thus these new producers will have increased their aggregate earnings by $a \cdot x \cdot r$, and their income-deposits by $a \cdot x \left(1 + \frac{2r-2}{2r-1}m\right)$; and the aggregate profit accruing to the entrepreneurs will have amounted to $a \cdot x \left\{ r - \left(1 + \frac{2r-2}{2r-1}\right)m \right\}$, since this represents the excess of the value of investment over the volume of saving. As we shall see below (p. 312 footnote), entrepreneurs will sacrifice a small part of their surplus in the 2rth week; so that the total surplus accruing to them in the end will be $a \cdot x\{r - (1 + m)\}$.

Working capital, output and employment have now all been raised to their maxima with such rise of prices as is compatible with our assumptions, in particular the assumption that the rates of money-wages are maintained at their previous levels.

This is the height of the boom and prices are at their maximum. If the percentage of unemployment amongst the factors of production requiring to be absorbed was originally 10 per cent and t is 90 per cent, prices will have risen by about 11 per cent. The second act of the drama now begins—namely, the slump.

In the 2rth time-interval from the beginning of the revival in employment, available output begins to emerge at the rate $a(t + x)$ instead of at the rate $a \cdot t$,

[1] The above argument excludes such contingencies as unemployed allowances, the effect of which is dealt with on p. 315 below.

and continues steadily thereafter at this increased rate. The price-level is, therefore, diminished in the proportion $\frac{x}{t}$ by which the available goods on the market are now increased. That is to say, since in the 2rth interval the expenditure is $a(t+x)$ and the available goods coming on to the market $\frac{a}{p}(t+x)$, the price-level abruptly falls to its initial value p.[1]

It will be noticed that the increase in the flow of available output just balances the fall in prices, so that income-deposits, at their increased figure of $k_1 \cdot a(1+x)$, are still in equilibrium with the new situation.

Under our present assumptions the slump is purely a price slump and carries with it no reaction in the volume of employment. The new position is one of equilibrium at the same price-level and the same wages-level as before the expansion of production, but with working capital, production and employment all increased in the proportion x.

(ii.) Eight Epilogues.

Before we abate the rigour of our assumptions, there are several points, most of them already made in previous chapters, which are worth repeating with special reference to the present case:

(1) The same result could have been brought about by keeping prices stable and progressively reducing money-wages in the same proportion as, in the above, prices have been supposed to rise; except that in this

---

[1] This is not strictly accurate. For the carry-forward at the end of the 2rth interval, namely, $a(1+x)(1+m)$, will be greater than at the end of the $(2r-1)$th interval, namely, $a(1+m)+a \cdot x(1+\frac{2r-2}{2r-1} \cdot m)$, so that this addition to the carry-forward will bring the fall of prices temporarily below p in the 2rth interval, so that they will not settle down at p until the $(2r+1)$th interval.

case the increment of wealth would accrue more to the new entrepreneurs entering into production and less to those with goods already in process when the increased production begins—with the result that this alternative cannot occur in competitive conditions.

(2) The same result could also have been brought about without any transference of wealth from consumers to entrepreneurs if the factors of production would accept a proportion of their money-wages in a deferred form, only to be exchanged for available output as and when new saving is available from other sources. For example, if the wage-interval is equal to the production-interval so that $r = 1$, or if the carry-forward is increased at every wage-interval by the appropriate amount, or if savings are sufficiently increased in some other way, there will be no rise in the price-level.

(3) The pre-cycle bank depositors will, if they sit tight throughout the credit cycle, suffer neither gain nor loss; their bank-deposits are worth the same amount at the end as at the beginning. The increment in working capital, most of which on the assumptions so far made belongs to the entrepreneurs, has accrued entirely at the expense of current incomes, which have diminished in purchasing power, and not at all at the expense of depositors.

(4) Whilst it is the producers who have to accept a smaller real income per unit of productive effort in the interests of raising the fund of working capital so as to enable the whole population to be fully employed, almost the whole of the resulting increment of wealth accrues, as a pure windfall, to the entrepreneurs.

If, however, we were to suppose that the Society under observation is a completely socialised State in which the State fixes wages, determines the volume of saving and is the sole entrepreneur, then no question of inequity would arise as a concomitant of the process of increasing the fund of working capital. For in such a case the temporary reduction of the level of real wages, which is an inevitable accompaniment of the full employment of the factors of production (as it would be of saving for any other purpose), means an increment of wealth which accrues to the community as a whole.

(5) Furthermore the increment of wealth accruing to entrepreneurs as a class will accrue mainly to those entrepreneurs who already have goods in process at the moment when employment begins to increase, and not at all to those who set on foot the increased volume of production, since these will obtain only normal prices for their output when it becomes available; in other words the forward price for a date ahead corresponding to the length of process will remain normal throughout, showing a backwardation as compared with the spot price, *i.e.* the latter will have risen to a premium over the forward price.

(6) The price p' of working capital, which is much the same as the index number of raw materials at wholesale, will, on the assumption of perfect forecasting, rise at once to a greater extent than p, which is the price-level of available output, *i.e.* of liquid consumption goods. For whilst the value of working capital, in the shape of goods which have been started into the productive process after the beginning of the credit cycle, will not rise, inasmuch as, when they are finished, they will only sell for the old price; nevertheless the value of working capital, in the shape of goods which, although still non-available, were already partly finished when the cycle began, will reflect the anticipated higher price for available output at the date when their process will be completed—that is to say p', the price-level of raw materials and half-finished goods, will on the average, assuming correct forecasting, rise much more sharply than p, namely to a level intermediate between p and $p(1 + \frac{x}{t})$.

CH. 20 PURE THEORY OF THE CREDIT CYCLE 315

(7) The argument assumes that factors of production receive larger money incomes, and consume correspondingly more, when they are employed than when they are unemployed, so that an increase in the volume of employment by involving larger incomes for the units previously unemployed means, during a period of time equal to the length of process, smaller real incomes for the units already employed. In so far as this is not the case (*e.g.* as the result of unemployed benefit) the increment of working capital required may be partly made good from the source out of which the incomes of the unemployed were previously paid.[1] This does not affect the character of the argument, but means that the amount of the necessary price rise is correspondingly diminished. If, for example, unemployed pay is half of employed pay, the above equations will still hold good with $\frac{x}{2}$ substituted throughout for x. And if the Society under consideration is one in which the factors of production receive exactly the same rate of wages whether they are employed or unemployed ("Work or Maintenance"), then, obviously, there will be no rise of price at all. On the other hand, prices will in these cases slump below the initial level at the end of the production-period, unless the funds, formerly used to pay the dole and subsequently used to replenish working capital, are then employed to augment consumption or investment in some other direction.

(8) There is one paradoxical fact of outstanding importance—already mentioned, but worth repeating. The addition to the accumulated wealth of the community over any given period of time depends on the decisions which are taken, mainly by entrepreneurs

---

[1] If payments to the unemployed are charged against industry, then the effect of increased employment is to decrease efficiency-wages, assuming that wages per factor employed are unchanged. Alternatively we may regard the expenditure of the unemployed as negative saving.

and financiers, during that period as to the amount of output in the shape of fixed or working capital, and not on the decisions of the body of individual citizens as to what part of their money-incomes they will save. When the cost of production of the new investment differs from the amount which individuals have saved out of their money incomes, then certain price changes *must* result. When it is a case of inflation, as in the example just considered, the wealth of the community increases, though no one is deliberately saving more—the increased wealth coming out of the diminished consumption of individuals due to the rise of prices. When, on the other hand, a deflation is in process, individuals may appear to "save", and indeed are able to do so to their own complete satisfaction inasmuch as they are in fact individually richer by the amount of their savings, yet in spite of this there will be no net addition whatever to the national wealth—the increased wealth of the "savers" being balanced by an equal loss of wealth by a section of entrepreneurs, and the consumption forgone by the "savers" being balanced by an equal increment of consumption by consumers generally.

Thus whether the earning and consuming public intend as individuals to be prudent or imprudent will not in fact make the slightest difference one way or the other to the amount of their aggregate consumption; for so far as current consumption is concerned, the intentions of individuals to reduce or to maintain consumption will always be defeated, in respect of any effect on the aggregate of current consumption as a whole, by an appropriate movement of prices upwards or downwards. Thus the net effect of the prudence or imprudence of individual members of the public will be seen, not in the aggregate consumption of the public, but in the price-level and in who owns the increased non-available wealth of the community. In short, "prudence" by the public will in such circumstances be, for them, cheap and useful; for it will, without diminishing their aggregate consumption, entitle them to wealth which would otherwise accrue to the entrepreneurs.

(iii.) THE GENERALISED CASE

We must now endeavour to remove some of the limitations by assuming which we have been simplifying our argument.

(1) *Assumption Alpha.*

If current savings are greater than is here assumed, the rise of prices is correspondingly less—since the increment of buying for consumption will be less than the amount of $\frac{ax}{2r-1}$ per week which is assumed above; and correspondingly, if current savings are less. But this does not alter the character of the argument; it merely means that we must substitute for $\frac{ax}{2r-1}$ in our calculations a term which is either less or greater than this.

Similarly, if net new investment, apart from the addition to working capital, is diminished or increased without any corresponding change in savings, the effects on prices, etc., as given above, will be either mitigated or aggravated, without being changed in character. In so far, for example, as the growth of working capital can be offset by a diminution of the Foreign Balance, the mitigating effects come under this head.

In short, the phenomena of the Credit Cycle are more or less violent than in the Standard Case, according as the actual disequilibrium between Savings and Investment exceeds or falls short of Assumption Alpha.

The main difference, however, in the development

318   A TREATISE ON MONEY   BK. IV

of the Cycle, which results from the non-fulfilment of Assumption Alpha, is that the Cycle does not last for just one, and only one, production period. It becomes much more complicated, and one can only describe its exact course if one first makes an assumption as to its exact character.

To take a particular case of the non-fulfilment of Assumption Alpha let us assume that the entrepreneurs increase their expenditure on personal consumption by the whole amount of their windfall profits in the previous "week", in which case their "savings" as defined above are negative. As before, the new purchasing power will effectively reach the consumers one week late, so that the situations in the first and second weeks are as before; but in each later successive week there will come on the market as purchasing power for finished goods not only the increased expenditure of the newly employed but also the equivalent of the windfall of the entrepreneurs in the previous week.[1] Thus in the third week prices will rise to

$$p\left(1 + \frac{x(2-m)}{t(2r-1)} + \frac{x(1-m)}{t(2r-1)}\right), \text{ i.e. to } p\left(1 + \frac{x(3-2m)}{t(2r-1)}\right),$$

in the fourth week to $p\left(1 + \frac{x(3-m)}{t(2r-1)} + \frac{x(3-2m)}{t(2r-1)}\right)$, i.e. to $p\left(1 + \frac{x(6-3m)}{t(2r-1)}\right)$, and so on, until (as is apparent by easy algebra[2]) in the qth week prices are

$$p\left(1 + \frac{(q-1)(q-2m)}{2} \frac{x}{t(2r-1)}\right)$$

[1] It is assumed that the recipients do not regard their successive windfalls as part of their regular income, and therefore do not increase the carry-forward of their income-deposits proportionately to them.

[2] For if prices in the qth interval are $p\left(1 + s_q \frac{x}{t(2r-1)}\right)$, we have $s_q - s_{q-1} = q - 1 - m$. Therefore $s_q = \overset{q}{\underset{2}{\Sigma}}(q-1-m) = \frac{q-1}{2}\{(1-m) + (q-1-m)\} = \frac{(q-1)(q-2m)}{2}$.

instead of $p\left(1 + \dfrac{(q-1-m)x}{t(2r-1)}\right)$ as in the Standard Case; and finally in the $(2r-1)$th week

$$p\left\{1 + (r-1)(2r-1-2m)\dfrac{x}{t(2r-1)}\right\}.$$

If, intermediately, we assume that the old entrepreneurs in receipt of windfalls retain part of their windfalls but not all, then the rise of prices lies between the results of the two formulae compared above. Thus the increase of bank-credit and consequently of retail prices in the successive time-intervals must be greater than in the Standard Case—how much greater depending on how much of the windfalls is consumed by those receiving them; but the argument is not otherwise affected. The enforced diminution in the consumption of existing consumers must now be sufficient to equal the new consumption of the profiteers as well as the consumption of the new producers, and the fall in the real value of money-incomes must be proportionately greater. For this reason the absorption into production of 10 per cent unemployment is capable of requiring a much greater increase in the price-level than the 11 per cent which was the maximum required in the Standard Case. For example, if x is 10 per cent, t is 90 per cent, m is 1 and $2r$ is 50, prices rise in the Standard Case from 100 to 110·6, and in the case where entrepreneurs consume their windfall, from 100 to 350. The result is the same if consumers try to do what it is impossible for them to accomplish as a body, namely, to maintain their former rate of consumption per unit of output by drawing on their savings.

On the other hand, there is a way—apart from the increase of the Income Deposits—in which the phenomena of the Credit Cycle may stimulate increased saving which would not have occurred spontaneously. Since the value of money is falling during the upward phase of the cycle but will afterwards rise again to its previous level, any individual by postponing the date of his consumption and transferring the equivalent to his savings-deposits can gain not only the normal rate of money interest but, in addition, the equivalent of the prospective increase in the value of money calculated as a rate per cent per annum. Thus there may be a substantial motive in operation influencing individuals to modify the time-distribution of their consumption. In the earlier stages of the price rise this stimulus will be small, both because prices will not have risen much and because the date of the prospective fall of prices will still be remote. But in the later stages, when the prospective fall is both large in amount and near in time, it will become substantial. Thus, given correct forecasting, this factor may do something to smooth away the hump at the top of the price curve.

(2) *Assumption Beta.*

In the same sort of way, various irregularities are introduced, which it would not be difficult to describe in any particular case, but which do not lend themselves to a generalised description, if the banking system facilitate the increase of employment and aggregate earnings, at a faster or a slower rate than that which has been assumed.

(3) *Assumption Gamma.*

We assumed that all available income is purchased and consumed as it is produced, the volume of liquid consumption capital (if any) remaining constant; that is to say, that there can be no hoarding of ready retail goods and that there are no initial stocks of them. This assumption would be unreservedly valid if, and in so far as, available output is perishable and therefore incapable of being hoarded. But in so far as available output is not perishable, obviously the prospect of a rising price-level will tend to evoke hoarding —unless the rate of cost of hoarding is greater than the rate at which the price-level is expected to rise —and the prospect of the restoration of the price-level to its previous lower figure will cause stocks to be cleared off. The removal of the no-hoarding assumption is therefore important.

If we assume that the course of the price-level is correctly foreseen, a certain proportion of the new bank-credit will be employed not to replenish working capital but to augment liquid hoards, with the result that the initial rise in the price-level will be greater than would otherwise be the case, because less liquid goods will be available for consumption. If hoarding cost nothing, the price-level would rise to its maximum in the first time-interval (instead of, as in the Standard Case, in the $(2r-1)$th time-interval), and this maximum will be the price which can be maintained without change throughout the $2r-1$ time-intervals. This price will be half-way between the initial price-level and the maximum price-level on our old no-hoarding hypothesis, that is to say approximately $p\left(1+\dfrac{x}{2t}\right)$.[1] In this case the volume of hoarding will continue to increase up to the rth time-interval and will diminish thereafter until the hoards have been completely absorbed in the $(2r-1)$th interval, after which, as before, the price-level falls back again to p.

It will be seen that the possibility of hoarding (if done at no cost) halves the amplitude of the price fluctuation, and is in the general interest since it brings about a better distribution of consumption through time. For hoarding to be practicable along with the increase of employment at the rate we have stipulated,

[1] For if there were to be a greater rise than this it would only be possible to sell at a loss in subsequent time-intervals some of the stocks taken off the market in the first time-interval.

the supply of money will have to be increased in a slightly greater degree in the earlier weeks and in a slightly less degree in the later weeks, since the amount of profits requiring to be financed will be increased in the early stages and decreased later on.

The above is what would occur if the course of the credit cycle is correctly foreseen. In practice, however, it may be that the initial price rise, so far from stimulating hoarding, will bring out into the market additional supplies, if this be possible, from such hoards or normal reserves as may already exist. The price rise may only provoke hoarding when it has lasted for some time and has thus created mistaken expectations about the prolonged continuance of rising prices. In this case the rise of prices will be less at first than in our Standard Case but subsequently it will be greater, and, since through their miscalculation the hoarders will still have stocks on hand at the $2r$th interval when the additional supplies come on the market, the collapse will bring prices in the first instance *below* the normal level p.

We must next take account of the fact that hoarding normally costs something. If this cost is greater than the rate at which prices would rise in the absence of hoarding, then no hoarding will take place. That is to say, there will be no hoarding if the cost of hoarding per time-interval is greater than $\dfrac{px}{t(2r-1)}$. If, on the other hand, the cost of hoarding per time-interval is less than $\dfrac{px}{t(2r-1)}$, hoarding will take place. In this case prices will be higher in the earlier time-intervals after hoarding begins and lower in the later ones than in the Standard Case. As before, however, the maximum price-level will be reached immediately before the $2r$th interval and will slump back to p in the $2r$th interval.

(4) *Assumption Delta.*

We have assumed in the Standard Case that the rates of remuneration of the factors of production remain the same in terms of money throughout the cycle, *i.e.* that the Commodity Inflation is not accompanied by an Income Inflation. If this assumption is not fulfilled, there will be a further increase in the consumption price-level, superimposed on the rise due to the Commodity Inflation, to the precise extent and for the precise period that Income Inflation is present.

(5) *Assumption Epsilon.*

Let us next dispense with the assumption that the length of process is the same for all commodities. In this case the price-level will be composed of commodities of which some have not yet reached their maximum price and some have already passed it. The curve of the composite price-level will then take on the familiar shape

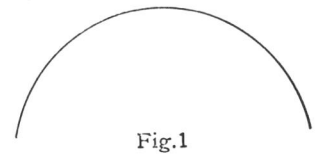

Fig.1

instead of a straight line suddenly declining as in the Standard Case, where there is no hoarding:

Fig.2

or a curve rising more rapidly at first, and then suddenly declining where there is hoarding:

Fig.3

For, as more and more commodities reach their peak and decline, the rate of increase of the composite price-level will be, in the case of Fig. 1, slower and slower, until a point comes when the commodities of which the price has declined outweigh those of which the price is still rising.

There is also a further qualification to our previous conclusions, if we relax our assumption as to uniform length of process but not our assumption as to perfect forecasting. For if the rate of input of a commodity having a short production-period is increased in the same proportion as that of everything else, its price will fall below the normal at the end of its production-period, because the purchasing power available for it will not yet have increased in as large a proportion as its output. It follows that the rate of input of commodities having a relatively short production-period should be increased somewhat more slowly than that of the others. On the other hand, as a partially balancing factor to the above, there will be some diversion of consumption from articles of long production-period to articles of short production-period, to take advantage of the lower price of the latter.

(6) *Assumption Zeta.*

Any departure from this assumption has the same effect as a variation of the rate of saving already considered with reference to Assumption Alpha.

(7) *Assumption Eta.*

In practice Credit Cycles have a strong inherent tendency to be " overdone " as compared with the Standard Case.

So far we have presumed accurate forecasting and have only made a few passing allusions to the results of imperfect forecasting. But in fact forecasting is certain to be imperfect, and likely, moreover, in the present state of ignorance, to have a bias in one direction. For, with the existing mentality of entrepreneurs, to-day's spot price for finished goods, which is certain, has far more influence in determining entrepreneurs' decisions as to the rate of new input into the machine of process than the prospective price at the end of the production-time, which is to them quite uncertain ; whereas it is wholly the latter price and not at all the former which ought to influence them. The result is that, when spot prices are rising, especially if they have been rising steadily for some six months, the rate of input is unduly accelerated, and if they have been falling it is unduly retarded—with obvious subsequent consequences.

Moreover, where there are a number of entrepreneurs making independent decisions, which they take pains to conceal from one another, involving an increased rate of input, it is quite impossible for any of them to foresee with accuracy the increased rate of output, and consequently the reaction on prices by the time that one production-period has passed by.

Evidently the possible ramifications and extensions of the foregoing argument are so numerous that one could continue for many more pages amplifying, qualifying and generalising it. Perhaps, however, it has been carried far enough to enable a reader, who has entered into the general system of thought here exemplified, to apply it for himself to any further interesting cases which may occur to him.

CHAPTER 21

CHANGES DUE TO INTERNATIONAL DISEQUILIBRIUM

IT is outside the scope of this book to deal thoroughly with the Theory of International Values. But there are certain brief *prolegomena* to such a theory, which are necessarily in place in a treatise on Money.

(i.) *Relative Price-levels and Relative Interest-rates as Causes of Monetary Disequilibrium*

We have seen that equilibrium in an international currency system requires that for each country its rate of foreign lending should be equal to its foreign balance. Now this involves *two* sets of conditions. For the rate of foreign lending depends on relative interest-rates at home and abroad ; whilst the foreign balance depends on relative price-levels at home and abroad.

There is, however, a radical difference between a disequilibrium which is set up by the relative price-levels falling out of gear from a disequilibrium which is set up by the relative interest-rates falling out of gear. In the first case, the disequilibrium can be cured by a change in price-levels (or, rather, of income-levels) without any permanent change in interest-rates, though a temporary change in interest-rates will be necessary as a means of bringing about the change in income-levels. In the second case, on the other hand, the restoration of equilibrium may require not only a change in interest-rates, but also a lasting change in income-levels (and probably in price-levels). That is to say, a country's price-level and income-level are affected not only by changes in the price-level abroad, *but also by changes in the interest-rate, due to a change in the demand for investment abroad relatively to the demand at home.*

(i.) Let us begin with the first and simpler case, where the disturbance of equilibrium comes about solely through a change, let us say a fall, in the price-level abroad. This will result in a falling off in the foreign balance B without a corresponding change in the volume of foreign lending L, with the consequence that L will exceed B and gold flows out of the country. Temporarily bank-rate must be raised; but when the process, which this sets up, towards a fall, first of prices and then of money-incomes, has been completed, the bank-rate can be safely restored to its previous level. For the conditions of equilibrium will be satisfied by a fall in Π, the price-level of output as a whole, and also in S_1, L, I_1, and B, below what they were measured in terms of money before prices fell abroad (though they will be unchanged in terms of purchasing power), corresponding to the fall in the foreign price-level. Apart from money-values, the new equilibrium once established will differ in no significant respect from the old—the character of production will be unchanged.[1]

(ii.) Next let us suppose that the disturbance of equilibrium is due to a rise in the rate of interest abroad, whereas S and I_1 at home remain the same functions of the rate of interest as before. This will result in an increase of L, with the consequence that L will exceed B and gold flows out of the country. As in the previous case, bank-rate must be raised, which

---

[1] This involves certain tacit assumptions, such as that the money-earnings of the different factors of production are all changed in the same proportion.

retards both home investment I_1 and foreign lending L, so that S exceeds I and prices Π fall. The fall of Π causes losses to entrepreneurs at the old cost of production, so that they tend to reduce the rates of money-earnings which they offer to the factors of production and eventually the first term of the Fundamental Equation falls. Meanwhile the fall of Π, occasioned initially by the fall of the second term and subsequently by the fall of the first term of the Fundamental Equation, will have served to increase B, whilst the rise of bank-rate will have abated L. The process continues until once more L = B, when gold ceases to flow out of the country. At the new position of equilibrium L is a greater proportion of S than before and S_1 is a less proportion. What will have happened to Π ?

B will have had to increase, which means that exports must have increased or imports diminished or both ; so that the necessary increase of B can only come about as a result of a fall in the price of foreign-trade goods produced at home, leading to a diversion of production, and a reduction in I_1. Now at one stage of the process outlined above all three of these things will have happened. For the outflow of gold will have *pro tanto* raised the prices of foreign-produced goods and reduced the prices of home-produced goods, whilst the rise in the rate of interest will have diminished I_1. Thus at the new point of equilibrium, the prices of all home-produced goods will have fallen relatively to the prices of all foreign-produced goods. The *amount* of this relative fall will depend—as we shall see below (p. 333)—on the change in the terms of trade resulting from the physical characteristics of the productive forces at home and abroad.

As regards Π itself some of its constituents will have fallen and some will have risen. If all the articles consumed within the country enter into international trade without hindrance, then Π cannot change relatively to a similar price-level abroad. Since, however, this condition is never fulfilled in practice and, besides, most countries predominantly consume their own output, there will, as a rule, be an absolute fall in Π on balance. This is the essence of the argument. But we must now elaborate it further, for reasons which will appear.

(ii.) *The Relationships between Foreign Lending and Movements of Gold*

The foregoing argument has implicitly assumed that B is a function of relative price-levels at home and abroad, and that it is not *directly* a function of L. That is to say, the mere fact of L's increasing—so we have assumed—does not influence the foreign situation, whether in respect of foreign price-levels, or in respect of the volume of the foreign demand for our country's goods at a given price-level, in such a way as to increase B to the same extent that L has been increased, *without* any appreciable disturbance of the level of prices or of incomes at home. On the contrary, we have assumed that, for the most part, approximate equality between L and B is preserved, not by an increase of L directly stimulating an increase of B, but because an excess of L over B brings about either the threat or the fact of a movement of gold, which induces the Banking Authorities of the countries concerned so to alter their terms of lending as temporarily to reduce the net amount of L and ultimately to increase B (by when the temporary reduction of L will be no longer necessary) through the medium of a disturbance of the existing investment equilibrium in both countries leading to appropriate changes in relative prices at home and abroad.

Now, in so far as the above reasoning depends on actual movements of gold, it is in accordance with the traditional Ricardian doctrine, extended so as to cover international capital transactions of which Ricardo himself took little account, as it is expounded in relation to the facts of to-day by, for example, Professor Taussig.[1] But it is not quite in accordance with another traditional doctrine which was widely held in Great Britain, mainly on empirical grounds, during the nineteenth century, and is still held to-day. According to this view foreign lending stimulates the foreign balance directly and almost automatically, and the actual movement of gold plays quite a minor part. This conclusion was, I think, based much more on British experience during the nineteenth century than on *à priori* reasoning. But recently—especially in connection with the German Transfer Problem—it has been supported by argument also, notably by Professor Ohlin.

Professor Taussig has endeavoured, in his *International Trade*, to put the question to the inductive test by examining a number of nineteenth- and early twentieth-century examples drawn from the countries which have at various dates suffered an important ebb and flow in the value of L. He finds, naturally enough—indeed inevitably—that B and L tend to move together. But when he comes to the question how far monetary movements have been necessary to make B obey the direction of L, the result is more inconclusive. Sometimes the facts seem to support the Ricardian view, and sometimes it is difficult to detect monetary changes on a scale sufficient to verify the essentials of the theory. Moreover, the inflow of gold may sometimes follow, instead of preceding, a rise of prices.

In a controversy between Professor Ohlin and myself in the pages of the *Economic Journal* (1929), with special reference to the German Transfer Problem, I was not able to make clear the theoretical basis underlying my view, because the analysis of the pre-

[1] Cf. his *International Trade* (1927) *passim*.

ceding chapters had not then been published. But with the aid of this analysis I can, I hope, resolve the difficulty, and show in what circumstances the facts will appear to conform to Professor Ohlin's thesis and in what circumstances to the Ricardo-Taussig thesis.

There are two contingencies which we must first of all put on one side as not being relevant to the essence of the argument. There is the case where foreign lending is bound up with a contract or understanding that the proceeds shall be employed in making purchases at home, although, failing such an arrangement, they would in ordinary course have been made abroad;—for such arrangements, apart from their being, in fact, negligible in aggregate quantity, are equivalent to subsidising the cost of the goods supplied, which is tantamount to reducing their price, at the expense of the rate of interest which might have been charged.

Secondly, there is the case where Gold Exchange Management is present in some shape or form, so that movements of foreign liquid assets take the place of movements of actual gold. We shall regard such changes as equivalent to movements of gold for the purposes of this discussion.

Let us call the value of a country's market-rate of interest which would obviate gold movements (*i.e.* which is such that $G = 0$) its *international-rate*. (The international-rates of different members of the same currency system are, of course, not independent of one another.)

Let us begin with the case where there are only two countries, A and B, in question, thus avoiding the complications of roundabout trade.

Let us assume that we start from a position of equilibrium with $G = 0$ and $I = S$ in both countries. This means that in each country :

Its Market-rate = its International-rate
= its Natural-rate.

(The reader should remember that this does not mean, unless there is complete mobility of international lending, that the rate of interest is *the same* in both countries. But if there is equality between the market-rate and the international-rate in one of the countries, then—when there are only two countries in question—there must necessarily be equality between the market-rate and the international-rate in the other country also.)

Let us then suppose that the attractions of investment increase in country A but not in country B. Two questions now arise for discussion—the characteristics of the new position of equilibrium when it has been reached, and the nature of the transition from the old position of equilibrium to the new. (It will simplify the exposition, without altering the essence of the argument, if we assume that the rise which takes place in the market-rate of interest does not materially affect the rate of saving in either country.)

1. *First, the Characteristics of the New Position of Equilibrium.*—In each country the market-rate, the international-rate, and the natural-rate will have returned to equality with one another, but at a somewhat higher level than before, corresponding to the increased marginal attractiveness of investment in the two countries taken together—and a level, moreover, which is higher in B and lower in A than if there was no mobility of international lending; and B and L will be again equal, but with higher values than before. In other words, there will be a displacement of investment, which was previously taking place in B, in favour of increased investment in country A. What will be the effect of this displacement on the levels of money-earnings in the two countries?

There will have to be a change-over on the part of the factors of production, which were previously producing new investments in country B, to produce something else which is calculated to facilitate new investment in country A. This may come about by the factors in B producing goods previously imported from A, thus releasing factors in A to produce for investment in A, or by factors in B producing goods for export to A which were previously produced in A, thus releasing factors in A to produce for investment in A, or by factors in B producing goods for export to A, which can be directly utilised for the purpose of the additional new investment which is now taking place in A.

If this change-over in the character of production can be effected without any loss of efficiency, *e.g.* if country B can produce goods, previously produced in A, to sell in B or in A, as the case may be, at the same price as before, without any reduction in the money-earnings of the factors of production as compared with what they were getting in their previous employment or any loss to the entrepreneurs, then there is no reason why rates of money-earnings in the two countries should be any different in the new position of equilibrium from what they were in the old. In so far as country B is specially efficient in the direct production of materials for the new investment-goods required for use in A, there may well be not only no loss of efficiency as compared with producing these goods in A, but actually a gain of efficiency ; and in this case, so far from money-earnings in B falling relatively to those in A, they might, in conceivable circumstances, actually rise as a result of the increased attractiveness of kinds of investment in A, which can only be efficiently supplied by factors of production in B. If, on the other hand, the new investment-goods in A have to be produced by factors of production in A, which factors are made available by being released from producing goods hitherto exported to B or henceforward imported from B, then the presumption is the other way round ; for it is unlikely that A would have previously exported the goods in question to B or refrained from importing them unless there was some gain in doing so. Thus, generally speaking, money-rates of earnings in B will have to fall relatively to money-rates of earnings in A in the new position of equilibrium as compared with the old.[1]

This is usually expressed by saying that there will be a change in the "terms of trade" between the countries, adverse to country B. The change in the terms of trade is measured by the proportionate change in the price of goods exported by B relatively to the proportionate change in the price of goods imported. This ratio will not be equal to the ratio of the proportionate change in average rates of actual earnings in B to that in A, except in so far as there is internal mobility of the factors of production within a country, so that their rates of remuneration in domestic-trade industries are the same as in international-trade industries. Perhaps we should add that, of course, the changes in real earnings will not be so great as the changes in money-earnings, and also that the less the importance of foreign trade in a country's economy the less will be the change in real earnings.

Now the amount of the alteration in the terms of trade between A and B, due to the increased attractiveness of investment in A, is independent of the character of the transition and of the means by which it is brought about. It depends on non-monetary factors —on physical facts and capacities, and on the elasticities of demand in each of the two countries for

[1] Professor Taussig has, in his *International Trade*, collected a good deal of evidence to show that fact bears out this theory. That is to say, when foreign investment is increasing, the terms of trade turn against the lending country and in favour of the borrowing, wages falling in the former and rising in the latter—in his terminology the gross and net barter terms of trade tend to move in the same direction. Professor Taussig is, I think, a little too ready to assume that exports and imports adjust themselves to the other factors in the situation, rather than—in part—the other way round. But his treatment of the influence of international investment on the price-levels in different countries is far in advance of any other discussion of the subject.

goods which the other can produce with physical efficiency.

This alteration in the terms of trade may sometimes be very small, as, for example, when Great Britain made loans for railway developments abroad during the nineteenth century, and was herself the only efficient producer of much of the materials required for these new investments. Nor does it follow that the new situation is necessarily disadvantageous to country B on balance. For, as a set-off against the deterioration in the terms of trade, B has three possible sources of gain, namely, the higher rate of interest on part of her savings, a subsequent reversal of the change in the terms of trade when the interest on the new loans is being remitted or when the new loans are ultimately paid off, and a possible future cheapening as a result of the new investment of the cost of goods which she is in the habit of purchasing from A.

But in some circumstances, on the other hand, the change in the terms of trade adversely to B may be substantial; and this is particularly likely if A puts a high tariff on B's goods, and if B is not capable of supplying directly the materials required by the new investment in A.

The change in the terms of trade is also likely to be large in the short period, when there is a *sudden* change in the relative attractions of lending at home and abroad, because the factors of production require time if they are to effect a change-over in the character of their activities without serious loss of efficiency. It is for this reason that the so-called "flight" from a currency can be so disastrous—that is to say, the situation which arises when, for some reason, there is an overpowering motive to a country's nationals to lend their resources abroad. There were some remarkable examples in the post-War period of the extraordinary effect on the terms of trade over the short period, of a sudden distrust, leading to a sudden change in the relative attractions of lending at home and abroad.

The neglect to allow for the effect of changes in the terms of trade is, perhaps, the most unsatisfactory characteristic of Prof. Cassel's *Purchasing Power Parity Theory of the Foreign Exchanges*. For this not only upsets the validity of his conclusions over the long period, but renders them even more deceptive over the short period, whenever the short period is characterised by a sharp change in the attractions of foreign lending.

2. *Second, the Characteristics of the Transition.*— We have seen that the international-rate cannot return to equality with the natural-rate in *both* countries until an appropriate change has taken place in the *relative* rates of money-earnings in the two countries. But this relative change could come about either by one country bearing the whole brunt of change by modifying its own absolute rate, leaving the absolute rate of the other country unchanged, or by the two sharing the burden of change.

If each of the countries is determined to keep a quantity of gold reserves, which bears a constant proportion to the level of its money-income, the share of change to be borne by each is predetermined, the major part of the change being borne by the smaller of the two countries. But if the countries are prepared to allow some variation in this proportion (and the changes which actually occur as the result of increased foreign investment would generally involve only a *small* change in the proportion of gold reserves to total income, even if no gold at all moves from one country to the other), then the proportionate sharing between the two countries of the burden of the change in absolute rates of earnings is indeterminate, and depends on the course of events and on the policies of the two central banks during the period of transition.

To illustrate this let us take the extreme cases.

Let us suppose that country A has no objection to receiving more gold, and fixes its market-rate at an equality with its natural-rate regardless of the policy of country B, but that country B is reluctant to lose gold and keeps its market-rate at an equality with its international-rate (which latter largely depends, of course, on the market-rate fixed by country A). In this case country A suffers no period of inequality between its market-rate, its natural-rate, and its international-rate, and no alteration in its stock of gold, and there is, therefore, no need for any alteration in its rate of earnings. Thus the whole brunt of the change is thrown on the rate of earnings in country B, which will be forced, in order to retain its gold, to keep its market-rate above its natural-rate until the process of deflation thereby set up has brought its rate of earnings down to the necessary extent.

If, on the other hand, country B is prepared to lose any amount of gold rather than raise its market-rate above its natural-rate, then it is country A which will have to bear the brunt of the change by undergoing an inflation until its rate of money-earnings has been raised to the necessary extent relatively to the rate in country B, which will have remained constant throughout.

The amount of the flow of gold between the countries, if any, is, in a sense, quite non-essential to the process. For the same results can be brought about by the potentiality of a flow of gold as by the actuality. The amount of absolute change in rates of earnings in A and B depends on the policies of the central banks of the two countries as to the relationships which they respectively maintain between their natural-rate and their market-rate. The one whose policy is most independent of the policy of the other, and keeps its market-rate nearest to its natural-rate throughout the transition, will suffer least absolute change in its rate of earnings.

Now, since there is generally much more reluctance to lose gold than to receive it, this means that the lending country will often have to bear the brunt of the change. Only if the lending country is willing and able to take up an independent attitude towards the risk of losing gold can it throw the brunt of the change on the borrowing country.

When, however, it is a case of an old country lending to a new country, the necessary conditions may exist which will tend to ease the difficulties of the transition for the lending country. For the foreign loan may be the consequence (and the symptom) of a tendency of the natural-rate of interest in the borrowing country to rise relatively to that market-rate, which is dictated by conditions in the outside world; and in this case the loan may be preceded and accompanied by a rise in the rate of earnings in the borrowing country, which, in the absence of a loan, would set up a state of disequilibrium with the outside world. In short, the foreign loan allows an increase of home investment relatively to home saving in the borrowing country *without* this development being nipped in the bud, as it would be otherwise, by rising prices, a loss of gold, and a consequent increase in market-rate leading to a reaction in the volume of home investment. But the reader must please note that all this only occurs if for some other reason there is already in existence a tendency for the natural-rate of interest in the borrowing country to rise relatively to the rate abroad. Thus it makes a difference whether the loan is required to preserve the existing equilibrium in face of a spontaneously rising tide of new home investment or whether it involves an induced transition to a new equilibrium.

If, on the other hand, the loan is due to a rise in the market-rate of interest in the borrowing country, without there being a corresponding tendency in the natural-rate, then we must expect a deflationary effect on the lending country unless it can afford to allow substantial gold-movements to ensue. Such a situation may be due to deliberate policy on the part of the banking authority of the borrowing country, because they wish to increase their stock of gold. Or they may have been forced into it for one reason or another as a result of the character of their banking system, *e.g.* the loan may be due to a rising market-rate of interest in the borrowing country due, not to a rising natural-rate, but to meet the increasing requirements of the financial circulation. For example, the change in the value of L between the United States and the rest of the world in 1928-29 was probably due more to financial factors in the United States, which were increasing the requirements of the financial circulation, than to investment factors; whereas, if dear money in the United States had been due to a rising natural-rate of interest in that country relatively to other countries, the dear money policy need not have occasioned any serious embarrassment to the rest of the world or have depressed world-prices for commodities, since there would have been a concurrent tendency for it to be accompanied by a foreign balance increasingly unfavourable to America.

Thus in the case where the responsibility lies with financial, rather than with investment, factors in the borrowing country, the gold movements will tend to continue or—to avoid this—the market-rate of interest will have to be raised in the rest of the world to a level in excess of the natural-rate, with the result of causing the rate of investment to fall below that of saving everywhere and so establishing a régime of Profit Deflation. This serves to illustrate the way in which Profit Deflations (and similarly Inflations) tend to spread sympathetically from one member of an international system to another; and this may occur without any material movement of gold, if the other members are not able or willing to let their stocks of gold fall to any great extent, the effort to keep their gold necessarily involving them in a sympathetic deflation. It will also occur, in spite of a material movement of gold, if the country which initiates the movement is able to absorb large quantities of gold without being compelled to bring its market-rate down to equilibrium with its natural-rate.[1]

I have said enough to indicate the nature of the process and of the argument. It is evident that many illustrations could be given. For example, a lending country, which is not willing to lose much gold and whose rate of earnings is not sensitive to deflationary forces, may suffer a long and painful transition between one position of equilibrium and another. But it would lead me too far into the intricacies of the theory of international trade, which would fill a book in itself, if I were to pursue the matter further. I must leave the reader to carry on the line of thought for himself, if it interests him.

Perhaps, however, I may be allowed, in parenthesis, to apply the above to my discussion with Professor Ohlin about the German Transfer Problem in the *Economic Journal* (1929). The payment of Reparations by Germany operates in the year in which it takes place, much in the same way as a compulsory process of foreign investment of equal amount, except that Germany will not enjoy the cumulative off-sets in subsequent years which foreign investment affords, and the investment does not correspond to a spontaneous change abroad, such as would lead directly to a demand for Germany's exports. Now I conceive Professor Ohlin's standpoint to have been, that, given an appropriate credit policy in the receiving countries,

[1] As we shall see in Vol. ii. Chap. 30, Great Britain in the 1890's deflated every other country in the world by refusing to lend abroad on the scale to which international economic relations had become adjusted. At the end of 1929 it looked as if France might be playing somewhat the same rôle, and was provoking a world-wide deflation by her reluctance to lend abroad on the appropriate scale (*i.e.* to allow L to accommodate itself to B).

the new equilibrium could be brought about without throwing on Germany the brunt of any change whatever in her current rate of earnings, and without any movement of gold.

This is quite true. Such a thing is not theoretically impossible. But I contend that it is highly improbable in the conditions of the actual problem, and that to establish the opposite, Professor Ohlin must explore more fully the conditions which have to be satisfied before his conclusion can hold good.

To begin with, this line of argument is quite irrelevant to the amount of change which will be required in the terms of trade, and therefore in the *relative* rates of earnings in Germany and elsewhere and in the rate of German real wages. It is only concerned with the question whether this relative change will be brought about mainly by an absolute fall in the rate of money-wages in Germany, or mainly by an absolute rise in the rate of money-wages elsewhere. Now it would be difficult to find a case where the conditions for the former alternative to be probable are better fulfilled. For Germany is not in a position to part with enough gold to have a sensible effect on the credit policies of the rest of the world, there is no preexisting tendency for the natural-rate of interest in the recipient countries to rise relatively to the natural-rate in Germany, and she is not in a position to resort to the expedient of regulating the rate of growth of her foreign investment to suit the rate at which relative money-earnings can be adjusted (or rather she only can do this by increasing her own borrowing from abroad, which is a more difficult task than diminishing her own lending would be). I conclude that, *if* the payment of Reparations involves a substantial change in the terms of trade (which depends not on monetary considerations but on physical facts relating to the nature of the productive forces of Germany and the rest of the world), then it will probably be necessary to force down the rate of money-earnings in Germany by means of a painful (and perhaps impracticable) process of deflation. It will be necessary to qualify this, only if the rest of the world, deliberately or by a fortunate coincidence, encourage tendencies leading to an income inflation with the result of easing the practical difficulties of Germany's problem of reaching a relative adjustment, or if new extraneous conditions come to pass which naturally lead the rest of the world towards a higher level of money-incomes.

Borrowing from the now familiar terminology of the German Reparation Problem, we might use similar language in the general case, meaning by the " Transfer Problem " the problem of transition which occurs when there is a change in the locality where investment takes place. Thus, when international equilibrium (*i.e.* the equality of the international-rate of interest in every country with its natural-rate) requires a change in the relative rates of earnings in different countries, the amount of the absolute change in the rate of earnings in each country depends, in general, on the two following factors:

(1) The *total* amount of the relative change required. This depends on what degree of difficulty and what loss of efficiency is involved in the change-over of production from goods required for a particular kind of investment in one place to a different kind of investment in another place, *i.e.* the amount of necessary change in the terms of trade.

(2) The *proportion* of the total amount of the relative change which has to fall on each country. This depends on the policy and comparative skill and strength to support changes in its proportion of gold to circulating money possessed by each of the central banks respectively.

(iii.) *The Net National Advantages of Foreign Investment*

We have seen that, when a change in the terms of trade occurs as a concomitant of increased foreign investment, this is due to the factors of production in the lending country having to change over to a kind of output in which they are less effective (having regard both to technical efficiency and to the various elasticities of demand involved) relatively to the factors of production in the borrowing country, than they were in respect of the output which they were producing before the change-over. That is to say, their marginal efficiency is reduced for obtaining foreign-trade products by exchange. This means that the terms of exchange alter to their disadvantage, not only in respect of that part of their foreign trade which corresponds to the *increased* volume of foreign investment, but over the whole field of their foreign trade—assuming, of course, competitive conditions. Since, in accordance with our definitions, we measure the output of the factors which are working to exchange exports for imports by the quantity of imports which are obtainable in exchange, it follows that the total output of the factors of production in the lending country is reduced by an amount corresponding to the loss involved in giving more exports for a given quantity of imports or in replacing goods previously imported by goods produced at home.

In the new position of equilibrium actual rates of money-earnings will be reduced and real earnings will also be reduced, though to a less extent. But real efficiency-earnings will be unchanged, since in a position of equilibrium efficiency-earnings in terms of money and the price-level must necessarily have changed in the same proportion. In other words, $\dfrac{E}{O \cdot \Pi}$, the rate of real efficiency-earnings, will be unchanged; but O, the output, and $\frac{E}{\Pi}$, the actual real earnings of the factors of production, will both be reduced and in the same proportion, corresponding to the loss of efficiency of the factors of production in their new situation as compared with their efficiency in the old.

On the other hand, the efficiency of capital engaged in foreign investment is increased by reason of the higher rate of interest earned. Whether on balance there is a national gain or loss as a result of the increased proportion of investment abroad depends on a comparison between the prospective gain of increased future income from foreign investment and of improved terms of trade when this income is being paid and the immediate loss occasioned by the deterioration in the terms of trade whilst the foreign investment is taking place; *i.e.* on the elasticity of demand for investment at home in terms of the rate of interest and the elasticity of the world's demand for our goods and our demand for theirs.

Subject to the simplifying assumptions that earnings in the export trades are the same as in other trades, that there are constant returns to industry within the range of variation in question, and that the total volume of saving is unchanged, the loss through the fall in prices of exports relatively to those of imports is measured by $E_2(p_1 - p_2) - F_2(q_1 - q_2)$, where E_2 is the volume of exports and F_2 of imports in the new position;[1] p_1, q_1 the prices of exports and imports respectively in the old position; and p_2, q_2 their prices in the new position. On the other hand, the gain in the advantage of current foreign lending by reason of the rise in the rate of interest is measured by $s.L'$, where s is the proportionate rise in the rate of interest and L' the amount of foreign

---

[1] This ignores loss of consumer's surplus through substitution of home-produced goods for imports.

lending in the new position. Thus the net national gain (or loss) to our country, in respect of these two elements in the calculation, is

$$s.L' - E_2(p_1 - p_2) + F_2(q_1 - q_2).$$

I see no presumption in favour of this quantity being positive rather than negative. In the case of a country for which the elasticity for investment at home is large and the elasticity of demand for exports and imports is small, one would expect it to be negative. The orthodox doctrine that the volume of foreign investment under a free play of forces is always at a social optimum for the investing country is probably based on the assumption that a very small fall in the prices of exports will develop an adequate increase of B.

The above makes no allowance, on the one hand, for the subsequent effects of foreign investment in turning the terms of trade the other way when interest comes to be paid, or for any indirect advantages accruing to the lending country through the development of the world's resources—which advantages, however, would accrue to it equally if the foreign investment were undertaken by some other country. On the other hand, it also makes no allowance for the inevitable losses of any transition. As a rule, money-earnings will not fall to the necessary extent *immediately*; with the result that there will be an intervening period when the market-rate of interest exceeds the natural-rate, so that, total investment falling short of savings, business losses and unemployment ensue.

If the above piece of analysis is applied to Germany's "transfer problem" in the payment of reparations, there is no set-off corresponding to the higher rate of interest earned or to the subsequent improvement in the terms of trade; so that the loss to Germany occasioned by the strain of establishing the new equilibrium is measured by $E_2(p_1 - p_2) - F_2(q_1 - q_2)$, together with the pains and difficulties of the transition,—over and above the amount of the actual reparation payments themselves.

(iv.) *The Awkwardness of Changes due to International Factors*

The importance of the foregoing discussion is this. A mere change in the demand-schedule of borrowers abroad is capable, without any change in the monetary situation proper, of setting up a disequilibrium in the existing level of money-incomes at home. If borrowers abroad are ready and able to offer better terms than before, whilst the demand-schedule of borrowers at home is unchanged, this means that foreign lending is increased. Consequently gold will flow until money-earnings have fallen sufficiently, relatively to similar earnings abroad (which may be rising a little as a result of the movement of gold), for the foreign balance also to be correspondingly increased. The extent to which real incomes will fall at home will depend partly on the elasticity of demand for loans on the part of home borrowers and partly on the elasticity of the world's demand for our country's exports, and of our country's demand for its imports. If the demands of home investment are elastic and the foreign trade position is inelastic, the troubles and inconveniences of the transition may be very great.

At present public opinion—in Great Britain at least—is chiefly coloured by memories of nineteenth-century experience, when for various reasons the adverse reaction of foreign investment on the level of money-incomes at home was probably at a minimum. The significance of the above in the different circumstances of to-day in relation to the national benefits of a high degree of mobility for international loans is, as yet, scarcely appreciated.

In an old country, especially one in which the

population has ceased to expand rapidly, the rate of interest at which borrowers for home investment are able to absorb home savings must necessarily decline. Meanwhile in the new countries the rate will be maintained, and as these countries get over their early pioneer difficulties, the estimated risks of lending to them—provided they are careful about their reputation as borrowers—will decline. Consequently the old country will tend to lend abroad an ever-growing proportion of its total savings. This will be partly cared for by the interest on its previous foreign lending. But for the rest its costs of production must fall so as to stimulate its exports and increase its favourable balance on trading account. If there is a resistance to this fall, gold will flow, bank-rate will rise and unemployment become chronic. This is particularly likely to happen if the prevalence of tariffs against manufactured goods (and a readiness to raise them when imports of such goods are increasing) renders the foreign demand for the old country's exports inelastic, whilst at the same time Trade Unions in the old country present great obstacles to a reduction of money-wages.

I leave it to the reader to work out in detail what a pickle a country might get into if a higher rate of interest abroad than can be earned at home leads to most of its savings being lent abroad, whilst at the same time there are tariffs abroad against most of its exports and a tendency to raise these tariffs from time to time to balance the gradually rising level of costs in the protected countries due to the outflow of gold from the lending country.

Let him take, for example, as his imaginary case, a Great Britain where neither the government nor individuals are prepared to invest at home at a higher rate of interest than 5 per cent, and a socialised Australia where the government is ready to develop at 6 per cent, both on a gold standard and with complete mobility of lending between the two; let him suppose further that this imaginary Australia has a sliding-scale tariff on most British goods based on the difference between the costs of production in the two countries, and that in this imaginary Great Britain wages are virtually fixed in terms of money; and let him complete his imaginary picture by supposing a Thrift Campaign in Great Britain which raises savings to an unusual proportion of the national income, or, alternatively, a government ruled by financial virtue which taxes heavily in order to raise to a high figure the Sinking Fund for the extinction of the National Debt.[1]

Or let him take the case in which the Currency Authorities of the countries to which gold flows so manage their currency systems that the inflow of gold is not allowed to have any effect on their bank-rates or their volume of money.

All this, we must repeat, is subject to the assumption of a high degree of mobility of international lending. Where this does not exist, disequilibria due to changes in price-levels abroad may be more sudden and disagreeable than where it does exist (for changes in Bank-rate will not avail to break the impact); but, on the other hand, disequilibria due to changes in interest-rates abroad will be of secondary importance. Moreover, even when there is a fairly high degree of mobility of lending over long periods, our country need not necessarily subject itself—unless there are

[1] The reader will readily perceive that in writing the above I have partly in mind the position of Great Britain in 1929–30. I should, therefore, add that, whilst I regard the relative attractiveness of foreign lending as a serious aggravation of the difficulties, I do not regard this factor as so important a cause of the disequilibrium between Foreign Lending and the Foreign Balance as the factors decreasing the volume of the latter, due to the failure to deflate earnings and costs of production in as great a degree as the international value of sterling had been raised in the period ending in 1925. The actual situation was due to the combination of a tendency for foreign lending to increase, for long-period external reasons over which we had little control, with a tendency for the foreign balance to decrease as a short-period result of our post-War monetary policy.

other counterbalancing advantages to be gained—to a high degree of short-period mobility of international lending. If short-period mobility is absent, then short-period changes in interest-rates abroad need occasion no serious inconvenience. Methods of damping down an excessive short-period mobility of international lending will be discussed in Vol. ii. Book VII. Chapter 36.

The seriousness of the changes which are set up as the result of International Disequilibrium lies partly in their *inevitability*. If we are dealing with a closed system, so that there is only the condition of internal equilibrium to fulfil, an appropriate banking policy is always capable of preventing any serious disturbance to the *status quo* from developing at all. If the rate of creation of credit is so regulated as to avoid Profit Inflation, there will be no reason for the Purchasing Power of Money and the money-rate of efficiency earnings ever to be upset. But when the condition of external equilibrium must also be fulfilled, then there will be no banking policy capable of avoiding disturbance to the internal system.

This is due—quite apart from changes in the value of the international standard—to the lack of uniformity between home and abroad in respect of the demand schedules of borrowers. These schedules, for home and foreign borrowers respectively, can and do change differently from one another. When this happens, the existing rate of foreign lending is upset. Unless, therefore, a country is prepared to accept from time to time large quantities of gold and at other times to part with large quantities without modifying the terms and volume of lending at home— and in any case this cannot continue indefinitely— changes in foreign conditions are bound to set up disequilibria in home conditions. If, moreover, there is a high degree of mobility of foreign lending, a low degree of mobility of home wage-rates, an inelasticity in the demand-schedule for our country's exports and a high elasticity in the demand for borrowing for home investment, then the transition from one position of internal equilibrium to another required by the necessity for preserving external equilibrium may be difficult, dilatory and painful.

Even where a change in Bank-rate is only required as a temporary corrective to the rate of foreign lending, so as to preserve external equilibrium, it cannot be prevented from reacting on the rate of home lending, and, therefore—over a period too short to effect the establishment of a lower wage-level—on the volume of output and employment. Thus, what we have claimed in Chapter 13 as a virtue in Bank-rate regarded as an instrument for restoring long-period equilibrium— namely, that it works *both* ways, tending to decrease foreign lending and also to increase the foreign balance —becomes a vice, or at least an awkwardness, when we use it to check foreign lending, the excessiveness of which may be due to temporary causes without our having any wish to go through the painful readjustment of the wage-structure which must precede a material increase of the foreign balance. Since the influence of Bank-rate on foreign lending is both quick in taking effect and easy to understand, whereas its influence on the internal situation is slower in operation and difficult to analyse, the awkwardness of handling such a double-edged weapon is being but slowly realised.

(v.) *The same Phenomena under Gold-Exchange Management*

The virtue of gold movements under an old-fashioned international gold standard, not merely as an expedient, but as a stimulus towards the restoration of international equilibrium, has been rightly extolled as lying in their *double* effect—both on the country losing gold and on the country receiving gold, so that the two countries *share* the brunt of any necessary change. For just as the loss of gold stimulates a country to raise its interest rates at once and to lower its costs of production later on, so the receipt of gold has the opposite effect. Now, since L, the volume of foreign lending, depends on *relative* interest rates at home and abroad, and B, the amount of the foreign balance, depends on *relative* price-levels at home and abroad, this is important. For it means that the whole brunt of the change is not thrown on our own country; the flow of gold means that other countries are stimulated to meet us half-way.

But what if our Central Bank keeps its reserves, not in the form of actual gold, but in the form of liquid resources at a foreign financial centre? Does a change in the volume of such resources also operate for the restoration of equilibrium in a reciprocal fashion? Some critics of the methods of Gold-Exchange Management—though applauding them as a means of economising the demand for gold in the reserves of Central Banks—have argued that movements of liquid resources, other than gold, do not operate in reciprocal fashion, and that this is a very serious objection to the methods in question. When Central Bank A, which keeps liquid reserves in the country of Central Bank B, begins to draw on these reserves in order to maintain the parity of its exchanges, it is under the same motive, as if it were losing gold, to alter the terms of lending within its own country. But Central Bank B —so the argument runs—is under no such motive; for nothing has happened in country B to affect the terms of lending, since nothing is altered except the ownership of certain liquid resources.

Before we can say if there is a satisfactory answer to this criticism, we must probe into the whole matter somewhat more deeply. If Central Bank B is mainly influenced by the ratio of its gold-reserve to its liabilities, then it is clearly true that a change in the volume of foreign balances held within its system has no more *immediate* effect on its own behaviour than a change in the volume of net foreign lending (for that is what it amounts to) for any other cause. Again, a change in the volume of foreign balances will not, unless A's balances are held in the form of demand-deposits with Central Bank B, *force the hand* of Central Bank B to act in a manner which in its own unfettered judgment is prejudicial to the interests of its own internal equilibrium, in the way in which a movement of actual gold may force its hand. So in this case, it would seem, the charge of there being no reciprocal action is justified.

If, on the other hand, Central Bank B is in the habit of regarding a movement of actual gold, not primarily as a *disease* but mainly in the light of a *symptom* of the existing or prospective relationship between the incentives to foreign lending and the incentives governing the amount of the foreign balance, then a movement of liquid balances by Central Bank A to or from B may be just as important and significant a symptom as if Central Bank A were moving actual gold from or to B; and there is, therefore, just as much reason for Central Bank B to be influenced by the one as by the other in the determination of its monetary policy. But at this point we must pause a moment to notice that an increase of the balances of foreign Central Banks in the hands of Central Bank B is, on the above supposition, equivalent to a *loss* of gold by Central Bank B. If, therefore, Central Bank B is to treat the movements of the balances of foreign Central Banks exactly as if they were movements of gold, it will (*e.g.*) have to *raise* its bank-rate when the foreign balances in its hands are increasing, and will have to persist in this policy until it has attracted an amount of gold equal to the increment of the balances of the foreign Central Banks or, by attracting the resources of the nationals of the foreign Central Banks, has forced these Central Banks to part with their own balances;—and in either event there will be no economy of gold to the Central Banks of the world taken as a whole.

It would seem, therefore, at first sight that we cannot have it both ways. Either the complaint of the critics as to the lack of reciprocal action is justified, or there is no real economy of gold. But it is not necessarily so bad as this, for the following reason.

Suppose that the increase or decrease of the liquid foreign resources of Central Bank A with Central Bank B is at the expense of the decrease or increase of the resources of Central Bank A' with Central Bank B, then, although there is no reciprocal action so far as B is concerned, there *is* reciprocal action on the part of A' of a kind to help A towards its readjustment. Moreover, if Central Bank B is used as a Clearing House by the Central Banks of the rest of the world so that a change in the balances of one Central Bank with B is normally balanced by an equal and opposite change in the balances of some other Central Bank, then it will be reasonable for Central Bank B not to hold any important proportion of gold against the normal aggregate of foreign Central Bank balances held with it, though regarding any departure from this normal aggregate as a symptom requiring much the same treatment as if it were a movement of gold. In this case we should, up to the extent of the accepted size of this normal aggregate, secure for the world a real economy of gold, and also for individual Central Banks, when they vary the amounts of their foreign balances, the same reciprocal action on the part of other Central Banks, as if they were varying their stocks of gold.

In practice, however, the actual position is unfortunately not so good as this ideal case. For the ideal case requires the fulfilment of two conditions :—

first, that there should be a stable policy on the part of Central Banks as to what the normal aggregate of their gold-exchange reserves should be ; and, secondly, that these reserves should all be concentrated in a single centre, or, if divided between several centres, that the normal aggregate in each centre should be stable, so that there is no risk of movement (under the influence (*e.g.*) of differential rates of interest) between one centre and another. If these conditions are not fulfilled, then there must be some sacrifice either of reciprocal action or of economy of gold.

At any rate, a system must be liable to work in a precarious and unsatisfactory manner, in which the degree of reliance of the Central Banks of the world, taken as a whole, on gold-exchange reserves as compared with actual gold is highly variable, and in which such reserves are capable of moving in large amounts from one centre to another, *e.g.* between New York and London, under the influence of changes in the rate of interest, which changes may be determined by local and not by international considerations. Indeed the general effect of the above discussion is, I think, to lead up to the conclusion that the only satisfactory way of working the gold-exchange system would be under the aegis of an international bank, which would be the sole depository of Central Bank gold-exchange reserves ; the aggregate of whose balances in favour of Central Banks would be determined by considerations of international policy ; and the balances of which would not normally be withdrawn in gold but merely transferred from one Central Bank to another. In such a system the proportion of their reserves held by Central Banks at the International Bank would be truly a substitute for gold, whilst the benefits of reciprocal action between one country and another would be fully maintained. Further examination of the project of an International Bank must, however, be postponed to Vol. ii. Book VII. Chapter 38.

Turning to the practical considerations of the moment, one finds also certain other obstacles in the way of Gold-Exchange Management working out in an entirely satisfactory way. In the first place, there is not always accurate and up-to-date knowledge of the *amount* of liquid resources which one Banking System is holding as a reserve within the territory of another Banking System. Consequently changes in these amounts are not as overt and palpable as are movements of actual gold. Indeed, this greater secrecy, which allows a Central Bank's reserves to fluctuate in amount without this being generally known, is sometimes a recommendation in the eyes of the Bank in favour of its holding foreign liquid resources rather than gold in its own vaults.

In so far as the vagueness of our knowledge about the movements of foreign balances is due to the love of secrecy, Central Banks have only themselves to blame. But it may also be due to a certain vagueness as to what ought to be reckoned for the present purpose as a foreign banking reserve. One kind of asset shades off into another—from Central Bank Balances to Member Bank Balances, to Bank Bills, to Treasury Bills, to other Short-dated Securities, to Securities generally having a free international market. Nor is it clear that we should concentrate our attention solely on Central Bank assets in those cases where Member Banks also are accustomed to hold foreign liquid resources on an important scale. For the real distinction is between those resources which are held abroad for the purpose of affording reserves against contingencies to a country's banking system as a whole, and those resources which are held abroad because of the attraction which they offer as investments. The solution to this difficulty can only be found in Central Banks having in their possession the greatest possible amount of information under all the above headings, and then applying their practical judgment to the question of the degree of importance to be attached to changes under any one or more of them. Assuredly a Central Bank ought to be completely informed, both as to the absolute amount and as to the fluctuations of the foreign banking resources of whatever description held within its territory.

Another practical obstacle is the fact that, although methods of Gold-Exchange Management have been generally blessed as a means of economising gold, and have been put into actual practice on a fair scale, Central Banks are still accustomed, by force of habit, to pay a disproportionate amount of attention to movements of gold as compared with the attention they pay to other significant factors.

When all is said and done, moreover, it must necessarily be admitted that, in so far as national systems develop devices and maintain large liquid reserves with the express object of having the power to maintain internal equilibrium over the short period, without too sensitive a regard for external events, reciprocal action will necessarily become less dependable—except in the event of major movements and over the long period. For sensitive reciprocal action, of the kind which the pre-War gold standard was supposed to provide, involved every country in a subordination of internal equilibrium to every external change however trifling or transitory; and the wider the margin of safety in Central Banks' aggregate reserves, the less willing will each be to respond reciprocally to the vagaries of the others.

(vi.) *The same Phenomena in the Absence of an International Standard*

We have assumed so far that there is in existence an effective International Standard. In conclusion, we must consider the case where there is no such Standard—as, for example, in many countries of the world during the years immediately following the War, before the general return to the Gold Standard in 1924–29.

When a disparity between B, the Foreign Balance, and L, the volume of Foreign Lending, cannot be cured by allowing gold to move, the pressure on the foreign exchanges must obviously alter the rates between our own country and the rest of the world to whatever degree is necessary to cause the disparity to disappear. In short, the operative machinery for the preservation of external equilibrium is no longer, primarily, a change in bank-rate, but a change in the rates of foreign exchange. Bank-rate remains as a secondary instrument for external equilibrium and as a primary instrument for internal equilibrium. But the character of transitions due to external disturbances is considerably modified, compared with what has been described above on the assumption of an International Standard.

For the effect of a change in the rates of foreign exchange, though similar in a sense to that of a change in bank-rate, works—as we shall see—*the other way round*. It also brings into operation *at once* certain forces which are entirely absent, in the first instance at least, when a change of bank-rate is employed as a means of restoring equilibrium. The chief differences between the foreign-exchange method and the bank-rate method can be classified as follows:

(1) Let us call goods, which are capable of entering into foreign trade within the contemplated range of foreign-exchange rate changes, whether as imports or as exports, *foreign-trade goods*, including in this category goods which do not actually enter into foreign trade but are used at home, if they are the same in kind as foreign-trade goods in the above sense. Now an increase in B is the same thing as an increase in the surplus home-production of foreign-trade goods, meaning by *surplus home-production* the excess of the home-production of such goods over the home-utilisa-

tion of such goods, whether for home-investment or for home-consumption. Thus a country increases its foreign investment by increasing its surplus production of foreign-trade goods. Similarly we can call by the name of *home-trade goods* all other goods produced at home. Now when the rate of foreign exchange is altered, the prices of all foreign-trade goods are changed forthwith in terms of the local money, whereas in the first instance nothing will have happened to change the prices of home-trade goods. Let us suppose that the disequilibrium which we set out to cure is a deficiency of B relatively to L, and let us compare the working in this case of exchange-rate policy with that of bank-rate policy as a means of restoring equilibrium.

If the exchange-rate is altered so as to depreciate the local money to an appropriate extent, equilibrium is restored by *raising* the price of foreign-trade goods whilst leaving that of home-trade goods unchanged, thus attracting entrepreneurs towards an increased production of the former with the consequence of increasing the surplus production of foreign-trade goods, *i.e.* of B. If, on the other hand, bank-rate is raised to an appropriate extent, forces are set in motion tending to *lower* the price of home-trade goods whilst leaving the price of foreign-trade goods unchanged (I am speaking broadly and without reference to niceties). That is what we meant above by saying that the two methods work similarly but the other way round. In the case supposed the foreign-exchange method restores equilibrium by an act of inflation, whereas the bank-rate method would produce a similar relative change by an act of deflation. If, on the other hand, the disequilibrium had consisted in an excess of B relatively to L, then it would be the foreign-exchange method which would function by means of a deflation, whereas the bank-rate method would employ inflation. Thus —so far as friction is a serious trouble—the line of least resistance will be to employ the foreign-exchange method in the former case and the bank-rate method in the latter case (with the result, however, that if we were always to follow what was in the circumstances the line of least resistance the long-period trend of prices would always be upwards).

But this is not the only contrast between the two methods. The foreign-exchange method has the characteristic that it operates *directly* (whether upwards or downwards) on relative price-levels, whereas the bank-rate method only does so *indirectly*, and therefore with a time-lag. On the other hand, the bank-rate method has the characteristic that it operates *directly* on L. Which of these characteristics is the more advantageous depends on whether the disequilibrium between B and L is due to a change of interest rates in the outside world or to a change of price-levels in the outside world. In the former case, the new position of equilibrium cannot be reached merely by exchange-rate policy but must be accompanied sooner or later by a change in bank-rate also. Indeed, assuming that the average level of money-incomes at home and abroad remains finally unchanged, the new equilibrium rate of foreign exchange will only differ from the previous rate to an extent corresponding to the change in the terms of trade, the amount of which will depend, as before, on the physical facts of production and investment in the two countries. But in the latter case bank-rate method sets up a disturbance in the rate of investment, which is unnecessary and injurious in itself and is only applied in order to produce at long last an effect on the money-cost of production, after which it will have to be reversed again. Nothing is required in order to reach a new position of equilibrium with money-incomes at home at the same level as before, except an appropriate change in the rates of foreign-exchange.

We can now sum up the question of choice as follows. If the disequilibrium is due to changing price-levels abroad, the foreign-exchange method will have advantages because it preserves external equilibrium without upsetting internal equilibrium at all ; but if it is due to changing interest-rates abroad, then in the long run the bank-rate method will be essential, and there is only room for the foreign-exchange method as well (assuming stability of money-incomes at home to be our objective) if the change in relative interest-rates involves an important change in the terms of trade. In the second place, if the disequilibrium is purely temporary and needs no lasting readjustment, then a temporary use of the foreign-exchange method has the advantage that it operates quickly and directly on prices, whereas the bank-rate method may not have produced its desired results until they are too late to be useful. For, in this case, an oscillation in the price-levels of foreign-trade goods and home-trade goods relatively to one another may cause a sufficient modification in B to overcome the fleeting occasion of disequilibrium, without any serious disturbance either in money-incomes or in the equilibrium of savings and investment.

If, therefore, Central Banks could be assumed to be wise, it would seem—subject to the considerations in (2) below—that they ought to have both weapons in their armoury for use on the appropriate occasions.

(2) But there is a further important bye-product of the foreign-exchange method. The uncertainty as to the prospective rates of exchange with the outside world will have a far-reaching effect on the magnitude of L, tending to diminish the volume of foreign lending and equally (if our country is a borrowing country) the volume of foreign borrowing. Thus the choice between the two methods may be as much governed by the consideration whether, on grounds of general social and national policy, we desire to encourage or to discourage foreign lending (or borrowing), as by the technical monetary considerations adduced above.

(3) Furthermore, fluctuations in the volume of short-period lending, in so far as they are dependent on comparatively small differences between the rates of interest at home and abroad, will come to play a much smaller part in our country's internal economy. For there will come into existence another factor governing L, namely, the expectations which are entertained as to the *prospective* course of the foreign exchanges. This is so familiar a feature—as the result of post-War experience—that I need not expatiate on it. If the fluctuations in the foreign exchanges are expected to be short-period oscillations about a slowly moving norm, every excess or defect of L relatively to B will, as soon as it has had time to affect the foreign exchanges, tend to bring into operation corrective forces. For the prospect of profit or loss when the foreign loan is repaid will always tend to move L in what, from the standpoint of preserving external equilibrium, will be the desired direction.[1] But if a change in the foreign exchanges is believed to be a foretaste of a progressive and cumulative change in the same direction, then the effect will be to aggravate the disequilibrium and to move L in the opposite of the desired direction.

Let us in what follows neglect the case of a local *fiat* money, which has no objective standard and is at the mercy of impotent or misguided management; and let us assume, rather, that the management of the local money is governed in the long run by some sort of criterion of the internal stability of money-values.

On this assumption the salient differences between the behaviour of such a monetary system and that of a system under the International Standard is to be found, first, in a more immediate sensitiveness of B to external changes; secondly, in a more delayed

[1] We shall examine the technique of this in greater detail in Vol. ii. Bk. VII. Chapter 36.

sensitiveness of L to changes in the relative rates of interest at home and abroad; thirdly, in the introduction of a new means of influencing L other than changes in relative rates of interest (namely, changes in the rates of foreign exchange); and fourthly, in its being possible to have a change in the rate of foreign investment without a change in the average level of money-incomes.

I am not concerned in this chapter to weigh up finally the practical advantages of an international standard and of a local standard respectively—a topic which properly belongs to Volume ii., where I shall in fact propose something of a compromise between the two. But the most significant difference between them —wherever the advantage may lie on balance—seems to me to be as follows.

With a local standard the dilemma, which sometimes faces a Central Bank, that it may be impossible to preserve both internal equilibrium and external equilibrium at the same time, presents itself much less acutely. If the Central Bank is free to vary both the rate of foreign exchange and its market-rate of interest, applying appropriate doses of each at the right moment, there is much less risk of the loss of wealth and output due to the prevalence of general unemployment. For direct changes in the price of foreign-trade goods can be largely substituted for unemployment as the first link in the causal chain whereby external equilibrium is preserved and restored. Its disadvantage is to be found in the diminished mobility that it means (if that is a disadvantage) for foreign lending.

It is evident that no general answer can be given to the question where the balance of advantage lies. It depends partly on the relative importance of foreign-trade industries in our country's national economy. But not entirely. For it also depends on whether the potential fluctuations in the volume of foreign lending, in the absence of the artificial check of sharp changes in the local rates of interest, are likely to be large relatively to those corresponding fluctuations in the amount of the foreign balance which can be brought about quickly and with a moderate change in the terms of trade. The answer to the last point is not unaffected by the tariff policy of the rest of the world—for a high degree of sensitiveness in the rate of foreign lending to small changes may be inconvenient, and even dangerous, if it is not accompanied by an equally high degree of sensitiveness in the response of foreign trade to small changes.

END OF VOL.